The Social-Emotional
Learning Toolbox

The Social-Emotional Learning Toolbox
Practical Strategies to Support All Students

by

Kathy Perez

·P A U L·H·
BROOKES
PUBLISHING C<u>o</u>.®

Baltimore • London • Sydney

Paul H. Brookes Publishing Co.
Post Office Box 10624
Baltimore, Maryland 21285-0624
USA

www.brookespublishing.com

Typeset by Progressive Publishing Service, York, Pennsylvania.
Manufactured in the United States of America by
Kase Printing, Inc., Hudson, New Hampshire.

All examples in this book are composites. Any similarity to actual individuals or circumstances is coincidental, and
no implications should be inferred.

Library of Congress Cataloging-in-Publication Data

Names: Perez, Katherine D., author.
Title: The social-emotional learning toolbox : practical strategies to
    support all students / by Kathy Perez.
Description: Baltimore : Paul H. Brookes Publishing Co., [2022] | Includes
    bibliographical references and index.
Identifiers: LCCN 2021024765 (print) | LCCN 2021024766 (ebook) |
    ISBN 9781681254357 (paperback) | ISBN 9781681254364 (epub) |
    ISBN 9781681254371 (pdf)
Subjects: LCSH: Affective education. | Classroom environment. | Behavior
    modification.
Classification: LCC LB1072.P47 2022 (print) | LCC LB1072 (ebook) |
    DDC 370.15/34–dc23
LC record available at https://lccn.loc.gov/2021024765
LC ebook record available at https://lccn.loc.gov/2021024766

British Library Cataloguing in Publication data are available from the British Library.

2025   2024   2023   2022   2021

10   9   8   7   6   5   4   3   2   1

Table of Contents

About the Online Materials vii
About the Author ix
Acknowledgments xi

Chapter 1:   Making the Case for Social-Emotional Learning 1

Chapter 2:   Social-Emotional Learning and the Self:
             Emotional Intelligence 13

Chapter 3:   Self-Regulation: Helping Your Students Understand
             Their Emotions 33

Chapter 4:   Developing Executive Function Skills in Students 51

Chapter 5:   Mindfulness in the Classroom 71

Chapter 6:   Supporting a Growth Mindset 87

Chapter 7:   Social-Emotional Learning and Relationships: How to
             Create a Caring, Positive Classroom Environment 109

Chapter 8:   Fostering Empathy in the Classroom 131

Chapter 9:   Relationships: Strengthening Bonds 149

Appendix A: Additional Resources 173
Appendix B: Children's Books to Support Social-Emotional Learning 193
Appendix C: Resources for Continued Learning 199
Appendix D: Trauma-Informed Resources 201
Glossary 203
Study Guide 207
References 213
Index 221

About the Online Materials

Purchasers of this book may download, print, and/or photocopy the forms, worksheets, handouts, study guide, and printable classroom posters for professional and/or educational use.

To access the materials that come with this book:

1. Go to the Brookes Publishing Download Hub: http://downloads.brookespublishing.com

2. Register to create an account (or log in with an existing account).

3. Redeem the case-sensitive code **xIxnzYEBW** to access any locked materials.

About the Author

KATHY PEREZ, ED.D.

Dr. Kathy Perez is an international consultant, presenter, teacher, administrator, instructional coach, and author who has worked with students from preschoolers to university graduates. Dr. Kathy is Professor Emerita at Saint Mary's College of California. She has extensive teaching experience as a general and special educator, literacy/ESL coach, and administrative experience as a principal and curriculum/staff development coordinator.

Teachers from all grade levels and subject areas rave about Kathy Perez's dynamic approach to teaching. Her innovative and interactive workshops, books, articles, and blogs are loaded with teacher-tested materials and activities you can use immediately and share with others. Kathy provides lively and informative strategies to reinforce hands-on and minds-on learning. Participants learn from an experienced and informed educator who knows firsthand the daily instructional challenges of classroom teachers. Her enthusiasm is infectious!

Dr. Kathy has worked extensively with teachers, administrators, and parents throughout the United States, Canada, Europe, China, Qatar, Brazil, Britain, Colombia, the Caribbean, Africa, New Zealand, Australia, Thailand, Hong Kong, and Singapore. Kathy holds a bachelor's degree in Honors English from Holy Names University, a Master of Science degree in Educational Psychology from California State University East Bay, and a Doctorate of Education degree in Curriculum and Instruction from Brigham Young University.

To learn more about Kathy's work, visit drkathyperez.com; for professional development, contact her at kperez@stmarys-ca.edu.

Acknowledgments

Like any teacher, I am so grateful to the students that I have taught over the years. They have shown me the importance of integrating the heart as well as the mind in learning. I learned firsthand from these students of multiple ages, abilities, languages, and cultures that relationships are just as important as the curriculum in the classroom.

I have had the distinct privilege of working collaboratively with extraordinary educators, administrators, board members, parents, support staff, and other key personnel on the importance of educating the whole child. Each day, I am awed and inspired by the work that my colleagues do to help *all* learners achieve success—no matter what their entry point to learning is.

On a personal note, this book would not have been possible without the unwavering love and support of my family—my dedicated and loving husband, Robert; and my two amazing sons, Hart and Devon. Their patience and constant commitment and encouragement to my work made me a better wife, mom, educator, and person.

A heartfelt thank you goes out to the editorial team at Brookes Publishing with special recognition of the expertise shared by Rachel Word in fine-tuning the final product. Her broad knowledge and sharp insights in the editing process really strengthened the finished manuscript.

When I wrote this book, I was overwhelmed by the realization of what a vast variety of individuals and sources I utilized to synthesize the information presented in these pages. In addition, as I compiled my strategies for successful social-emotional development in the classroom, I was able to reflect on the various workshops, trainings, collaborations, and mentors from whom I have benefited.

CHAPTER 1

Making the Case for Social-Emotional Learning

Social-emotional learning (SEL) has been receiving more and more attention recently in the educational sphere, both from practitioners and researchers. SEL has been called the "missing piece" of education; the information and strategies we'll discuss throughout this book will allow you to complete the puzzle to providing exceptional learning experiences to your students.

KEY CONCEPTS

- What is social-emotional learning (SEL)?

- Why is it so important in our classroom today?

- How can SEL help you and your students?

- What are some strategies for integrating SEL to develop a more positive classroom culture?

- What are some misconceptions about SEL?

- How can we increase our students' SEL?

INTRODUCTION

Across the country, momentum is building for schools and districts to help students develop the social, emotional, and academic skills that evidence shows are needed for success both in school and in life. There's a deepening recognition that skills such as responsibility, problem solving, empathy, self-regulation, self-control, and persistence all form a solid foundation for academic achievement and personal growth. **The Every Student Succeeds Act (ESSA),** 2015, recognizes social-emotional education as a vital factor in helping students develop critical life skills that go well beyond academics.

Furthermore, emotions are of paramount importance for cognition: "We feel, therefore we learn" (Immordino-Yang & Damasio, 2007, p. 3). When there is damage to the emotional networks of the brain, even simple decisions can become challenging (Damasio, 1994). For educators who have dozens of students in their classrooms each day, it can feel overwhelming to support the range of students' emotional needs in addition to their diverse learning needs. Educators may feel inadequately prepared and need tools to support emotional learning.

There is also the time factor to consider. Teachers have concerns that there is not enough time to address the emotional needs of their students in addition to the cognitive content that must be covered in the curriculum. One teacher I spoke with said, "I cannot take time each day to talk about how each student feels." This is the challenge that many teachers experience daily.

However, while it is important to recognize that dilemma, educators cannot ignore the critical role of emotions in the classroom and their impact on learning. We must ask, What would it take to weave social and emotional learning into the daily routine and fabric of our nation's schools? For both adults and children, emotions drive our attention and are essential for cognitive skills such as memory and executive functioning. Emotions even influence basic perception (Zadra & Clore, 2011). If we are not addressing emotions in our classrooms, then we are not addressing how students learn.

The strategies shared in this book provide educators with engaging strategies that are research based and do not require a lot of time to implement. Using these classroom-tested techniques, teachers can design environments and lessons to support emotions for learning. These strategies are inclusive in nature and can be proactively integrated into the learning environment so that *any* student can access them, whether a student is just having a "bad day" or they have greater emotional or learning challenges.

What Is Social-Emotional Learning?

SEL has been defined in a number of ways (see Humphrey et al., 2020). In general, it focuses on a set of social, emotional, behavioral, and character skills that support success in school, the workplace, relationships, and the community. According to CASEL (Collaborative for Academic, Social and Emotional Learning,

> Social and emotional learning (SEL) is an integral part of education and human development. SEL is the process through which all young people and adults acquire and apply the knowledge, skills and attitudes to develop healthy identities, manage emotions and achieve personal and collective goals, feel and show empathy for others, establish and maintain supportive relationships, and make responsible and caring decisions. (CASEL, 2015)

Joan Duffell, executive director of the Committee for Children, summarizes the definition this way: "These are the skills that allow children to calm themselves when angry, make friends, resolve conflicts respectfully, and make ethical and safe choices" (Elias et al., 2017, p. 64).

On a broader scale, SEL includes recognizing and understanding emotions, strategies for managing emotions, developing the ability to recognize and understand emotions in others, and strategies for responding to the emotions of others. SEL also includes explicitly teaching and practicing strategies to develop **emotional resiliency**—the ability to bounce back after adversity. For years, many of us in education have assumed that **impulse control**, self-discipline, and sound decision making were taught in the home, that they are innate skills, or that teachers just do not have time to bother with them. Fortunately, educators are realizing that those assumptions were incorrect. Now, we look to schools to integrate these traits into the curriculum.

What Does the Research Say?

The concept of SEL and its importance in education have evolved over the years. In 1997, Elias et al. suggested that SEL comprises a set of competencies, which Durlak et al. (2011) further described as the ability to

- Recognize and manage emotions

- Set and achieve positive goals

- Appreciate the perspectives of others

- Establish and maintain positive relationships

- Make responsible decisions

- Handle interpersonal situations constructively (p. 406)

A few years later, the Collaborative for Academic, Social, and Emotional Learning (CASEL, 2005) identified five interrelated cognitive, affective, and behavioral competencies (see Figure 1.1):

1. *Self-awareness*—the capacity to reflect on one's own feelings, values, and behaviors

2. *Social awareness*—the ability to view situations from another perspective, respect the social and cultural norms of others, and celebrate diversity

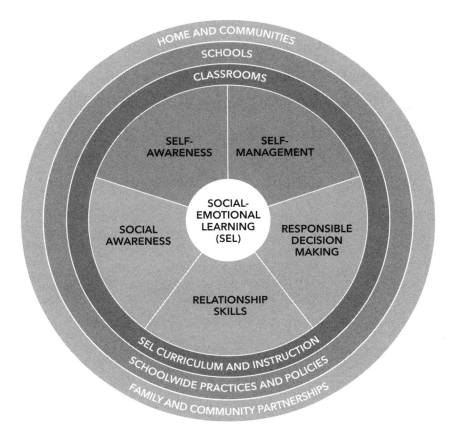

Figure 1.1. CASEL's five interrelated cognitive, affective, and behavioral competencies. (*Source:* ©2021 CASEL. All Rights Reserved. https://casel.org/sel-framework/)

3. *Relationship skills*—the ability to initiate and sustain positive connections with peers, teachers, families, and other groups

4. *Self-management*—the set of skills that includes **self-motivation**, goal setting, personal organization, self-discipline, impulse control, and use of strategies for coping with stress

5. *Responsible decision making*—the ability to make choices that consider the well-being of oneself and others

Furthermore, the Wallace Foundation model (Jones et al., 2018) identified three domains of SEL:

1. *Cognitive regulation*—attention control, inhibitory control, working memory and planning, and cognitive flexibility

2. *Emotional processes*—emotion knowledge and expression, emotion and behavior regulation, and empathy or perspective-taking

3. *Interpersonal skills*—understanding social cues, conflict resolution, and prosocial behavior

From their extensive study of effective SEL practices, *Navigating SEL from the Inside Out* (Jones et al., 2017), the Wallace Foundation identified key features that are essential for implementing effective SEL programs (see Figure 1.2):

• Set reasonable goals

• Incorporate SAFE elements

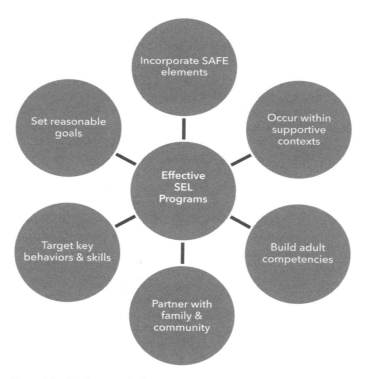

Figure 1.2.   Key features of effective SEL programs. (From Jones, Brush, Bailey, Brion-Meisels, McIntyre, Kahn, Nelson, & Stickle. [2017]. *Navigating social and emotional learning from the inside out* [p. 22]. The Wallace Foundation; reprinted with permission.)

- Occur within supportive contexts

- Build adult competencies

- Partner with family and community

- Target key behaviors and skills

Additionally, in an article titled "What Is Social Emotional Learning?" educator Samantha Cleaver (2013) reminds us that SEL is more than just classroom management and the development of social skills. In a school or classroom where SEL is purposefully included from the first day of class, it becomes an integral part of the day's lesson; it is not just an afterthought or an "add-on." The basic principles of SEL are merged into the curriculum so that they are continually reinforced.

When instruction on relationships, empathy, and emotional features are incorporated into lessons throughout the day, it can positively affect how students learn and feel about themselves and others. As a result, there may be a reduction in acting-out behaviors, giving teachers more time to effectively address curriculum-based teaching and learning.

WHY SOCIAL-EMOTIONAL LEARNING?

The Aspen Institute released a major report promoting SEL in education. The report *From a Nation at Risk to a Nation at Hope* (National Commission on Social, Emotional, and Academic Development, 2019) states

> The promotion of social, emotional, and academic learning is not a shifting educational fad; it is the substance of education itself. It is not a distraction from the "real work" of math and English instruction; it is how instruction can succeed. And it is not another reason for political polarization. It brings together a traditionally conservative emphasis on local control and on the character of all students, and a historically progressive emphasis on the creative and challenging art of teaching and the social and emotional needs of all students, especially those who have experienced the greatest challenges. (p. 6)

An emphasis on educating the "whole child" is understood to include mastery of social and emotional skills in addition to academic ones. Proponents of this broader view of learning believe explicit instruction focused on the social and emotional aspects of learning (SEL) will result in improved academic learning.

This reflects an ageless debate: the "what" of learning versus the "how" of learning. As Berman, Chaffee, and Sarmiento (2018) note, "*How* we teach is as instructive as *what* we teach. Just as the culture of the classroom must reflect social belonging and emotional safety, so can academic instruction embody and enhance these competencies and be enhanced by them" (p. 13). Teachers communicate these values every time they step in front of their class.

Current efforts to address the social and emotional needs of students can be traced to the work of Waters and Sroufe (1983), who describe competence as the ability "to generate and coordinate flexible, adaptive responses to demands and to generate and capitalize on opportunities in the environment" (p. 80).

In other words, competent people are adaptive—they respond to situations in their environment in appropriate ways, and they seek opportunities in their communities. Isn't that what we want our students to be able to do? Accordingly, it seems that schools should be invested in developing this type of skillset in students to prepare them for the colleges, careers, and communities they will live in.

Furthermore, over the last decade, increased attention has been paid to SEL needs of children. This area of learning is necessary and essential to address—for both children and adults. It is time that schools take responsibility for meeting the entire range of learning needs that educators also have—the need to use new technologies, understand and implement new standards, use new assessment strategies, and attend to their students' and their own SEL.

The evidence of the impact of SEL is compelling. Before they can learn academics, students need to know how to behave in a group. A thorough meta-analysis of the impact of SEL was conducted by Durlak et al. (2011). This study examined hundreds of programs involving more than 270,000 students in kindergarten through high school. In their findings, the authors noted, "SEL programs significantly improve students' skills, attitudes, and behaviors" (p. 2) on six factors:

1. *Social and emotional skills* such as goal setting, conflict resolution, and decision making

2. *Attitudes toward self and others* such as self-efficacy, school bonding, and helping others

3. *Positive social behavior* such as getting along with others

4. *Conduct problems* including bullying, noncompliance, and aggression

5. *Emotional distress* including stress, anxiety, and social withdrawal

6. *Academic performance* as measured by reading and math test scores and grades

How Social-Emotional Learning Will Help You and Your Students

While social and emotional learning may seem like a new development to be studied and adopted, it isn't about adding one more program or strategy to your already crowded curriculum. Rather, it's a comprehensive approach to teaching and learning that spans all grade levels and all content areas—one that has a positive impact on students and therefore important implications for professional learning. Research shows the importance of infusing social and emotional learning into the daily work of schools (CASEL, 2015; Jones & Kahn, 2017).

Students are more successful in school and daily life when they

- Learn how to self-regulate and manage themselves

- Understand how to empathize with the feelings of others and are able to relate better to them

- Make positive and proactive choices about their personal and social decisions

These social and emotional skills are a few of the short-term student outcomes that SEL programs foster and develop (Durlak et al., 2011; Farrington et al., 2012; Sklad et al., 2012). The other long-term benefits also include the following:

- Decreased emotional anxiety and stress

- Improved assessment scores and grades and increased attendance

- More positive attitudes toward oneself and others, as well as improved outcomes including positive self-efficacy, more confidence, resiliency and persistence, empathy, connection, compassion for others, and commitment to school, as well as an increased sense of purpose

- More positive interactions and relationships with peers and adults
- Reduced behavior problems

These far-reaching implications of greater social and emotional competence can also increase the students' readiness for not only graduation from high school but also postsecondary education and career success, as well as fostering more positive family and work relationships and overall better mental health condition (Jones et al., 2015).

Common Misconceptions About Integrating Social-Emotional Learning Practices in the Classroom

There are numerous studies that demonstrate how SEL builds the foundation for flourishing and thriving in life—inside and outside the classroom. In fact, students with strong social-emotional skills tend to

1. Get along more positively with others

2. Have an increased ability to cope with stress and anxiety

3. Be more likely to complete high school

4. Have key social skills that help them be better prepared for college and careers

Despite the research and increased presence in schools, there are still misconceptions about SEL. The following sections contain some of the most common misconceptions about SEL and some reasons to refute them.

Does Social-Emotional Learning Interfere With the Role of Academic Learning? The instructional minutes that teachers have with students are critical. They need to maximize the impact of that time to help all students succeed. Jones et al. (2018) explain, "Children who are able to effectively manage their thinking, attention, and behavior are also more likely to have better grades and higher standardized test scores" (p. 15). Further research confirms this claim that time spent on SEL can facilitate academic learning (e.g., Durlak et al., 2011; Hawkins et al., 2004). Therefore, when students develop prosocial behaviors and self-regulation skills, they learn more (e.g., Duncan et al., 2007); and the converse is also true that students with unaddressed problematic behavior learn less than their peers (Wilson et al., 2001).

What About the Role of Parents/Families in Implementing Social-Emotional Learning? When schools and teachers integrate SEL practices in a transparent way, parents and families can monitor and be involved in these efforts and reinforce SEL values at home.

Does Social-Emotional Learning Integrate Well With Classroom Structures? There is no single way of thinking about SEL in schools, and this book provides you with multiple options to integrate the principles and practices into your daily routine. SEL practices are not intended to be rules to which students must conform—instead, they are classroom conditions in which students and teachers need to work together in a productive, positive, and collaborative way.

The SEL techniques presented in this book are efforts to help students grow and develop socially and emotionally and to facilitate the skills of teachers to help their students be productive members of society. There is no single "recipe" or formula for SEL techniques that will work in every classroom. Educators need to select strategies that are congruent and compatible with their own classroom environment.

What About Issues of Equity and Social-Emotional Learning? It is important to realize that social and emotional learning is about much more than developing kids who are nice to one another, are collaborative in class, and have a positive mindset. SEL is also an equity issue.

Equity is the practice of recognizing the unique qualities of every individual and dismantling systems and structures that prevent students of certain demographics from achieving to their highest potential. Equity is not the same as *equality*. As Rufo and Causton (2022) note, "Whereas equality assumes equal treatment, inherent in the principle of equity is that [educators] may need to support students differently for them to be successful in an educational system" (p. 87).

Today's schools are increasingly diverse, with multicultural and multilingual students, as well as students with different learning needs and social and economic backgrounds. Therefore, educators are tasked with serving students from different backgrounds with a wide variety of entry points for learning. This may include a variety in students' academic performance, motivation for engaging in learning, perception of positive behavior expectations, and/or understanding of the cultural "norms" of the classroom (note that that expectations for what is "positive" behavior and strong academic performance are shaped by cultural norms).

As a result of diverse student populations, various inequities have arisen, including an academic achievement gap between students of color and white students (Merola & Jackson, 2019; National Center for Educational Statistics, 2018a-c); trouble or difficulty accessing the curriculum due to English language proficiency or other language barriers (Haycock, 2014; Genesee et al., 2005); lack of access to the general curriculum and inclusive classrooms, especially for students with disabilities (Rufo & Causton, 2022; Dessemontet & Bless, 2013; Hehir et al., 2012); and systematic biases in expectations for minoritized student populations (Scott et al., 2017; Cherng. 2017; Carlana, 2019); among others.

SEL provides a foundation for safe, supportive, and positive learning with equitable opportunities so that students can succeed in school, careers, and life. SEL meets students where they are by helping students to better understand themselves and others, to feel respected and valued based on their individuality, and be provided opportunities to receive the unique supports they might require to access learning.

Implementing SEL practices in schools *requires* equitable learning environments, therefore, SEL instruction must include the "explicit goal of promoting educational equity" (CASEL, n.d.). While SEL practices cannot dismantle the inequities inherent in educational systems, CASEL (n.d.) states that:

"When SEL is leveraged to promote equity:

- SEL is relevant for all students in all schools and affirms diverse cultures and backgrounds.

- SEL is a strategy for systemic improvement, not just an intervention for at-risk students.

- SEL is a way to uplift student voice and promote agency and civic engagement.

- SEL supports adults to strengthen practices that promote equity.

- Schools must engage students, families, and communities as authentic partners in social and emotional development."

SEL and equity are also inherently intertwined with complex subjects such as trauma, racism, identity, biases, opportunity gaps for certain populations (e.g. based on race, socio-economic status, sexual orientation, gender, ability, etc.), and much more. Throughout the book you will find SEL practices that help young students understand equity through the framework of valuing every individual within the school community for their unique identities, interests, backgrounds, and knowledge. However, certain topics are outside of the scope of the foundational SEL practices presented in this book (for a deeper exploration of some these topics, see Rufo & Causton, 2022; Jagers, 2016; Alexander, 2019; CASEL, 2021; García & Weiss, 2017; Duane, et al. 2021; Linder, 2021; Lund et al., 2021; Walls, 2021; Simmons, 2019; Simmons, 2021; Green et al., 2019).

STRATEGIES FOR YOUR CLASSROOM: CAPTURE THOSE "TEACHABLE MOMENTS"

According to CASEL (2013), SEL is the process through which children and adults acquire and effectively apply the knowledge, attitudes, and skills necessary to understand and manage emotions, set and achieve positive goals, feel and show empathy for others, establish and maintain positive relationships, and make responsible decisions. As a teacher you can be part of this process by learning to notice "teachable moments" throughout daily classroom routines.

Teachable moments can occur when we least expect them. Because class time is so precious and passes too quickly, strategies that impact small moments in instruction have great potential for helping students form a learning community. Imagine that your class is faced with a challenge or dilemma. It may be a conflict between students or a classroom procedure that has been compromised.

Teachers should strive to build a sense of a caring community in their classrooms; it's important to recognize that strengthening relationships between students isn't a one-time event—it needs to be routinely integrated. First, teachers can instruct strategically and systemically. You do not need to adopt an entire SEL curriculum to get started: all you need is a positive disposition and a desire to make a difference! Each chapter in this book will present strategies that you can integrate into your classroom norms so that identifying teachable moments becomes second nature to your teaching style. There is nothing to it . . . but to do it!

Class Meetings

Class meetings build a sense of creating a classroom community, collaborative problem solving, and clarifying communication. Take class meetings as opportunities to reinforce how SEL principles can be used to help reach a solution. During the class meeting time, you can use several questions to help frame problem-solving responses:

1. What is the problem our class is having?

2. Why is this a challenge for our class?

3. How does the issue make you feel?

4. What can we do about it? Brainstorm solutions.

5. What is our best solution? Why?

Effective teachers know that classroom and school climates influence the content learning that happens within them. Teachers who are themselves skilled in SEL recognize those teachable moments when a student is being challenged to apply what they have been learning about themselves. Those same teachers are responsive and assist students in working through a challenge, thereby further strengthening relationships.

Integrate Social-Emotional Learning to Develop a Positive Class Culture

An integrated approach to SEL amplifies program effectiveness because students receive many opportunities to apply the principles to their lives in a natural way. The insights they gain about themselves and others provide them with a new lens through which to see the world. The time dedicated to infusing SEL in meaningful ways into the curriculum isn't time wasted—it is an investment in our students to maximize their capacity to learn with and from others.

In our classrooms and schools, there are many things we cannot control. We cannot change the kinds of homes or economic situations from which our students come, the trauma they may have faced in the past, or the challenges they will likely face in the future. However, we *can* control our own school and classroom environments, and we can use our time with students to teach them necessary **coping** strategies and skills that will help them achieve both academic and real-world success. This is the goal of SEL.

SEL, then, is the first step toward developing a positive school climate, which can often result in fewer behavior problems, stronger social-emotional health, and higher academic motivation and achievement, especially for our students who are more likely to struggle in school. See Figure 1.3 for a list of simple ways to integrate SEL throughout the day.

What do all learners want and need to perform well? Maslow (1943) affirmed that next to one's basic physiological needs of safety, food, water, and so forth, learners require physical and mental security and safety. Furthermore, Muhammad (2009) contends that "substantial cultural change must precede technical change. When a school has a healthy culture, the professionals within it will seek the tools that they need to accomplish their goal of universal student achievement; they will give a school new life" (p. 16).

It goes without saying that *all* learners want a supportive relationship with the people around them. All learners deserve to know the performance expectations. It is all about lesson *mastery*, not lesson *mystery*. Furthermore, all learners desire to know how they are progressing (**formative assessment**) and ways to improve (**feedback**). The way in which educators cultivate a culture of well-being and trust is pivotal to such profound learning and self-awareness.

SUMMARY

Increase your own learning in SEL. A warm, caring teacher does wonders for our students! By educating the heart through SEL, teachers can encourage the development of positive habits in children. This will make a huge difference in schools and communities!

Understanding SEL and how it helps to support all students is an important issue of equity, of which all teachers need to be aware. When educators understand the social and emotional learning contexts and needs of students, their ability to make the curriculum accessible to every student improves. This book will cover techniques on how to integrate SEL successfully throughout the curriculum to support student success.

Overview of This Book

Answers to the following questions will be covered in this book:

- What can we do to make sure all of our students feel safe and welcome in our schools?

- What can schools and communities do to create inspiring and challenging learning opportunities for all students that address social, emotional, and academic skills simultaneously? Examples will be shared to demonstrate SEL in action.

Simple Ways to Integrate Social-Emotional Learning Throughout the Day

- Start the day with a check-in.
- Use story time for teachable moments.
- Work in partnerships.
- Teach students how to work collaboratively in a group.
- Nurture a culture of kindness.
- Teach students new words to support a growth mindset.
- Set up a peaceful place in the classroom.
- Teach your kids how to manage conflict with peer mediation.
- Use positive posters to teach social-emotional skills.
- Practice lots of role play to act out emotions.
- Allow for plenty of talk time.
- Play games to build community.
- Use cross-age tutors: Buddy up with an older or younger class.
- Build community with teams.
- Teach students to monitor their own progress.
- Hold regular class meetings.
- Make space for reflective writing.
- Encourage expression through art.
- Include interview projects.
- Create classroom jobs.
- End each day with a checkout and community circle.

Figure 1.3. Simple ways to integrate social-emotional learning throughout the day.

- How can we support educators to model these skills and foster them in their students?

- What can we learn from the communities, districts, and schools that have prioritized this work?

- How can schools partner with families and community organizations, knowing that schools can't do this work alone?

As a former classroom teacher, special educator, reading specialist, ESL teacher, administrator, instructional coach, and consultant, I have worked with thousands of students and teachers over the years, around the planet. I have worked across the general and special educational curriculum in elementary, middle, and high schools, and in nearly every configuration of schooling. Based on these experiences, and on my review of the research, I have concluded that because teachers dramatically influence students' social and emotional development, they have a responsibility to do so in a way that is positive and purposeful.

One idea that is a primary focus of this book is that classroom learning should always include cognitive, social, and emotional aspects. In this book, I offer real-life classroom examples, tools, and practical strategies that you can use to intentionally guide students' social and emotional development. It is essential to integrate SEL into the academic mainstream of learning.

I appeal to teachers and school leaders to consciously support the growth of every child, not just academically but also socially and emotionally. Together with their families and community, you can equip your students to realize their aspirations and contribute in positive ways to our society. What could be more meaningful and worthwhile? Give your students a voice and choice. Finding ways to design learning experiences that tap into what students value is at the very heart of learning.

Recapture the *joy* of learning—inspire to go higher!

CHAPTER 2

Social-Emotional Learning and the Self

Emotional Intelligence

It is critical that students learn to identify and express their feelings in a positive way to develop the skills they need to manage them effectively. As adults, we know this from our own personal experience. However, our students need tools to help them to become aware of their emotions and how to deal with them. Developing *emotional intelligence* in your students will help them understand and express their feelings and be ready to attend to the learning tasks.

KEY CONCEPTS

- What is emotional intelligence?
- Why is it important to share feelings?
- How do students identify emotions in themselves and others?
- What are some ways to teach and develop skills of self- and social awareness?
- How do teachers foster self-expression and recognizing strengths?
- Ways to celebrate positive emotions and self-confidence

INTRODUCTION

Expressing emotions isn't always easy. Most students keep emotions to themselves and don't share them with others. Being able to express their feelings will help your students to handle emotional triggers. For instance, a student who can say, "I'm mad at you" is less likely to act out aggressively. Similarly, a student who can say, "That hurts my feelings" is better equipped to resolve conflict peacefully. When children can identify their own feelings and the feelings of others as well as begin to understand experiences outside their own immediate reality, they can relate to others at a deeper level.

To support students in this way, educators must ask themselves a series of questions: What are some engaging techniques to teach **emotional intelligence** to kids? In so doing, how can we help them develop self-awareness and empathy? How can we help them relate better to others? This chapter explores these issues and gives you tools to use to help students get in touch with their feelings and express them in meaningful ways.

What Is Emotional Intelligence?

Emotional intelligence can be concisely defined as the ability to manage one's feelings and interact positively with other people. This is of paramount importance in the classroom because classrooms are inherently emotional settings.

Schools need to develop a culture in which teachers and students talk freely about their feelings. To have a caring conversation about emotions, it's important to recognize the feelings students have—in other words, students must be able to name the emotions they're feeling. Therefore, we need to focus on ways to teach students to identify different feelings.

What Does the Research Say?

As children grow, they're learning various emotional intelligence skills at different rates—there's no single pathway to summarize how emotional intelligence should look in children of different ages. However, there are a few findings that researchers apply to child development in general and, more specifically, have implications for how children make friends and exhibit impulse control.

These include, but aren't limited to, the following:

- Developing emotional awareness—first of their own feelings, then understanding the emotions in others

- Recognizing, identifying, or perceiving emotions—as well as understanding what feelings are, they'll learn to perceive what certain facial expressions mean, how to interpret body language, tone of voice, and so forth. They can generalize these and eventually label them as happy, angry, sad

- Describing feelings—as well as being able to name emotions, they'll learn how to use certain emotional vocabulary words to share how they feel

- Empathizing with others' feelings—related to their own expression of feelings, this will extend to feeling concern when others aren't feeling well or feeling sympathy for animals

- Controlling and managing their emotions—learning about when it's suitable to act or react when they feel something and how to express themselves appropriately

- Understanding what causes feelings—both in themselves and in others

- Understanding emotion–behavior linkages—how emotional reactions are triggered by certain events, for example, "My brother kicked the wall because he's mad" (Denham, 1998; Saarni, 1999)

In addition, Peter Salovey, one of the early pioneers in studying emotional intelligence, along with fellow Yale researcher John Mayer established a more formal theory of emotional intelligence in 1990. They coined the term *emotional intelligence* and described it as "the ability to recognize, understand, utilize, and regulate emotions effectively in everyday life" (Salovey & Mayer, 1990, p. 186).

According to Salovey and Mayer (1990), there are four distinct dimensions or "branches" of emotional intelligence that form a hierarchy of emotional skills and abilities:

1. Perceiving emotion

2. Using emotions to facilitate thought

3. Understanding emotions

4. Managing emotions

The first dimension, perceiving emotion, relates to being aware of and recognizing others' physical and/or psychological states (like being in physical pain or feeling anxious), identifying emotions/feelings in others, and being able to express one's own feelings/emotions and needs.

Using emotions to facilitate thought involves redirecting your thinking based on the feelings associated with those thoughts, which will facilitate better judgment so you can appreciate different points of view, and then using emotional states to improve your own problem-solving skills and creativity.

Understanding emotions includes understanding the relationships among various emotions and/or feelings and understanding the causes and consequences of emotions. For many children, this takes some time to develop.

The final dimension, managing emotions, refers to being open to both positive and negative feelings, being able to monitor and reflect on your own emotions, and managing those emotions (Emmerling et al., 2008; Salovey & Mayer, 1990). See Figure 2.1 to get a better idea of these facets of emotional intelligence and how they are integrated.

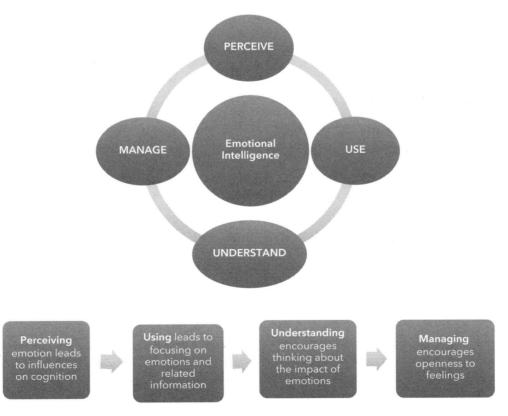

Figure 2.1. Emotional intelligence. (From Salovey, & Mayer. [1990.] Emotional intelligence. *Imagination, Cognition, and Personality* 9[3], 185–211; reprinted by permission.)

Other researchers and psychologists soon began to explore this concept of emotional intelligence. Daniel Goleman, a noted psychologist, published the national best-selling book *Emotional Intelligence* in 1995, which helped introduce the concept of emotional intelligence into the mainstream of public thought.

Goleman saw emotional intelligence as an important factor for success, especially for children. He proposed that promoting "social and emotional learning" in children to boost their emotional intelligence would not only improve their learning abilities but also help them succeed in school and in their future careers by reducing some of the more distracting and harmful behavioral and emotional problems, such as anger outbursts, defiant behavior, and sassy and disrespectful reactions to situations (Goleman, 1998).

According to Daniel Goleman, there are five components or elements of emotional intelligence:

1. Self-Awareness

2. Self-Regulation

3. Motivation

4. Empathy

5. Social Skills

These studies answered some important questions about emotional intelligence and also opened the door for subsequent, more in-depth studies. The results of all this research showed us that emotional intelligence is, indeed, a vital factor in a student's success and that emotional intelligence is also a vital factor in how they relate to one another and, in general, their mental health. The best news from all of these studies is that we can actually improve our own emotional intelligence and support our students in doing the same. Thus, it is not necessarily a fixed trait but something that we can build and boost with practice and specific strategies for success.

STRATEGIES FOR YOUR CLASSROOM

The Importance of Sharing Feelings

Discussion Questions and Prompts: *Note: Feel free to revise the following questions and prompts in language appropriate for sharing with the age of your students:*

1. Let's name as many feelings as we can.

2. Share feelings that you like and feelings that you don't like.

3. What do you do when you feel happy? What do you do when you feel sad?

4. What helps you feel better when you're feeling sad about something? How about feeling angry?

Benefits of Journal Writing

Students need to be given ample opportunities throughout the day to write. Writing is an excellent way for them to freely express their feelings and emotions. See Appendix A (also available online) of this book for additional ideas and strategies that will provide your children with daily practice in responding to journal prompts.

Other Activities to Help Students Share Their Feelings

Sharing one's feelings is essential in building emotional intelligence in students. The following activities will provide your students with the tools they need to effectively share their feelings.

Morning Meetings   It is important to set the tone for the day with a connection to mood and feelings. This process really helps to develop a student's self-awareness. Figures 2.2, 2.3, and 2.4 include prompts that can be used during morning meetings to boost a child's speaking and listening skills as well as developing writing skills if used as a writing prompt.

"Feelin' Good" Journal
Objectives   Students will
- Identify positive feelings

- List things that make them feel good

- Create a class book illustrating things that make them feel good

Materials
- Chart paper and markers or whiteboard

- Paper to draw and write on

- Pencils, crayons, markers

Class Time   20–30 minutes

Activity   There are many kinds of good feelings: You can feel happy, funny, silly, safe, relaxed, proud, or excited. What other types of feelings would you consider to be "good" feelings? What makes you feel good? Sometimes special events can make you feel good, like a vacation or birthday party. Little everyday things can make you feel good, too, like playing a game at recess, hanging out with your friends, being with your pet, or when someone shares toys and games with you. Let's make a list of things that make us feel good.

Then, we'll all have a chance to write these down and even make a class "Feelin' Good" Journal. Let's get started: draw a picture of something that makes you feel good, then describe your picture.

Note: younger students can dictate a sentence for the teacher to write under their pictures.

Face the Feelings
Objectives
- Students will identify and define these feelings in their own words: mad, embarrassed, concerned (worried), excited, surprised, sad.

- Identify and discuss how they'd feel if they were involved in a variety of scenarios provided by the teacher.

- Demonstrate the ability to listen to and appreciate classmates' opinions and feelings.

Materials
- "Face the Feeling" handout (see Appendix A of this book, which is also available online)

- Index cards (with each student's name)

Questions to Ask Kids

- Are you a good friend? Why do you think so?
- What does it mean to be a good friend?
- What is one thing you want to learn this year?
- What makes you special?
- Who is your hero?
- If you could have any superpower, what would you choose?
- What is something that makes your family special?
- What are you looking forward to this week?
- How would the world be different if animals could talk?
- What do you do to feel better when you're sad?
- If you could grow up to be famous, what would you want to be famous for?
- What is your favorite number and why?
- If you could be invisible for a day, what would you do?
- What is the best gift you have ever received? Why was it so special?
- What is your biggest dream?
- What accomplishment are you most proud of?
- If you were a teacher, and the kids in your class would not listen to you, what would you do?
- What is one thing you like to do every day?
- Where is your favorite place in the world?
- How do you show someone you care?
- What three words do you think best describe you?
- What could you do to make someone smile today?
- Describe your perfect day.
- When was a time that you felt lucky?
- What do you see when you look up at the sky?
- Where do you travel in your dreams?

- What are two of your least favorite things to do and why?
- What makes you feel loved?
- What do you want to learn this week?
- What do you like about your classmates?
- What can you learn from your mistakes today?
- What makes you feel proud of yourself?
- If you could be any animal for a day, what would you be? Why?
- What is something that you are confused about?
- What is the coolest place you ever visited?
- Name something that makes you laugh.
- What is something that scares you?
- What is something you wish others knew about you?
- What is your favorite thing to do when you have free time?
- How would you change the world?
- What is your happiest memory so far?
- If you could change one rule your family has, what would it be?
- What is your favorite thing about school?
- If you could give a gift to a friend, what would you give them? Why?
- What is something funny that has happened to you?
- What is your favorite thing to play outside?
- Name something you learned last year in school. Why was that important to you?
- What is the weirdest thing you've ever seen?
- If you could meet someone famous, who would it be?
- What is your favorite book? Why?
- What would you do if you had a million dollars?

Figure 2.2. Questions to ask kids.

Getting to Know You . . .

What are three of your greatest strengths?
1. _____
2. _____
3. _____

What are two things that seem hard for you?
1. _____
2. _____

How do you learn best? _____
_____

When do you feel most successful? _____
_____
_____

What are three of your favorite things to do?
1. _____
2. _____
3. _____

What are two of your *least* favorite things to do?
1. _____
2. _____

Think of three recent successes that you had.
What made them successful?
1. _____
2. _____
3. _____

List two things you recently did that were *not* successful, and you wish you could "do over."
1. _____
2. _____

What would you have done differently? _____
_____

When things get hard what do you do? _____
_____

Who do you turn to for help? Why? _____
_____

Do you think struggling with things makes you stronger?   Yes _____   No _____

If yes, in what ways do learning and making mistakes make you stronger? _____
_____

Figure 2.3.   Getting to know you worksheet.

Tell Me About Yourself . . .

What makes you special?

_____

_____

_____

What do you struggle with?

_____

_____

_____

What is your favorite thing about school?

_____

_____

_____

What would you like some help with?

_____

_____

_____

How do you learn best?

_____

_____

_____

Figure 2.4.   Tell me about yourself worksheet.

Class Time
- 30–45 minutes

Activity   Look at these faces. What feeling do you think each of these faces is showing? They are angry, embarrassed, concerned (worried), excited, surprised, and sad. Have you ever felt any of these feelings before? When? Why? Today, I'm going to share some short stories with you and you're going to think about how you'd feel if you were in each story. After you decide how you'd feel, come up to the board and tape your name card under the face that shows how you'd feel. After reading each story, ask yourself these questions: Why would I feel this way? Why do I think it's okay for other people to feel different than me?

Face the Feelings Variations   Students can make up other stories and share them with the class, or work in small groups and role-play each of the stories.

Feeling cards—activities for younger children:

- Have the children choose a card from a stack and ask them to guess what happened to this person to cause that particular emotion. (You can use the "Face the Feelings" images found in Appendix A of this book.)

- Choose a card, name the emotion, and discuss what you could do if someone around you was feeling this way.

- Set out several stuffed animals or dolls and put one of the feeling cards next to each one; ask the children to speak to the "stuffies" as if they were feeling those emotions. When children can identify their own feelings and the feelings of others and begin to understand what the feelings are like to experience outside their own immediate reality, they can relate to others at a deeper level.

Activities for older children:

- Have students work with a partner and ask them to pick a card they will "act out."

- Ask your child to select a card and tell a story about a time they saw someone else exhibiting the emotion displayed, how they felt, what they did (or what they could have done).

Situations/Stories to React To   Role-play is a great way to teach kids about interpersonal skills and self-awareness, self-expression, and more. In addition, role-play allows students time to practice, apply, and fine-tune their emotional intelligence with others. As they dramatize the scenarios, they will be able to draw upon their own empathetic vocabulary. It will also help them learn different ways to show empathy in real life.

Situation 1   You're at a carnival standing in line to go on your favorite ride that goes really fast and high. How do you feel?

Situation 2   The bell rings for recess! You're planning to play on the swings, but when you get to the playground, all the swings are being used already. How do you feel?

Situation 3   You and your friends are playing checkers. You are winning. Suddenly, your dog runs through the room and on top of your checkerboard. Checkers go flying everywhere and you lose your spot on the board. How do you feel?

Situation 4   You're at Disneyland and waiting in line to get a photo and autograph with your favorite character, Mickey Mouse. How do you feel?

Situation 5   Your friend invited you to play at her house on Saturday. But that morning, your friend's mom calls and says that your friend is sick and so you can't play anymore. How do you feel?

Situation 6   School is over. You are waiting at the curb to get picked up. Other parents have already picked up all your classmates, but your dad isn't here yet. They are late. How do you feel?

Situation 7   Your parents are going to go out to the movies and dinner, and a neighbor is coming to be with you while your parents are gone. How do you feel?

Situation 8   You painted a really pretty picture in art class and the teacher puts it up on the bulletin board after showing it to the class. How do you feel?

Simon Says   This simple and easy game is a favorite with the young children. It is a fun way to teach them about how to express their emotions. Give them a heads-up that they need to be extra good listeners to advance in this game. The game can have several rounds. During Round One get them ready by matching your verbal instructions with visual cues (use facial expressions, gestures, picture cues, etc.). For each round, students need to match your instructions but only when you say, "Simon says."

Because this version of the game is to help kids learn to express their emotions, start with them displaying a range of emotions. Start by telling the children what emotions to express by modeling the behavior yourself. The following is an example:

Round One:

- "Simon says: Do a mad face." (Squint your eyes, pout, and stick out your bottom lip.)

- "Simon says: Do a happy face." (Eyes light up, big grin.)

- "Simon says: Stand up tall and proud and be confident."

- "Simon says: Touch your toes." (Try to trick them and touch your nose instead.)

Round Two: During this round only give them occasional visual cues, depending more on verbal directions.

- "Simon says: Your feelings are hurt."

- "Simon says: You are confused and don't know which way to go." (Scratch your head, look both ways, and hesitate before moving.)

- "Simon says: you're excited and wide awake!" (Surprise them and look drowsy and bewildered and yawn to trick them.)

Rounds Three, Four, Five, and more: Gradually decrease the visual cues and modeling and continue to try and trick them by occasionally giving them one instruction but doing something totally different instead.

Ask the kids to express various emotions, such as

- Surprise

- Worry

- Joy

- Fright

- Amusement

- Impatience

Each of these instructions encourages the kids to express different thoughts, feelings, and emotions in a risk-free and fun way. By expressing this range of emotional states, they can learn to develop emotional awareness and empathy.

Feelings Balloons

Objective   Students will identify feelings and relieve stress through tactile learning.

Materials (see Figure 2.5).
- Assorted colored balloons

- Permanent black marker

- Homemade playdough (recipe below)

    Playdough ingredients:

1. 2 cups all-purpose flour

2. 3/4 cup salt

3. 4 teaspoons cream of tartar

4. 2 cups lukewarm water

5. 2 tablespoons of vegetable oil (coconut oil works too)

6. Food coloring, optional

7. Quart-size bags

    - Make playdough recipe and stuff assorted balloons with mixture

    - On outside of balloons, draw a face on each that depicts various emotions

Figure 2.5. Feelings balloons.

Class Time   15–20 minutes

Activity   There are many kinds of feelings. What feelings do you see on the faces of these "stress ball balloons"?

Gently toss the balloons out to the students. As they catch them, have them do a shout-out of the feeling expressed on the balloon.

Plastic Egg Faces   Acquire a variety of colored, plastic Easter eggs. Put a variety of different eye expressions on the top half of the plastic eggs. On the bottom half, draw various expressions of the mouth with a fine-lined, permanent black marker. The children will have fun interchanging the tops and bottoms to make all sorts of different faces and emotional expressions. Have them talk about the feelings and what might have happened to cause that facial expression.

Puppets and Feelings   Use simple sock puppets to act out different situations, for example, one puppet takes a toy from another puppet; ask the children what emotion(s) the puppets might be feeling (have them choose from pictures of children showing different emotions). After labeling the emotions, have children practice making the emotion with their own faces. Then ask what the puppet should do next to help when feeling that emotion. Have the puppet model coping with the emotion. Then have the children role-play their own reaction.

Have each child make a hand puppet. Then you can ask them to use the puppets to convey their feelings during a role-play activity. Examples could include brother and sister cleaning up their room (taking responsibility); or one puppet is playing on the swing and pushes the other puppet away (not sharing). After the role-play activities, have each puppet talk about what it was like not to share or not to listen to the other. What happened?

Feeling Cubes   Children learn about their feelings by acting them out. Get a small tissue box. Paste pictures of feeling faces on each side of the box. The students take turns turning the box and whatever feeling face shows up on top is the one they must act out.

Feeling With Your Feet   Play an emotion walking game while outside. Sound a chime and have students walk around the playground like they are angry. Ring the bell again and have the children walk like they are happy. Repeat the activity until you have practiced several emotions. See Figure 2.6.

Sing It With Feeling!   Sing an "emotion hello song" to start the day. Start with singing the following in a lively, responsive and rhythmic way: "Hello, Hello, Hello and, how are you? I'm glad, I'm glad, and I hope you are too." Ask the students to share other ways they could feel and/or show them pictures of feeling faces to choose from. Sing the song with that emotion in your expressions, voice, and actions.

"If You're Happy and Know It" . . . Remixed!   Sing the classic song "If You're Happy and You Know It" using new verses substituting other emotions and feelings: mad, sad, excited, scared, and so forth. Include the actions you might do when you are feeling each emotion. For example, "If you're mad and you know it, give a growl." Have children share different ideas and moves. Here are some suggestions to get them started:

- "If you're sleepy and you know it, close your eyes."

- "If you're surprised and you know it, say, "'Oh my.'"

A Rainbow of Feelings . . .

A colorful rainbow helps make a beautiful world. Using your favorite colors, write things that bring you joy on the bands of the rainbow. Here are some ideas to get you started:

- Singing
- Family

- Learning
- Reading

- Friends
- Love

- Kindness
- Eating

- Playing

- Sunshine

Figure 2.6. Rainbow of feelings worksheet.

- "If you're angry and you know it, stomp your feet."

- "If you're scared and you know it, shiver and tremble."

- "If you're sad and you know it, say 'waaa-waaa.'"

It might be helpful to have pictures showing each emotion and use them as visual cues.

The Wonder of Words: Teaching Feeling Words   Depending on the age of your students, expand their "emotional vocabulary" by teaching more robust feeling words. Your students should learn to express and act out these words and be able to identify situations in which they might experience them:

- Peaceful

- Cheerful

- Confused

- Disappointed

- Brave

- Curious

- Overwhelmed

- Tense

- Satisfied

- Stubborn

- Frustrated

- Awkward

- Surprised

- Fantastic

- Generous

- Embarrassed

- Generous

- Relieved

- Uncomfortable

- Proud

- Bored

- Impatient

- Jealous

- Envious

- Ignored

Which Emotion Am I?   Once children understand emotional vocabulary and "feeling words," try this acting game.

Objectives
- Help students react to one another's emotions better.

- Teach kids to distinguish emotions through facial expressions.

Materials   Print the emotions that you want to use on index cards. You will also need a large rubber band or elastic band that the kids can use to keep the feeling card attached to their heads.

Class Time   20–30 minutes

Activity   Shuffle the feeling cards and place them in the center of the group. Ask each child to choose a card and place it in their headband without looking at it. The goal is for everyone to see the feeling card except for the child wearing it. The game proceeds in a clockwise fashion around the circle.

When it is a player's turn, they ask one "yes" or "no" question at a time to the others, without using emotion names directly. For instance, "Would I feel this way if I fell on the playground?" or "Would I feel like this at my birthday party?" The other students respond with a "yes" or "no" answer.

Once a child thinks they are ready to guess the emotion on their secret card, they share their response. The game continues until all the emotions have been guessed.

Mirror, Mirror, on the Wall . . .   Duplicate Figure 2.7 for each student. Have them pretend that they are looking into a different mirror for each of the prompts, and they are to do a quick sketch in the mirror that reflects the emotion they are feeling to the following:

- You are at the beach.

- Your friend is sick and can't play with you.

- You are eating an ice cream cone.

- You are playing with your pet or a favorite toy.

Teaching Self-Awareness and Relationship Skills

Design instructional conversations and collaborative activities that allow students to share ideas, discuss their thinking, share their feelings, and problem solve together. For example, a teacher might pose a problem to the class, have students discuss and problem solve in mixed-ability groups, and then reconvene the class to share common themes among the groups' ideas so that all voices are heard and students help one another build social competence.

Community-Building Questions   There are many ways to use questions to help develop social-awareness and relationship skills. Some examples include the following:

- You could use one or more of the prompts in Figure 2.8 in your morning meeting or community circle time.

Mirror, Mirror, on the Wall . . .

Reflections on Feelings

Everyone has feelings.
Sometimes you are happy, sad, or mad.
Look into the mirrors.
Draw your face showing how you feel when . . .

You are at the park.

Your friend is sick and can't play.

You are eating ice cream.

You are playing with your pet.

Figure 2.7.   Mirror, mirror on the wall worksheet.

Classroom Curiosity Questions

Answer these questions and don't forget to share why.

1. What is your favorite hobby?
2. What is your favorite food to eat?
3. If you could be any animal, what would you be?
4. What is your favorite flavor of ice cream?
5. What food do you dislike the most?
6. If you could have any pet, what would it be?
7. If you could change one thing about yourself, what would it be?
8. What is your favorite game to play?
9. What is your favorite type of candy?
10. What do you want to be when you grow up?
11. What is your favorite thing about school?
12. What is something that you are most proud of?
13. What is your favorite television show?
14. What is your favorite color?
15. If you could live anywhere in the world, where would you live?
16. What is your dream job?
17. What is your favorite movie?
18. What are you most afraid of?
19. What is your greatest success?
20. What is your favorite book?
21. If you could change your name, what would you like to be called?
22. What are you most thankful for?
23. What is your favorite thing to do at recess?
24. What do you like to do on a rainy, stormy day?
25. What is your favorite fairytale?
26. What is an adventure you took with your family or friends? What happened?
27. What superpower would you like to have?
28. Who is your hero?
29. What do you like best about yourself?
30. If you had three wishes, what would they be?
31. What do you like to do with your family?
32. How can you be a good friend today?
33. What makes you unique?
34. Where do you travel in your dreams?
35. What makes you feel loved?
36. How will you grow to be a better person this week?
37. When was a time that you felt lucky?
38. If you were a flower or tree, what kind would you be?
39. If you could be someone else for a day, who would you be?
40. What is your favorite season of the year?
41. What is something that made you really happy recently?
42. What are you looking forward to this year?
43. What is something you did recently for the first time?
44. What is something you have never done, but would like to try?
45. Imagine yourself ten years from today. What are you doing?
46. Pick a word to describe your future. What would it be?
47. If you could be someone else for a day, who would you be?
48. What are you excited about today?
49. If you could meet someone from any period in time, who would it be?
50. What makes a good friend?
51. What is something that your friends like about you?
52. What is your favorite thing to do on weekends?
53. What do you do to calm yourself down?

Figure 2.8. Classroom curiosity questions.

- The questions in Figure 2.8 are numbered and students could randomly pick a number and answer that question.

- Try doing an inside-outside rotating circle where students rotate and share with numerous partners around the circle.

- Think-pair-share

- Writing responses

The questions in Figure 2.8 can also be used to help establish classroom routines, students' speaking and listening skills, and also to practice expectations and taking turns. The possibilities are endless. Feel free to add your own questions that are pertinent to the unique needs of your students.

Good Things   This is a quick and easy activity for children of all ages; consider using it during your morning meeting because it gets your day started in a positive way. Ask each student to turn to a partner and share with them "something good." Here are some sample sentence stems to use:

- One good thing in my life is . . .

- Something good that happened is . . .

- One good thing I am looking forward to is . . .

After they have shared with a partner, ask for volunteers to share with the class.

Stepping Up to Learning   Using the staircase Figure 2.9 as a template, have students jot down a skill they would like to develop on each step (e.g., "be a better speller," "do more math problems on my own").

SUMMARY

How can our students make better choices if they don't have the skills to express themselves when things are not going well for them? How can we as educators be even more proactive? When working on students' self-confidence, and self-expression, it is important that you, the teacher, do a few things to help your students along. Follow these tips:

- Offer praise and acknowledgment for students' accomplishments. If you are going to provide constructive criticism, then make sure that you always start and end with positive feedback.

- Set attainable goals for the student. Make sure that the goals are believable and doable.

- Create opportunities for students to succeed by building on their strengths. For example, if a student knows a lot about their favorite hobby, then ask them to tell you about it.

- Give students the opportunity to choose what they learn. By doing so, it will help them build their own self-worth. Try using a learning menu or choice board, where students get to choose which activities they want to learn about.

- Always express a positive attitude to all of your students, not just those who lack confidence. This will show them that you are on their side and that they are worth your attention.

Stepping Up to Learning . . .

What are some things that interest you that you would like to do better? On each step write a skill that you would like to develop. Trying new skills and learning new things will make us feel good about ourselves as we try to get better. The first step, "math," is an example.

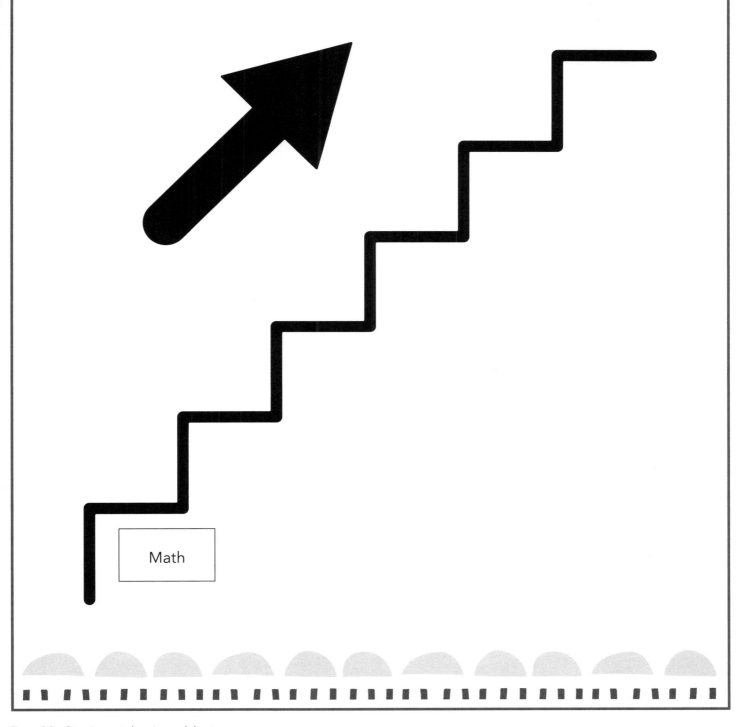

Figure 2.9. Stepping up to learning worksheet.

Being able to express their feelings will help your students be able to handle emotional triggers. Kids experience complex feelings just like adults do. They get frustrated, anxious, excited, sad, angry, worried, and joyful. However, children need support to develop their vocabulary so that they can more effectively share how they are feeling. Giving kids the opportunity to develop their emotions, empathy, and social skills is one of the best ways to prepare them for life ahead. It helps them find their own best ways of coping and leads to positive attitudes and behaviors later in life.

CHAPTER 3

Self-Regulation

Helping Your Students
Understand Their Emotions

Billy, a third-grade student, was doing well in all of his subjects—all, that is, except math. His teacher, Ms. Potter, was confused about why Billy was struggling in this subject when he excelled during reading and science instruction. When it came time for math instruction, however, Billy seemed to turn into a completely different student. He would become agitated and fidget in his seat; he would also often ignore Ms. Potter if she asked him a question or occasionally show signs of aggression toward his classmates during group-oriented math instruction.

To see if they could improve Billy's understanding of the math concepts and ensure he stayed on track with age-appropriate curriculum, Ms. Potter and the classroom aide decided to provide Billy with extra learning support during recess. Within a few weeks, Billy's understanding of the concepts had increased exponentially. He was performing better on assignments and was more focused and attentive during instruction when the rest of the class came in from recess.

Feeling as if the extra time was all Billy needed to get caught up, Ms. Potter told Billy that he could come in once a week for additional instruction. But as soon as Billy returned to his usual routine, Ms. Potter noticed that the behaviors returned, and Billy started to fall behind again. However, Ms. Potter soon realized a pattern in this behavior: on days where he would come in during recess for extra instruction, Billy would do well during full-class math instruction. On days when he was coming in with his peers from recess, he would be more agitated and less likely to engage in learning.

Having learned about dysregulation and how it affects students' learning, Ms. Potter determined that the reason Billy was struggling in math was because that instruction time came right after recess. Billy was very active and loved playing sports. When recess ended, he didn't want to go back to class and wanted instead to keep playing. Billy was dysregulated—he wasn't able to settle his body and his thoughts after recess, so he could not focus on the math lesson. To help Billy, and all her students, transition from recess to math instruction, Ms. Potter began implementing calming practices like stretching, deep breathing, and journaling to help students regulate their emotions from the excitement of recess and prepare themselves for learning. Billy quickly accommodated to this routine and his understanding of the math curriculum improved.

KEY CONCEPTS

- How do you connect emotions, behavior, and attention to learning?

- How do you create a caring learning community within the classroom?

- What are some coping skills to manage emotions and build resilience in students?

- What are some strategies to use to support the development of self-regulation skills in students?

- Why do you need to look at the "what" versus the "how" of learning?

- What are some ways of using children's literature to teach about emotions?

- What are some ways to help students understand their emotions in a deeper and more meaningful way?

INTRODUCTION

As adults, we have learned to manage our feelings throughout the day. Whether it's by taking a walk or stepping away from work for some deep breaths, there are many techniques adults use to overcome emotional distress and return to work. However, many children don't have these coping skills. That management, known as **emotional self-regulation,** takes place deep inside the emotional center of our brain. When we manage our emotions, we can go smoothly from one event to another, managing the different emotions that arise throughout the transitions and obstacles we may face.

However, if we do not have coping skills, and we have difficulty managing our emotions, each new event or activity can bring seemingly impossible difficulties and challenges. For students, this makes relationships and friendships challenging and can impede learning. Simply put: emotions drive behavior, behavior drives attention, and attention drives learning. Therefore, teachers need to first understand *emotional regulation* so they can then provide students with the strategies and tools they need to realize that they're in control of their feelings and the resulting actions.

What Is Self-Regulation?

Self-regulation can be defined as the ability to regulate feelings and actions in a socially appropriate manner. More specifically, **self-regulation** "refers to the self-directive process through which learners transform their mental abilities into task related skills" (Schunk & Zimmerman, 2012). This is the method or procedure that learners use to manage and organize their thoughts and convert them into skills used for learning. In a classroom setting, this includes students' ability to control their emotions, stay focused, and be able to adjust to change. Therefore, it is so important for teachers to be patient because the students who often have the most difficulty managing their behavior may have gaps in their knowledge and struggle academically. For instance, when students may appear to be off task or daydreaming or refuse to complete their work, there may be an underlying reason unrelated to the student's ability to do or understand the work.

Teaching Emotional Regulation

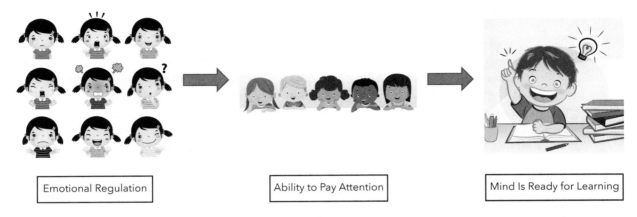

| Emotional Regulation | Ability to Pay Attention | Mind Is Ready for Learning |

Why Is Self-Regulation Important?

Self-regulation is a critical part of childhood development, and successful self-regulation can result in

- Improved self-esteem

- Increased learning

- Improved self-control

- Increased positive relationships

- Increased engagement

- Improved self-direction

Self-regulation is important, therefore, because it allows children to do better in school and relate with friends and family at home. It also helps children feel better about themselves and about what they can handle.

As a teacher, it is so important to be patient because the students who often have the most difficulty managing their behavior may also be facing personal struggles or have gaps in their academic knowledge.

What Does the Research Say?

Self-regulation is an essential aspect of the SEL curriculum. Teachers need to provide opportunities to model when and how to practice managing emotions and behaviors. Teachers need to set up their classrooms to provide specific procedures and routines that provide the important structure and learning tools necessary to help model and teach self-regulation throughout the grades. The ability for children to self-regulate needs to begin in the early years and continue to be reinforced (Shanker, 2009). In infancy, the brain is primed to create connections that support the beginnings of self-regulation. Across early childhood, brain-based capacity for self-regulation increases rapidly. Learning to self-regulate is a key milestone in child development; these foundations are laid in the earliest years of life. School-age children need to be taught about controlling their own wants and needs, imagining other people's perspectives, and seeing both sides of a situation. This means, for example, that they might be able to disagree with other children without having an argument. Teachers can set up their classroom to provide the structure and learning tools needed to help model and teach self-regulation with their students (Parrish, 2018).

In addition, it was previously thought that a child's adaptability to school was determined by their intelligence (IQ) and could not be altered, but recent research has identified effective self-regulation as the key for better school performance (Blair & Diamond, 2008; Shanker, 2009; Shonkoff & Phillips, 2000). These studies demonstrate the important role of self-regulation in both brain development and fostering effective relationships with others. It is also a significant factor for a student's sense of well-being and contributes to developing sustained attention that results in deep learning because a student who is self-regulated can sit and listen in the classroom as well as manage stress and be able to cope with strong feelings and calm themselves down (Laevers, 2000).

Furthermore, there have been other studies that focus on self-control, with evidence now showing that a child's ability to regulate their emotions is critical to their ability to develop and use the skills that underpin self-control (Casenhiser et al., 2012). This is significant because it is likely to affect the way a teacher thinks a child might behave or react in a particular situation in the classroom.

Self-regulation in school involves the ability to express feelings and to communicate with others effectively: self-regulation is the mastery of thinking. Therefore, language development is an important process in the development of self-regulatory skills (Cheyney et al., 2013). Explicit instruction in oral communication skills supports children in developing friendships and problem-solving skills and cultivates the ability to cope and the stamina to complete tasks (Mustard & Rowcliffe, 2009).

Children who are self-regulated are ready to learn. They are focused, able to regulate emotions, maintain impulse control, assess the consequences of a situation, understand what others are feeling, understand how their behaviors affect others, and feel empathetic toward others (Shanker, 2013). Using this body of research, this chapter will address strategies to teach self-regulation, stress reduction, and develop an inclusive, caring classroom.

Using Stories to Communicate Feelings

"Teachers are expected to deliver an academic curriculum in addition to meeting the social and emotional needs of their students" (de La Riva & Ryan, 2015, p. 71).

Teachers have the responsibility to educate the *whole child*, academically as well as socially and emotionally. When students can regulate their emotions and behaviors and communicate when they need support with regulating their emotions, they are more successful in school and life (Shanker, 2013).

Children typically learn how to communicate effectively through social stories they hear from parents and teachers. Another important aspect of high-quality instruction that promotes the development of self-regulation involves the process of incorporating books to teach social norms and explore feelings and emotions. Teacher read-alouds of quality children's literature have been found to increase students' overall language ability (de La Riva & Ryan, 2015).

Teachers and parents need to use clear and consistent communication with children for emotional well-being to be sustained. De La Riva and Ryan (2015) suggest using visual cues as reminders, setting clear expectations, and having everything at eye level in the classroom. Students who struggle with self-regulation need positive and consistent visual reminders to help them communicate information clearly and concisely.

As educators, we don't hesitate to teach our students the reading or math skills they need to be successful, and emotional and behavioral skills should be no different. Students with adverse childhood experiences (ACEs) may come to school with very little experience controlling impulses and regulating emotions. They also may have difficulty paying attention; these executive function skills affect our students' need to be academically, socially, and emotionally successful. Executive function skills are addressed in detail in Chapter 4.

STRATEGIES FOR YOUR CLASSROOM

This section provides many practical tools and strategies that can be shared with your students to incorporate self-regulation in the classroom. These strategies provide a foundation for well-being and involved learning. Keep in mind that working on self-regulation skills doesn't just happen overnight. Especially for those students who struggle with them, these abilities must be worked on and improved over time. The good news is that kids and young adults can learn techniques and strategies to improve their self-regulation and coping skills.

It might be helpful to have the students reflect on their own coping skills by having them complete the "Self-Regulation in the Classroom Checklist" (see Figure 3.1). This is a goal-setting activity so that students can begin to be more responsible for their own actions and reactions to various classroom situations.

Building a Positive Environment

Teachers can design their classrooms in a way that provides the structure and learning tools necessary to help create a caring learning community and to model and teach self-regulation. The classroom should feel like a safe space where strengths are emphasized and students feel supported.

Set Clear Expectations   Having clearly defined procedures and routines helps students understand what to expect and creates an environment that feels structured and safe. Examples include posting a schedule, daily activities, a poster of procedures and routines, conditions needed to work together, and what to expect throughout the day, which all help to promote a sense of order in the classroom. One way to develop students' sense of responsibility is to have them reflect on their current practices and reactions to challenging situations so they realize that they can control their feelings and subsequent actions. Teachers often focus on the content of the curriculum; however, to access this content, students need the self-regulation skills to organize their materials, manage their time, prioritize their tasks, stay focused, and retain and practice what is learned for later use.

Stress Detectors   The goal of fostering emotional self-regulation in children is to make them independent as individuals in the future. There are some situations or events that might create particular stress in some children, for example, getting scolded by a teacher, someone taking away their favorite toy, or someone calling them names on the playground.

If we help our students identify those occurrences that trigger certain emotions or spark unpleasant feelings, it can help them become more aware of their stressors and provide them with the emotional strength to effectively address with their feelings at the time and as they grow up.

Instruction on Study Skills   As teachers, we often focus on the content of the curriculum we are teaching—the "what" of learning—and overlook the "how" of learning. To access content and make meaning of what is being taught, students need some basic study skills,

Self-Regulation in the Classroom Checklist

Please rate how often you do the listed actions: Always, Sometimes, or Not at all. Then, look at your list and decide what you can do better. In what ways can you improve?	Always	Sometimes	Not at all
I can . . .			
1. Wait for my turn in class.			
2. Be ready and prepared for each lesson (pencils, books, etc.).			
3. Ignore distractions during class.			
4. Participate in small and large group activities.			
5. Complete my work on time.			
6. Stay focused on my work.			
7. Complete my best work.			
8. Use appropriate language.			
9. Cooperate with others.			
10. Ask for help when I need it.			
11. Follow the classroom routines.			
12. Do my own work.			
13. Raise my hand to ask or answer questions.			
14. Use a polite and respectful tone of voice.			
15. Accept feedback.			
16. Keep my hands and feet to myself.			
17. Stay in my seat when asked.			
18. Organize my belongings.			
19. Follow directions.			
20. Answer politely.			

Figure 3.1. Self-regulation in the classroom checklist.

such as the ability to organize their materials, manage their time, stay on task, read with comprehension, and retain what is learned. Therefore, teaching successful study strategies to the whole class will help all students to become more independent learners. Chapter 4 discusses this in more detail along with executive functioning skills that are necessary for self-regulation

Starting the Day Off Right

Start the school day in a positive manner to set the tone for the rest of the day. A morning greeting establishes warmth and trust. Consider starting each day by greeting every student at the door. A warm, individual welcome establishes your expectations for the day and gives you a chance to check in with each student and feel the pulse of the group before the day begins.

You could also consider ways to calm down any students who might be experiencing stress or anxiety. Have soft music playing as they enter the classroom. Kids who arrive at school upset often calm down if classical music is playing as they arrive. You could also begin each day with a short reading such as a brief poem, a funny quote, or a surprising fact. Try turning the lights down and projecting the morning activity onto the board. This helps focus students' attention on the day ahead, gets their brain in gear, and settles them in.

Another strategy that has been successful is to set up a Morning Center and stock it with activities students can do as soon as they arrive. This could include paper and the suggestion that students write to a friend or a relative, for example. For a fun, brain-activating activity, write the day's events in coded language and instruct students to work in partners to decode it. Laminate an assortment of word searches or number puzzles and provide washable markers. Fill a Challenge Box with extra-credit activities that the students can complete independently.

Morning Mood Message/Emotional Planner Begin the day by asking students what might be bothering them and ask them to write their answers in a private journal. Some prompts to get the discussion started might be issues with homework completion, no time to eat breakfast, or a fight with a brother or sister. After the students have had time for self-reflection and journaling, ask them the kind of feeling(s) this elicited and list the answers on a chart or whiteboard or in their journals. Then, ask everyone to share strategies they can use to deal with these events and create another list. Another extension of this strategy is to go over the day's schedule and identify emotions that are tied up to these events for some of the students. This gives your students an opportunity to think about and anticipate triggers that might get them upset and strategies to help them deal with these potential challenges.

Begin With an Attitude One of my favorite "activators" in the morning is to share with the students a list of robust vocabulary words that describe feelings as they enter the classroom. Some of these words you will need to unpack and explain their meaning before they choose the word that best describes how they are feeling. After defining some of the more complex words, play a brief segment of upbeat music and invite the students to "high 5" at least three to five of their classmates and share with them how they are feeling and the feeling word they chose.

This is a great way to enhance the sense of a learning community in your class and also expands their vocabulary at the same time. For primary students, introduce three to five new words per week; with intermediate students you could use six to eight new feeling words.

Boost Emotional Vocabulary

Self-expression works great for emotional self-regulation in children. Sometimes, students experience something that they are unable to name or explain, and this leads to frustration. Why not create a chart with facial expressions for multiple emotions, with examples of how that emotion makes us feel? Being able to name the feelings they are experiencing makes children more aware and reduces the chances of escalated emotional outbursts.

When I was a teacher, I taught emotional literacy explicitly to my students. Each week, my students learned a new "feeling" word and its meaning. They drew a picture depicting the word and used it in a sentence. At the end of the year, we created a book of all the new "feeling" words we learned. The best part was how appreciative the parents were because their children were better able to share and communicate what they were truly feeling at home as well as in school.

Today I Feel . . .   Use Figure 3.2 as an anchor chart or reproducible activity sheet for the children to check in with their feelings. After they select their feeling, students can illustrate and draw a picture in the space provided to show how they feel. This can be used as a daily activity (e.g., part of the morning meeting) or you can choose to do it weekly.

Daily Check-In: Maintenance of Coping Skills   Build time into your morning meeting for a "Daily Check-In" to allow the students a 5-minute break to discuss or private journal their coping skills in real-life situations. You could also consider checking in with the children informally and offering support to those who need it. Emphasize to the students that coping skills are flexible, and if one doesn't seem to work, then try another.

Following these techniques will demonstrate to students that coping skills are a powerful way to build their self-awareness and self-regulatory skills as they face the stressors of life.

Preparing a Safe, Calming Classroom

Stress and pressure can shut down the "thinking brain," which is the prefrontal cortex that helps students with self-regulation skills including focusing attention, calming down, and setting goals. When a child is in a state of emotional overload, it is challenging to get them to calm down. It is during these periods of emotional upset that the amygdala interferes with the other parts of the brain. The prefrontal cortex is not available to solve the problem (Tsujimoto, 2008); the amygdala will stay in charge until the child feels safe and is comforted.

Therefore, teachers need to set a positive tone by creating a supportive and safe classroom environment. Being able to calm oneself is foundational to getting along with others, as well as being able to follow directions, function fully in the classroom, and focus on a task. Practicing the skills of calming down helps to train the brain to notice when a big emotion is coming on and respond rather than react. Even in early childhood, children can begin to learn these skills and get better at them as they practice and as they continue developing.

Feeling Barometer—All Day Long   Don't forget the importance of checking in throughout the day with your students to do a "regulation check." Support student sharing if they have lingering emotions that an activity at school or an event at home might have caused. Consider giving your students a "moment of mindfulness"; mindfulness will be discussed in greater detail in Chapter 5. It doesn't take long to press the "pause button" and encourage students to spend a minute to do some quiet breathing to clear the mind. You can also use one of my suggested "brain breaks" to help them burn off some energy and anxiety. (These can be found in Appendix A, which is also available online.)

Feelings Check-In Anchor Chart

	Today I feel _____	because _____ .
	Happy	cheery, joyful, satisfied, pleased, glad
	Really happy	overjoyed, ecstatic, blissful, thrilled
	Excited	fired up, eager, wired, wild
	Sad	blue, down, low, out of sorts, bitter
	Worried	bothered, nervous, uneasy, tense

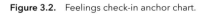

Figure 3.2. Feelings check-in anchor chart.

Feelings Word Wall   Bring emotions and feelings to life by creating a different kind of word wall that captures a plethora of possibilities to help your students name the emotions they are feeling (see Figure 3.3). It gets them beyond the pedantic refrain: "How are you feeling today?" "Mad," "Sad," "Glad," or "Bad."

"Cool-Down Corner"/Peace Place   Gather students in a group and have them brainstorm a very special place for them. Then do a round-robin response: "A special place that I find peaceful is . . ." Be sure to share your own special "peace place" with them.

Ask: "What is the value of having a special, peaceful place?"

A "cool-down corner" is a designated space in the classroom where the kids can go to take a break and to regulate their emotions. This is a special place that they can go to when they are upset, angry, or having difficulty focusing on work. Remind them often that this is NOT a "time-out" corner or a form of punishment. Instead of a "time-out" corner, make it a cozy, comfortable "cool-down" corner to which students can retreat when they need a brief break from the stresses of class so they can reset and then be ready to work. It is voluntary and should be used when they need it. I find it helpful to keep it to one student at a time and to have a time limit (5 minutes or use a timer).

This "cool-down corner" needs to be introduced and shared with your students prior to allowing students to use the space. This needs to be an area in the classroom that is easily accessible and that they can go to without disturbing other students. Once you have selected a spot, you might want to think about what should go in this space. Some items I found helpful were pillows, a bean bag chair, fidget items, stress balls, glitter jars, children's books about feelings, and "happy" posters. Talk to students about the purpose and what it should look and sound like. Make an anchor chart of their responses of what students might see, hear, and do in a calm-down corner (see Figure 3.4).

Remember to provide choices for the students because their individual needs are unique. You should also include some calm-down tools (not toys). One vital tool is a sand timer (one that marks 3–5 minutes is best and provides a great visual for the students). Students start the timer when they begin their calm-down strategy. When the sand timer runs out, they stop, clean up, and return to their seat in class.

Share Your Own Feelings First   Don't forget to share your own emotions as they occur throughout the day. Teachers get rattled too—when the copier jams, the faculty meeting goes too long, or you are getting ready for report card time. It is reassuring to students to know that you are not "superhuman." When you share your emotions with the students, it helps them understand the connection between feelings and behavior. Keep in mind that you need to use your own best judgment regarding which emotions to share to be transparent with your feelings. After all, what better model of emotional regulation is there?

Furthermore, emotions are contagious, and when a teacher can model a calm presence through voice, facial expression, and even posture, students are less likely to react defensively. Similarly, when the teacher takes time to focus on what feelings might be causing the behavior of the student who is acting out, this type of validation says to the child that the teacher understands and cares. Don't forget to show them how you take a deep breath, or get a drink of water, and create space for reflection for a minute or two. In this way, you are modeling the regulation skills you want to see from your students.

Use a Singing Bowl   Consider using a Tibetan singing bowl as part of your morning circle time—students listen to the gentle sound the bowl creates and take three deep breaths. In my own experience, sometimes we play the bowl and students close their eyes

My Feelings Word Wall

Angry	Excited	Happy	Sad
aggravated	beaming	cheerful	ashamed
annoyed	delighted	delighted	blue
bitter	eager	elated	depressed
cranky	enthusiastic	glad	down
frustrated	inspired	hopeful	gloomy
fuming	interested	jolly	glum
furious	overjoyed	merry	heartbroken
mad	thrilled	pleased	miserable
outraged		proud	unhappy
sore			
unhappy			

Silly	Scared	Surprised	Upset
childish	afraid	alarmed	angry
crazy	alarmed	amazed	confused
foolish	anxious	astonished	grouchy
goofy	fearful	dazed	hurt
wacky	frightened	frightened	low
zany	nervous	shocked	nervous
	panicked	speechless	unhappy
	petrified	startled	unsure
	spooked	stunned	worried
	terrified		
	worried		

Figure 3.3. My feelings word wall.

The Cool-Down Corner

One student at a time, please.

1. Set the timer for 5 minutes.

2. Think about what you did that made you upset, and what you can do better next time.

3. You may draw a picture or write about how you're feeling.

4. Choose a calm-down activity:

    - Squeeze a stress ball.

    - Blow or touch a feather.

    - Look at a glitter jar.

    - Close your eyes and think of something you like (birthdays, recess, sunshine, etc.).

    - Take deep breaths slowly in through your nose and out through your mouth three times.

5. Calmly return to your work.

Figure 3.4. The cool-down corner instructions poster.

and listen to the tone until they can't hear it any longer. When this happens, they raise their hands in the air one at a time. This patterned activity works with the body's rhythms and is calming to the nervous system as the sound reverberates through the air.

Mindful Breathing With a Pinwheel Many children succeed with mindful breathing exercises when they are able to engage with something visual and/or hands-on. Providing each child with a pinwheel on which to focus while practicing breathing exercises keeps them engaged and aware. Consider using this activity to settle the students down after lunch or recess. They blow on the pinwheel and take deep breaths until the pinwheel comes to a stop.

Building Resilience With Your Students

Self-regulation is the ability to control and manage our thoughts, feelings, and emotions in relation to the demands put on us. Research shows self-regulation is a good predictor of resilience. Resilience is the ability not only to cope and handle adversity but also to be able to learn from it and adapt to challenging life situations. In other words, learning from mistakes (**self-regulation**) is a predictor of coping, confidence, and tolerance in responding to negative situations (**resilience**).

Therefore, students who have learned skills of self-regulation tend to be more *resilient* to stressful situations in the classroom. Resiliency is a critical skill that needs to be nurtured and developed in all children. Educators understand the importance of building resilience in children, but knowing exactly how to promote resiliency in the classroom can be a challenge. To build the resilience needed to succeed in life, students need to develop self-awareness while teachers provide them with a way to discover positive, self-regulatory skills. When students have resilience, they are much more open to learning because they believe they *can* learn.

Help Students Identify Their Own Stressors It's important that students learn to identify and share how they feel and why they feel that way. Ask students to name the things that make them feel stressed, angry, and sad. (See the "Focus on Your Feelings . . ." worksheet in Appendix A, also available online.) Afterward, students share stressors with one another to start building a collaborative, caring community of trust where they feel safe and heard. In my own experience, I have shared my own stressors with students to set the tone of the activity and to model this strategy with them.

Identify Reactions to Stressors Next, invite students to write down or share orally their reactions to the stressors. This helps the students develop self-awareness. Again, in my own experience, I shared my reactions to stressors as an example.

Brainstorm Alternative Ways to Respond to Stressors During this phase of the process of self-awareness and self-regulation, introduce the concept of coping skills as a positive way to minimize feelings of stress or conflict. Once the feelings and stressors have been identified, it's important now that students learn how to handle their emotions.

Furthermore, discuss the concept of coping skills (what they are and what strategies to use to respond to negative feelings). Encourage students to compile a list of their "go-to" coping strategies that work for them, and together make a coping skills poster for all to see. This list of various coping strategies is a great visual reminder for the whole class of positive reactions to stressors and gives students additional ideas they might not have considered. This process is powerful because it shows students how to take charge of their own reactions.

Use Children's Picture Books to Teach About Feelings

Stories have the power to bring feelings to life and can help children understand their own emotions and those of others. Books and stories are great tools for teaching children emotional literacy skills. Through stories, characters show what feelings look like and model how to react to emotions, which helps students understand the importance of self-regulation. Reading a book together lets you engage with your students about feelings. A study by Maria Nikolajeva (2015) found that reading fiction provides an excellent way for students to develop empathy and understand how other people think and feel.

When children read stories that contain emotions, they can understand and accept their own feelings. It also helps them realize that there are other children who feel the same way and that they are not alone. It is important to watch their responses to the feelings of the characters in the stories because that might give you some insights about how a child feels and thinks about certain situations and emotions. (Please refer to recommended titles to share in the Resources section of this book.)

Use the following process to help reinforce the character trait featured in each story:

Describe   After you read the story, talk with your students, and have them talk with one another, about what they think the main idea of the story was. What character trait did the story focus on? How do you know? Why is it important? Can you make a connection to your own life? Make a poster together, or have the students write or draw in their journals about this character trait.

Demonstrate   Have a few students act out what the character trait looks like and sounds like. Having students role-play this character trait will help reinforce the emotion and the reaction to it.

Practice   Plan activities in which each child has to take a turn to practice the featured character trait.

Think Positive: Gratitude Journals

Nurturing gratitude has numerous benefits for adults and students alike. Consider dedicating a block of time each day to write positive thoughts in a *gratitude journal*. Ask students to write down at least one thing they are thankful for every day and/or draw a picture of it. When students became overwhelmed by negative thoughts or anxiety, encourage them to read their journals to affirm the positive things in their lives and redirect their thoughts and feelings.

Here are some sample prompts to get them started:

- Something beautiful I am thankful for . . .

- An event I am thankful for . . .

- A skill I am thankful for . . .

- Something outside I am thankful for . . .

- Something inside I am thankful for . . .

- A friend I am thankful for . . .

- Something fun I am thankful for . . .

Managing Expectations

Remember, "lesson mastery, *NOT* lesson mystery" is our goal as teachers. Students often learn best when you show them how to do something through direct instruction, modeling, and guided practice. The same is true with behavior. If students are not displaying productive behavior, teachers can demonstrate what the effective behavior would look like through modeling activities such as "think-alouds" or role playing.

Allow time for children to practice new behaviors they're learning in a low-stakes way that breaks down the desirable behavior into achievable steps. As a classroom teacher, I practiced improving transitions with a group by providing a visual and auditory cue (flicking the lights and clapping my hands). Students knew to stop what they were doing and return to their seat. At first, I gave them several minutes to do this and rewarded students who were in their seats, even if they were a bit loud getting there. Gradually, I decreased the time given and only gave rewards to students who were sitting quietly and listening for directions with their materials out, ready to work.

I found that thinking about behavior objectively, as a skill to be taught rather than simply as acting "good" or "bad," was immensely helpful in my ability to guide children in learning to control their behavior. Some children enter school without the self-regulation skills necessary for school success. Educators need to meet these children where they are and teach them the skills they need to be successful in the classroom.

One way to develop the students' responsibilities as well as managing expectations in the classroom is to have them reflect on their current practices and reactions to challenging situations. Using this technique helps them to realize that they can control their feelings and subsequent actions. Refer to Figure 3.1 ("Self-Regulation in the Classroom Checklist") for a goal-setting activity designed to help students understand appropriate expectations in the classroom and their reactions to these situations.

Helping Students Understand How Mind and Body Work Together

Introducing students to the mind–body connection will help them recognize the importance of taking care of both their mental and physical selves. Knowing how our emotions cause a physical response deepens self-awareness and understanding of emotions, coping skills, and self-regulation. Learning to maintain health (both physical and mental) is one of the most important things you can teach your students. Furthermore, many studies suggest a link between a child's mental and physical health with successful learning. Integrating the mind and body connection for children enhances self-regulation and affects everything from a child's behavior to their ability to focus on tasks.

Regulate Responses With Rhythm   Using rhythm is a natural way for students to help regulate their emotions. Why? Our heart beats in rhythms, we sleep and breathe in rhythms, and our breath can regulate our nervous systems. However, when these rhythms are missing or interrupted, our sensory and motor systems may be compromised, which can negatively affect a student's ability to learn or perform a task. Natural rocking exercises help even the youngest children to quiet down and refocus their attention.

Teachers can create a beat and have students mimic the rhythm using drumsticks or chimes from soft to loud, rapid to slow, or even move their body in rhythm with the drumbeats. Another twist to this is the technique of having your students use crayons and craft paper to visualize the beats as colors and shapes.

Transition Technique: Body-Breathing   Transitions are great opportunities for students to practice their empathy skills. As an extra benefit, these activities keep them engaged while moving from one activity or place to the next.

- Tell students to breathe up (this means breathing in and lifting their hands up, by their sides, and then stretched above their heads with their hands touching together, such as you might see in a yoga practice).

- Then students breathe out and bring their hands down, touching together, past their faces to the center of their chests.

- Then students breathe up again, but instead of bringing their hands above their head, they lift their hands to the sides of their bodies.

- Finally, students breathe out and cross their arms in front of their chests over their "heart center."

- Students walk silently to the line and out the door, through the hallway, and to their next destination or recess.

Get Outside   Being out in fresh air and nature can have a calming effect on the anxious brain. Maybe it is just a change of scenery that makes the difference. Breathing the fresh air or taking time to notice subtle sounds of nature like birds chirping can also soothe the students' stress and worries. Helping your students to observe the sights and sounds of nature around them might help to redirect their focus away from their worries. You could ask, "How many different kinds of trees do you see?" "How many shapes of clouds do you see?" "How many different bird sounds do you hear?" "How many different shades of blue are there in the sky?"

Get Kids Moving: Shake It Out!   Movement and exercise help anyone who is feeling anxious or stressed. Anxiety can end up looking like anger and be disruptive in the classroom. Even the simple "walk and talk" method helps to calm students down. Once, on yard duty, a student was upset because all the swings were in use, so I invited her to take a couple of laps around the playground with me and everything would feel a little better. Our walk also removed her from the situation, and she had a chance to explain the situation to me, which really calmed her down.

SUMMARY

Self-regulation is the ability to remain calm, cope with emotions, adapt, and respond appropriately to our environment. Self-regulation is important because it allows children to think before they act, thereby doing well in school and better relating with friends and family in school and at home. It helps children feel good about themselves and what they can handle. As educators, our goal is to help students build the resilience and self-regulation skills they need to be successful in school and in life. I invite you to try the strategies in this chapter and the rest of the book that provide your students with multiple pathways to discover positive, self-regulatory coping skills. (See Figure 3.5 for a cheat sheet with tips for teaching self-regulation to your students.) My wish for you is that you will use these techniques successfully with your students and be inspired to create and share your own ideas with others.

They key is to remember that we need to teach our students the connection between *how they feel* and *how they act.*

Research-Based Ways to Teach Self-Regulation

- Help your student recognize the higher goal (e.g., empathy and learning).

- Use familiar situations to teach self-regulation strategies (e.g., taking turns, using timers).

- Validate the challenge of self-regulation.

- Have your students make choices and practice decision-making skills every day.

- Design activities that focus on self-regulation skills.

- Remember that self-regulation skills gradually develop over a lifetime.

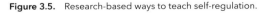

Figure 3.5. Research-based ways to teach self-regulation.

CHAPTER 4

Developing Executive Function Skills in Students

As children develop, they are increasingly able to consider and think about multiple aspects of a problem or situation, plan a course of action, and act on it. They also develop the ability to discern when something is in error, modify their actions, and respond appropriately. As children grow and gain new life experiences, they are increasingly able to engage in organized, planned, and goal-directed actions.

However, this goal-directed activity depends on several mental processes including the skills of organization, inhibiting impulses, selective attention, sustaining, shifting, and planning memory. The ability to engage in purposeful, goal-directed activity, along with the mental processes that make this possible, can be described as **executive functioning (EF).**

KEY CONCEPTS

- What are executive functioning (EF) skills?

- Why are EF skills important in learning?

- What are techniques for teaching students the importance of EF skills?

- What are some positive behavioral supports teachers can use in the classroom?

- How do social skills fit into EF?

- How can teachers strengthen EF skills with students who struggle?

INTRODUCTION

We have all worked with students who have challenges with EF skills—we just might not have called it by that name. *Executive functioning (EF)* is an umbrella term used in neuroscience to describe processes that many of us take for granted involving mental control and self-regulation. Students who have EF difficulties may exhibit some of the following traits:

- Difficulty paying attention
- Impulsive behavior
- Tendency to be persistently late
- Poor test-taking and study skills
- Difficulty planning and organizing time and materials
- Challenges with setting priorities
- Responding appropriately to social situations
- Tendency to lose things
- Inability to start in-class assignments
- Difficulty in taking turns
- Tendency to be negative
- Responding appropriately to stressful situations
- Difficulty in asking for help
- Inability to finish assignments in a timely manner
- Interrupting or making impulsive remarks
- Inability to manage emotions
- Tendency to be inflexible in thinking outside the box
- Demonstrating low tolerance for frustration
- Tendency to be overly anxious
- Problems when settling down after recess
- Inability to multitask
- Having a cluttered workspace or desk
- Having difficulty in generating information independently

Let's take a closer look at the facets that make up the comprehensive idea of EF skills:

- *Attentional control:* the ability to focus on a specific task, even if we find it uninteresting.
- *Cognitive inhibition:* the ability to tune out the stimuli that are not relevant to our task.
- *Working memory:* the ability to temporarily hold information needed for decision making and reasoning.
- *Inhibitory control:* the ability to curb impulses and select behaviors appropriate for completing a goal.
- *Cognitive flexibility:* the ability to adapt when rules or circumstances change.

You can probably understand why these skills are important for, well, pretty much everything we do! These indicators of EF difficulties can be categorized into the following five major domains that are often problem areas with our students:

1. Attention, concentration, and focus

2. Organization of materials, belongings, workspace, and tasks

3. Time management

4. Memory

5. Emotional regulation

Many children and young adults struggle with EF challenges. These difficulties are typically easy to spot, such as when a child can't focus on a lesson or a story or comes to class without their homework or a pencil. Maybe a child might take twice as long to understand directions or appears totally "zoned out" when given a task to do. Students have a finite pool of mental energy to draw upon as they work to succeed in school. As educators, we can help our students focus on the important things, including learning the content and practicing essential EF skills. Students need to be able to quickly negotiate, implement, and apply these specific abilities in a variety of contexts, as shown in Figure 4.1.

Understand the teacher's goal	Plan actions (*workspace, attention, focus, language*)	Sequence actions	Prioritize
Organize (*belongings, workspace, and materials*)	Initiate the task	Inhibit responses	Pace oneself (*manage time, frustration, emotional control*)
Shift attention (*to the teacher's goal, task, and its completion*)	Self-monitor (*time, emotions, attention/focus*)	Exert emotional control	Complete the task

Figure 4.1.   Cognitive skills in task completion.

Why Are Executive Functioning Skills Important?

Some students do not develop these EF skills to the same degree as their peers. For students with deficits, additional support and interventions may improve their development of EF skills. Consider those students in your class who never seem to be aware of due dates, are easily distracted during independent work time, or maybe wait until the last minute to get things done. These are the students for whom explicit instruction, practice, and real-life opportunities to learn EF skills are needed. Here are some ways that educators can reinforce these skills with seamless integration into the curriculum:

- Share the purpose behind any activity through learning objectives. Understanding the purpose helps the students retrieve their background knowledge of the topic and establish a readiness for learning.

- Model and provide explicit instruction and guided practice of strategies. This helps the students get a sense of the teacher's mental processing and helps them to develop their own metacognitive processing.

- Use prompts, cues, and questions to guides students toward responsibility for their own learning.

- Teach priority EF skills such as organization, flexibility, and attention.

- Guide and support students on how to develop their own strategy styles to help them succeed.

- Provide time for independent practice. Encourage students to identify strategies that work best for them in real-world situations.

- Create systems to promote greater organizational skills, scaffold, and review strategies often, using them in context.

- Give students an opportunity to review strategies prior to needing them in a higher-stakes learning situation (tests, quizzes). Practice, repetition, and review are important to activate students' memory systems.

What Does the Research Say?

Executive functions, as they are understood in the scientific sense, are defined as "the brain-based, cognitive processes that help us to regulate our behavior, make decisions, and set and achieve goals" (Dawson & Guare, 2009, p. 4). In other words, *executive function* in neuroscience is generally used to describe neurological processes and self-regulation. Experts have found that EFs are regulated in the frontal lobe of the brain (the prefrontal cortex). Children are not born with these skills, but they have the potential to develop them. Children with deficits might need additional support in the classroom to develop these skills.

Furthermore, researchers have not arrived at a universally accepted definition of EF, nor of the multitude of mental processes that are included under the EF umbrella. However, there is agreement that these functions do indeed help us to plan, organize, manage, and emotionally regulate our lives (Katz, 2014). There has been a lot of attention on EF because it is an important predictor of which students will succeed in school and those who will not (Katz, 2011). Students with weak EF skills might also exhibit exceptional strengths, such as in creativity and inquiry. Conversely, students with EF challenges will often know what they are supposed to do but have difficulty carrying that task out to completion (Goldstein & Barkley, 2010).

The research shows that EF provides a valuable lens for examining the challenges that some students may face in learning and mastering specific skills. Therefore, effective approaches to fostering EF skills are particularly important in the early stages of learning and development because these skills allow children to acquire knowledge more easily. A growing body of intervention studies has established that the acquisition of EF skills can be enhanced through specific strategies and repeated practice in the process of reflecting on and using specific EF functions and processes. This research supports the importance of keeping children motivated to practice EF skills and to integrate those skills continually throughout the school day.

We all—not just our students—are surrounded daily by so much data at any given moment. However, our brain can only process so much at a time. The reticular activating system (RAS), located in the lower part of the brain, filters almost all the incoming data and selects the necessary information to which we consciously attend (Willis, 2010). The RAS responds to and gives priority to novelty, which means novel stimuli have a better chance of entering the brain and getting our attention. Therefore, implications for the classroom include the importance of engaging the students in novel, unique ways at the onset of the lesson you are about to teach; you have to ensure that the information is put forth in an original way. This surge of focus and attention, in turn, helps to develop a sense of optimal arousal. "Optimal arousal enables brains to be alert, receptive, and ready to attend and learn" (Littman, 2007, p. 2), and once the students are at this state of optimal arousal, educators need to keep their interest alive as they continue to teach them the lesson.

By teaching these skills, educators can provide a critical foundation for school readiness, academic achievement, and lifelong success. EFs form a foundation for self-regulation and help children build social-emotional skills throughout their lives. EF skills help children stay on task, make plans, set goals, and carry them out successfully—even when faced with challenges (Willis, 2017). While some children seem to develop these skills naturally, many struggle and thus benefit from specific interventions and direct instruction and support. The strategies in this chapter will provide you with practical techniques for your instructional toolkit to foster and develop EF skills in your students.

STRATEGIES FOR YOUR CLASSROOM

Whether your students struggle with EF deficits or not, you can help *all* of your learners develop more orderly dispositions with the following simple techniques:

1. *Make assignment details memorable.* Unorganized students will repeatedly ask, "What do we need to do?" Try to make the details more vivid and reinforce with pictures where appropriate. For example, it might be helpful to offer a visual checklist of assignment details or a bookmark with reading reminders.

2. *Help students feel in charge.* If students ask what to do next, pause and reflect, not giving them a quick answer—ask them what they think comes next. Use motivational techniques discussed in Chapter 4. Find out the interests and/or hobbies of your students and use them in conjunction with specific instruction in organizational skills. Praise them for their improvement and for trying. This might encourage them to try out these skills.

3. *Be cautious about introducing long-term projects.* It is best to break down large projects into smaller assignments and then help students with backward planning so that they are proceeding with the end in mind. Disorganized learners often underestimate how much time and effort a task will take. Therefore, it's helpful to break it up and check in with students at frequent intervals so they experience incremental progress.

4. *Discuss organization in class.* What does *being organized* mean to them? Who has an organized backpack, desk, cubby who can share their organizational tricks with the class?

5. *Show students how to pre-plan homework.* For older students, ask them to write down when, where, and for how long they will do their homework. Then show them how they can make a homework menu of what they will study and in what order. This helps them get the big picture.

6. *Help students visualize "to-dos" so they do not become overwhelmed.* This can take the form of lists with visual icons to increase memory.

There are multiple ways to help students develop and refine their EF skills. But first you need to be able to assess students' EF skills. Your anecdotal notes gleaned from informal student assessment can uncover valuable information about your students' learning behaviors and patterns and brain functions. In addition, take note of students' responses to a thinking intervention or strategy used in the classroom. These are all indicators of their cognitive abilities. Furthermore, there are checklists, evaluations, and scenario diagrams that are effective resources to help organize classroom brain-training practices.

It is important to note that an intervention or strategy won't work in the same way for each student. For example, some students respond better to visual cues and others to auditory stimulus. Therefore, it might be necessary to differentiate thinking strategies for each student to help them achieve their potential. One way to keep track of your students' targeted EF skills is to use a checklist (see Figure 4.2). In this way, you can identify those students who are struggling with EF skills, keep track of strategies used and the results, and use data keeping and sharing with the student and/or their parents at parent–teacher meetings.

To develop EF skills, practices to use might range from technology devices to improve memory skills and reflexes, to working on gross-motor skills to improve balance and brain–motor functions. Here are a few examples of what I have found helpful in working with my students to improve their EF skills.

Organization and Planning Skills

As adults, we sometimes take for granted the skills needed to plan and organize our day. It is important to support students in mastering these tasks by establishing procedures and routines within your classroom (i.e., where do they hang their jacket, put their backpack, stash their lunch box, get to their desks, and start their work to launch their learning?). To facilitate this process, you can number certain stations in the classrooms to cue students on a routine for entering the classroom, accessing materials, and so forth. For example, you can use this method for students to gather their worksheets for the day at Station 1 and to pick up their binders and workbooks at Station 2. Adding visual cues with photos will facilitate students' execution of these daily routines, especially for younger students.

Another tip is to set aside a portion of your school day dedicated to specifically supporting your students to focus on these strategies. Even 5 to 10 minutes of discussion on these skills on a daily basis will add to the routines that you have established and help students focus on these important daily skills of self-control, being focused, and improving memory. The chart in Figure 4.3 might be a helpful tool for your students to use to prioritize their "To-Do Checklist" and keep in mind the steps to get ready to learn. Additional organization strategies to teach your students could include the following:

- Color-coding subjects and materials

- Providing seating charts with flexible arrangements

NAME: _____

Executive Functioning Skills				
A. Organization	B. Time management	C. Attention	D. Working memory	E. Emotional regulation

Figure 4.2. Student EF skills tracking checklist.

To-Do Checklist

Please stop
talking

Focus

Please get
started now

Do you know
what to do?

Do you need
any help?

First _____ Then

Figure 4.3. To-do checklist for students.

- Using "in" and "out" boxes for completed homework and classwork

- Posting a chart with group agreements and expected procedures and routines

- Writing assignments and a daily schedule/agenda on the board and referring to it

- Encouraging students to develop their own reminder systems

- Making assignment details memorable—use a visual checklist

- Helping students feel in charge. If they ask what to do next, don't just give them a quick response—ask them what they think comes next.

- Using motivation techniques—praise them for improvement and effort.

- Introducing long-term projects with care. Give them visual prompts and teach them the importance of "backward planning." Chunk the elements due so that it is not so overwhelming.

- Helping students visualize "to-dos"

Organization Worksheet   Using the "Make a Plan" worksheet in Figure 4.4, instruct students to draw tasks that need to be accomplished in the speech bubbles provided. Then have students number the tasks in the order they need to be completed.

Sustained Attention

Many of our students have difficulty controlling their emotions, and this interferes with their ability to sustain attention. I found it helpful to have a "fidget box" of small manipulatives including stress balls, play putty, pipe cleaners, and more. These items help students to refocus and direct their attention to the task they are working on. Students can also use these resources during class time in a "quiet corner" or at their desk or in the hallway. Additional tips for helping students maintain their attention on the tasks at hand include the following:

- Using music to help students focus or transition from one activity to another

- Integrating movement exercises with directions and learning outcomes

- Using nonverbal cues (such as hand gestures, facial expressions, written clue cards) to gain attention

- Creating simple visual signals for students to use to indicate need for assistance, such as a tongue depressor with a stop sign on it, colored cups or dots, or note cards

- Using "triple talk": repeating key phrases three times during a lesson and having students do a choral response

- Using classroom timers to help with time on task

- Connecting new learning with past experiences

- Providing opportunities for engaging stimulation, games, videos, and electronics

- Interspersing active tasks with quiet tasks

- Allowing students to use word windows or erasable highlighters to focus on key ideas in text

- Allowing for regular brain breaks as well as water and movement breaks (see Appendix A of this book for additional ideas of "brain breaks")

Make a Plan

What can I do next time?

Figure 4.4. "Make a plan" worksheet.

- Providing visual cues for workspaces in the classroom

- Explicitly teaching expectations and providing finished samples for each project or assignment

- Using a peer check-in system ("Checkmate")

- Providing headphones and listening centers for the auditory learner

- Breaking down assignments into smaller tasks

- Providing flexible seating structures (stand-up work stations, desks in pods and clusters, yoga balls, study carrels, individual desks, clusters)

Controlling Impulses

One technique I have found very helpful is implementing regular breathing exercises to show students how to pause and take control of their body and brain and to be mindful in the present. With younger, primary students I have used "breathing buddies" (previously described in Chapter 2) to help them regulate their breathing and become more mindful. Each student brings a stuffed animal from home and lies down on the floor, placing the stuffed animal on their chest. They take a deep breath in and out and watch the stuffed animal rise and fall on their chest with their breath. This provides tangible feedback to them of the importance of deep breathing.

Teaching Behavioral Expectations

It is important to be explicit in the elementary grades about behavioral expectations. This might include having a reward system and careful monitoring procedures so that these skills are sustainable. Administrative support, communication, and data-based decision making were all found to be important characteristics for long-term sustainability of these traits (Doolittle, 2006). You can use the list of "Prevention Pointers" (Figure 4.5) to help you and your students succeed in integrating EF skills throughout the day.

Teachers can provide many opportunities for students to build their EF skills through meaningful social interactions and implementing specific procedures and routines as an integral part of the school day. A gradual release of responsibility approach (I do, we do, you do) can help support EF learning as the teacher provides specific instruction and gives students an explanation of the strategies or skills involved in assignments and then allows them to practice independently.

Be aware that EF skills take years to fully develop and mature. These EF skills contribute to student achievement because they support learning as students develop specific coping skills and learn to focus on tasks and pay attention, solve problems, persist amid challenges, and resist distractions.

Time Management

Effectively managing time is an essential part of EF skills. The following list includes ways to help students become masters of time management:

- Help students become aware of their time habits.

- Use a variety of different classroom timers.

- On the glass or plastic cover of an analog clock, color a section on the clock with a dry erase marker to indicate passage of time.

- *Break cards*—Provide students with a specific number of cards that can be used to request their need for a break for a specific amount of time.

- *Quick-writes/journaling*—Provide time for students to do a quick-write or journal entry using a prompt, or for self-expression and reflection.

- *Active listening*—Listen to students carefully and paraphrase back to clarify what is being said and to validate their need to be heard.

- *"Cool-down corner" pass*—This "chill pass" can be used as a ticket to the class's quiet space when a child is feeling stressed or in need of some mindful moments.

- *Positive practice*—Provide time and an opportunity for students to practice a skill, then provide verbal and validating feedback.

- *Visual supports*—Provide a visual strategy that will help students perform the desired behavior (T-chart, feelings chart, choice board).

- *Behavioral momentum*—Deliver a set of easy-to-accomplish tasks or requests before asking students to engage in a more challenging task.

- *Prompting*—Remind students of appropriate and expected behavior *before* the activity takes place.

- *Offer assistance*—Rather than emphasizing completion of academic tasks when there is obvious frustration or anxiety, offer assistance to make instructional adjustments and scaffold the task to be completed.

- *Traffic lights*—This is an example of a visual sign for help when a student needs assistance. You can use different colored index cards, for example. A red sign means to "stop," and help is needed, the green card means all is okay, and the yellow card indicates that the student is "cautious" and some help may be needed to complete task.

Figure 4.5. Prevention pointers list.

- Use signs to indicate the half-way point of assignments and activities ("You have _____ minutes left").

- Break more complex tasks into smaller ones.

- Schedule frequent short breaks.

- Incorporate cooperative learning experiences with specific roles and responsibilities for the team, including a timekeeper.

- Encourage relaxation and focusing skills.

- Provide learning menus that build in choice of tasks to be accomplished in a specific time.

- Provide students with checklists of what needs to be done by when.

- Schedule frequent short breaks to keep them focused and attentive.

- Encourage *quality* not *quantity* or speed.

- Use peer checkers for early finishers.

Memory

It is important to remember that human memory consists of many different levels: **sensory memory, short-term memory,** and **long-term memory** as depicted in Figure 4.6.

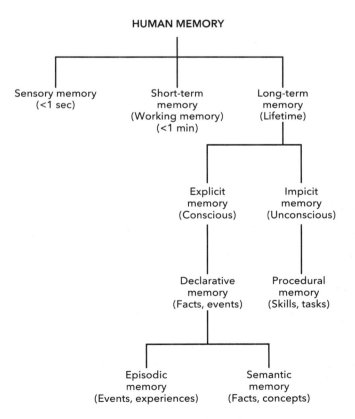

Figure 4.6. Human memory.

Here are some other helpful ways to support your students with memory skills:

- Provide visual checklists for students.
- Create word banks with the students about the topic or story.
- Give directions in multimodality formats: written, visual, recorded, rhythmic, tactile.
- Model the use of graphic organizers to remember key points of lessons.
- Use card games to further develop short-term memory (concentration).
- Teach students strategies through mind maps and word webs to retain key ideas.
- Develop and use student-constructed flash cards.
- Have students work with peers to recite, rehearse, and review key information to remember.
- Keep directions simple and use gestures to increase memory.
- Break larger ideas into smaller chunks to boost retention.
- Develop photo cards of routines and appropriate behaviors and display them for all to see.
- Teach students to visualize information.
- Incorporate movements into academic concepts.
- Teach and use rhymes, rhythms, and raps.
- Reinforce concepts with visual posters.
- Provide sentence starters to boost language development.
- Give clear, written, and numbered directions.
- Pause frequently during lessons and check for understanding: "What have we learned so far?"
- Have students do "mindstreaming" (i.e., brief sharing with peers of what they have learned so far).
- Ask students to paraphrase directions.
- Teach highlighting techniques.
- Color-code new words when teaching (e.g., nouns are green, verbs are red).
- Use picture cues, diagrams, and graphs.

Emotional Regulation

Teachers must guide students to understand the connection between how they feel and how they act. That's what emotional regulation is all about. Emotional regulation skills help children manage and control their emotional reactions. It is important to note that students who learn these coping strategies at a young age are better prepared to deal with more difficult emotions and successfully handle life's challenges. Here are a few techniques that teachers can use and help students to include them in their "emotional toolbox":

- Take a digital photo of the student demonstrating the appropriate behavior you are wishing to teach (students can role-play this) and display the photos with the desired task labeled.

- Teach and model the correct behavior and responses to a situation (choose one behavior at a time).

- Develop a list or menu of positive incentives that are motivating to the students.

- Create unique ways of allowing students to choose rewards (roll of the die, random drawing of a ticket from a jar).

- Work with the students to identify positive self-talk statements they can use when faced with a challenging situation.

- Create a "calming box" with personal objects that reduce anxiety.

- Teach deep-breathing techniques such as the concept of "breathing buddies."

- Encourage students to use self-calming exercises.

- Positively reinforce the students by using specific praise statements.

- Teach the specific expectations for activities ahead of time.

- Provide options (i.e., when to do something and how to do it).

- Redirect and avoid power struggles.

- Suggest the students hear you out before they say "no"; be brief and clear.

- Visually post schedules of the day.

Games and Activities to Use to Teach Executive Functioning Skills

When students play games that involve strategy, they have an opportunity to pause and think, get organized, and make a plan of action, and then they can adjust those plans in response to what happens during the course of the gameplay. This taps into students' sense of **cognitive flexibility**, working memory, turn taking, and inhibition control, which are all EF skills used to support playing the game.

The use of games to develop students' EF skills can be quite simple and provide healthy and fun challenges while practicing coping skills; these can include card games, board games, physical games and activities, and movement and song games. Even some popular commercial games, such as Connect Four or Jenga, as well as checkers, dominoes, and chess, can develop EF skills in the classroom.

Weekly Report   The "Weekly Report" form (Figure 4.7) can be a handy communication tool to keep parents informed about their child's progress with mastering EF skills and to celebrate their successes on a weekly basis. You can also encourage parents to follow up and reinforce these skills in the home environment as well.

Backpack Luggage Tag   This handy tag (Figure 4.8) is not only a useful label for identification purposes. It can also serve as a subtle checklist to help the student remember certain things on a daily basis until they become routine. You need to inform the parent of this tag so that they can reinforce the checklist at home as well, so the child comes prepared with the necessary supplies daily.

Guessing Games   Guessing games require players to use their working memory and flexible thinking as they retain a number of details. Popular children's games like 20 Questions or I Spy teach kids how to think in categories ("I spy something blue . . ."), and they need to use their memory to keep track of the description or criteria for the object they are

Weekly Report

Daily/weekly report

Name: _____   Date: _____

Teacher: _____

Homework turned in this week? [ ] Yes [ ] No

Comments: (*write something positive*)

_____

_____

_____

_____

_____

_____

_____

_____

Figure 4.7. Weekly report form.

Backpack Luggage Tag

Name: _____

Phone: _____

School: _____

Parents' phone: _____

In case of emergency: _____

Call: _____

IF FOUND – PLEASE RETURN – REWARD

Remember:

1. _____

2. _____

3. _____

4. _____

5. _____

6. _____

Figure 4.8. Backpack luggage tag.

trying to guess. Another example is Guess My Rule, which can be played with blocks or other items of different colors, sizes, and shapes so that children guess which attribute, or set of attributes, defines the rule for the set.

Card Games   There are lots of simple card games that can develop EF skills, and one of my favorites is Uno—it's a game where kids have to keep track of colors and numbers. There are other commercial card games like Memory and Spot It! that also emphasize memory skills.

Simon Says   This is a classic children's game that emphasizes listening skills, inhibitory control, and cognitive flexibility: "I didn't say 'Simon says'!" Kids need to resist the impulse to move unless they hear the requisite, "Simon says."

Board Games   Yes, even classic board games in your closet can be used to develop EF skills. For instance, games like Taboo, Apples to Apples, and Risk all require complex thinking and inhibition control.

Play Games That Require Fast Responses   Children develop attentional skills and control inhibition when they play games that require quick responses and monitoring. For example, flash cards can be used in a modified version of Snap or Slapjack.

Repeat Instructions in a Variety of Ways   Help students remember instructions by keeping them short and simple and by sharing them using multiple modalities: orally, visually, and even with gestures. You can also partner students and ask them to repeat the directions to each other.

OTHER CONSIDERATIONS FOR TEACHERS

Creating a Positive Environment

The most important thing that teachers can do to reinforce EF skills is to *model positive behaviors and create a positive classroom environment.* This environmental support means creating a space where children can thrive. Here are some more important ideas to keep in mind to help students develop EF skills:

- *Modify the physical layout of the classroom.* Simplify the classroom by reducing clutter, adding helpful physical barriers, reducing distractions, using homework bins, and arranging seats to promote attention.

- *Explicitly teach EF skills.* Do not assume that students will learn these skills by themselves intuitively. Model the skills, name them, break tasks down into small steps, and provide time to practice.

- *Present information in multiple ways for all learning styles.* Adjust lessons and/or strategies to match students' strengths. Consider how a lesson can appeal to students who are primarily visual learners (focus on what they can observe, give visual clues), auditory learners (takes in information by listening), or kinesthetic learners (learns best by movement and hands-on approaches).

- *Consider student readiness and attention span.* It is important to consider students' developmental level and age in designing tasks to complete. For example, think about using brain breaks or frequently engage younger students in the task to retain their focus.

- *Outline steps.* Use checklists and visual charts that outline steps and procedures.

- *Reward success.* Provide praise and positive feedback. Seek advice from the child regarding preferred rewards.

- *Evaluate and monitor.* Involve the student in the process and make changes as needed.

- *Reduce/withdraw support gradually.* It may take time. It is best to decrease the quantity and frequency of prompts slowly.

Creating a Positive Environment

Develop and Practice Routines   Being consistent is a huge factor for student success. Try to make a predictable, systematic daily routine in your classroom. Remember, it is not enough just to have a routine . . . you need to practice the procedures with the students frequently.

Keep Daily Schedule Posted   A daily agenda/plan for the day is not only important for the students, it is also helpful to keep you on track. It can be general, but such visual schedules help the students mentally prepare for class and give them previews of coming attractions. Don't forget to schedule time in the day for kids to get organized and to prioritize their personal planning.

Preview Changes   For students who struggle with flexibility and organization, a change of schedule or plans can be an obstacle and might set them off. If there is a change of schedule coming up, let the students know in advance to give them a heads-up. This will help reduce their stress and increase their coping skills.

Show Respect   It is important to listen to your students and show them you care about things that are important to them. For example, in my own classroom I apologize to students when I have forgotten to do something I said I would do, when I make a mistake, or even when I lose my temper or become impatient with them. I also encourage respectful responses from the students through classroom discussions and by role-playing how to show respect to others. We discuss what makes various interactions respectful or disrespectful. I also support respectful behavior by providing positive feedback when students show respect to each other.

Thinking Out Loud   Students need to know how to think through a problem, so I think out loud with my students. Whether you are demonstrating the solution to a math problem or you are sharing your solution to an everyday dilemma that you are facing, it is meaningful and memorable for you to share your thinking out loud to your students so that they know the thought processes you use to solve a problem. Here's a great way to get the students more involved in this thinking process—why not have them come up with the lesson idea? For example, in the past I have told students the goal of the lesson and ask them for ideas about possible ways to accomplish it. Then, as a group we weigh the pros and cons of each idea, then we decide the best way to start the work. This is an engaging way to demonstrate thinking out loud with your students.

Showing Your Human Side   Find out about your students' skills, interests, and hobbies. Let them know that their individuality is valued along with the academics. Turn these interests into possible "passion projects" for students to pursue. Ask them about different aspects of their lives and don't forget to share some of yours as well. For example, I share stories of my dogs, my puppets, my travels, and lots more. I feel that when teachers talk about their lives outside of school, it fosters a safe environment for students to show their unique personalities and helps you develop a personal connection with your students. It's also a great opportunity to model how to talk in positive ways about oneself. Students need to feel important. Such personal stories and discussions help students think and talk in positive ways about themselves.

Sharing Responsibility   You know that our students are observing us ALL the time; being a role model can be daunting. However, it is also a wonderful opportunity to show students a positive way of looking at themselves. Try modeling behaviors you would like to see in your students by demonstrating respect, kindness, and empathy. Along with classroom discussions, this modeling will give your students an opportunity to learn and practice skills they will need to succeed in life beyond school.

SUMMARY

In conclusion, keep in mind that students watch and learn when you least expect it. They watch and listen to how you treat other students and adults throughout the day. They watch how you treat them in good times and through struggles. They are watching and learning how to act toward others and how to take care of themselves.

Helping students develop essential EF skills during a school year takes time—not just out of your daily routine, but over weeks and months. As with any skill acquisition, EF skills develop at different rates in different children. There are many reasons why students struggle, both at home and in school, and many ways that teachers can support them through classroom strategies, modeling, and support.

Here are some planning pointers to keep in mind when integrating EF skills in your elementary curriculum:

- Teach fundamental EF skills of organization, flexibility, and focused attention first.

- Model and provide explicit instruction and guided practice of the strategies to support your students.

- Create specific systems, scaffold, and review strategies often and in context.

- Encourage students to develop their own EF strategy styles.

CHAPTER 5

Mindfulness in the Classroom

To help your students grow in SEL, it is essential that they understand their emotions in a deeper and more meaningful way. Teaching strategies that support mindfulness can have dramatic effects on your students' overall emotional state and growth. Therefore, it is helpful to become familiar with the meaning of mindfulness and how it can enhance your classroom practices. Mindfulness is the quality of being fully present in the moment and engaged in whatever you are doing—free from distraction, and still aware of our thoughts and feelings without getting "caught up in them" (Kabat-Zinn, 2009). **Mindfulness** in education then is exactly what it sounds like: including mindfulness practices and principles into the education program. Furthermore, studies have shown that mindfulness helps reduce stress, boosts memory, and can even help children focus and improve their attention span.

KEY CONCEPTS

- Why is mindfulness important to the well-being of your students?

- How do you help kids relax?

- What are some ways to help students focus on the present moment?

- How do you incorporate breathing techniques to reduce stress?

- What are some techniques to improve attention with students using mindfulness?

INTRODUCTION

The purpose of teaching mindfulness to students is to give them skills to develop their awareness of inner and outer experiences, to recognize their thoughts as "just thoughts," to understand how emotions manifest in their bodies, to recognize when their attention has wandered, and to provide tools for impulse and anxiety control.

Educators know that children learn best when they are comfortable, safe, and relaxed. Imagine if, along with giving our students the gift of lifelong learning and the tools to become kind and productive adults, we could also give them the gift of mindfulness—using their breath and mind to lead a happy and healthy life. In turn, teachers will reap the benefits of mindfulness as well—we all know that a happy teacher with happy students has a happy classroom.

Furthermore, mindfulness restores a state of calmness in the classroom by helping students develop a sense of inner peace. Some of the benefits of mindfulness include decreasing stress and anxiety, improving self-esteem and self-regulation, and increasing calm.

What Does the Research Say?

What does "mindfulness" really mean in terms of neuroscience and the brain? What are the implications for the classroom and learning? Scholarly research finds that mindfulness practice in the classroom decreases student stress and anxiety and helps increase attention, ability to focus, interpersonal relationships, empathy, compassion, and other benefits. Such benefits likely lead to long-term improvements in their quality of life.

What follows is a summary of key research findings with implications relevant to educators:

- *Improved attention*—Several studies demonstrated that students showed improved attention (Chiesa & Serretti, 2009; Sedlmeier et al., 2012), including longer concentration span on and performance of objective tasks (Jha et al., 2007).

- *Reduction of stress and anxiety*—Research supports that mindfulness reduces the feeling of stress in students (Chiesa & Serretti, 2009) and diminishes the sense of anxiety and distress that is felt when one is placed in a stressful situation (Hoge et al., 2013).

- *Improve mental health and well-being*—Emotional health and a positive sense of well-being are important components of childhood development. Not only does mindfulness help students manage stress, but it also leads to a deeper sense of overall well-being. According to a study by Schonert-Reichl and Lawlor (2010), mindfulness practice leads to positive emotions in elementary school students.

- *Emotional*—The effects of mindfulness on emotional regulation have been documented in numerous studies (Roemer et al., 2015). Mindfulness creates changes in the brain that correspond to less reactivity in certain tasks (Goldin & Gross, 2010) and better ability to sustain attention and engage in tasks even when emotions are activated (Ortner et al., 2007).

- *Executive function*—EF skills include the mental dexterity of sustaining attention, the ability to switch focus, make plans, manage time, stay organized, and remember details. Research in education suggests that mindfulness practice in the classroom can lead to improvements of EFs in students (Flook et al., 2015).

- *Greater compassion and empathy*—Children who have participated in mindfulness practices are more likely to demonstrate empathy and help someone in need (Condon et al., 2013) and demonstrate greater self-compassion (Birnie et al., 2010).

Mindfulness and the Developing Brain

Being present in the current moment can be very empowering. It means focusing a student's awareness on the here and now. While being in the present moment can be very transformative, what does it do to their brain? Interestingly, mindfulness does in fact change the brain (Lutz et al., 2008). See Figure 5.1 for a summary of these findings.

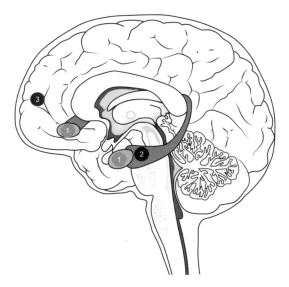

1. The amygdala—This area of the brain is activated when reacting to strong emotions such as fear or anger. Studies show that this part of the brain becomes less activated following mindfulness sessions (Desbordes et al., 2012; Lutz et al., 2008).

2. The hippocampus—This part of the brain is important for learning and memory functions and helps regulate the amygdala. It is a structure of the brain that is shaped somewhat like a seahorse. The hippocampus becomes more activated following mindfulness practice (Goldin & Gross, 2010). It is responsible for the regulation of emotions, spatial orientation, and learning.

3. The prefrontal cortex—This part of the brain also plays a role in mindfulness. This region of the brain is associated with memory, maturity, regulating emotions, behavior, and the ability to make wise decisions. Following a mindfulness session, this part of the brain is more activated and developed, which helps increase the child's attention span and focus (Chiesa & Serretti, 2009), as well as the processing of complex and abstract information.

Figure 5.1. Effects of mindfulness on the brain. (From MindfulSchool.org; adapted by permission.)

The more you can integrate a practice of mindfulness into your classroom, the more you will strengthen your students' brain synapses and improve their learning and attention. Joining together the fields of neuroscience and mindfulness, you can bridge the gap between how the brain really works and how the daily practices described in this chapter can impact the lives of your students. By practicing mindfulness, you can help your students more fully understand how emotions, thoughts, and feelings really make a difference in their lives and their capacity to learn.

STRATEGIES FOR YOUR CLASSROOM

Getting Started

Here are some foundational strategies to get you started in mindfulness practices.

Set a Goal to Relax   During your first session with your students, introduce the idea of mindfulness and how it can help them be better leaners and members of the classroom community. Your goal may be to teach the students how to relax and how their emotions affect their bodies' awareness.

Keep It Simple   Mindfulness is noticing our thoughts, what our body feels like, what our ears are hearing, what we are smelling, and anything else that is around us and happening right now. Consider using the words *noticing* or *being aware of* with students instead of more complicated definitions of mindfulness, which they may not understand.

Take It One Step at a Time   The first technique that is important to teach students is how to breathe. This sounds so simple . . . and yet, children do not usually pay attention to their breath. Here is an example of how to teach your students how to focus on just their breath:

- Start by having your students sit comfortably in their chairs with their feet on the floor and their hands resting gently in their laps.

- Next, have students close their eyes and focus on their breath. Instruct them to listen as they inhale and exhale. Have them try to lengthen their breath each time they inhale and each time they exhale.

- If they feel they are unfocused, instruct them to count up to 10 each time that they inhale and exhale or listen to a Tibetan chime to give them an auditory cue. Have them practice this technique on their own.

- Once you notice they have mastered this step, then you can gradually increase the amount of time they practice breathing each day. After each session, you might want to ask students to process their experience by writing about it in their journals.

Know Your Role: Silent Guide on the Side   Your role is to gently guide students into peaceful awareness. For a mindfulness practice to be truly effective, it must include periods of silence where students do not hear you talking the entire time. Students need to be able to engage in their own experience in silence. It is fine to begin the session with a few guiding words, then it's time for you to remain quiet. Your role is the facilitator and the guide to help them become more mindful.

Process the Experience   Allow time for your students to process what they have experienced and how they feel after the mindfulness exercise. This is best done with a partner and not as a total class discussion because each experience is unique. An alternative activity is to have them write about it privately in a journal. Mindfulness takes practice, and the more you practice and model this for your students, the better they get at it, and everyone experiences a positive result.

Use Stories as a Springboard

For younger children, storytime can be a natural move from reading aloud to the beginning of a mindfulness practice. Ask students to sit cross-legged and close their eyes. Start by asking them to pay attention to the way their bellies expand as they breathe slowly in through their noses and the way their bellies come in as they breathe slowly out through their noses.

In the past, I have read the book *Lemonade Hurricane* to introduce mindfulness to my students. There are many other recommended books that introduce the meaning of mindfulness even for younger students. (See Appendix B of this book for additional suggested titles.)

Check Your Personal Weather Report

During your morning meeting encourage your students to share their "personal weather report" (Figure 5.2) to describe how they are feeling. A book you could use to introduce this activity is *Sitting Still Like a Frog* by Eline Snel. This story encourages children to "summon the weather report that best describes [their] feelings: sunny, rainy, stormy, calm, windy, cloudy" (2013, p. 3).

My Personal Weather Report

Name: _____

Sit down and close your eyes. What is the weather like inside you right now? Do you feel relaxed and sunny or cloudy and sad?

What does the weather inside you feel like?

_____

_____

_____

_____

_____

Figure 5.2. Personal weather report worksheet.

This activity allows children to share their present emotional state in a safe and supportive way. They can't change the weather outside, and we can't change our emotions or feelings either. However, be sure to emphasize that *what we can change is how we relate to our feelings.* As the author Snel describes it, children can recognize their feelings in new ways: "Mindfulness is feeling sun on your skin, feeling the salty tears rolling down your cheeks, feeling a ripple of frustration in your body. Mindfulness is experiencing both joy and misery . . ." (Snel, 2013, p. 3).

Breathing and Mindfulness

Practicing mindfulness typically begins with simple breathing exercises. When kids notice their thoughts drifting and then bring their attention back to the breath, it can help them build their self-regulation skills and focus. The goal is to concentrate on each breath, in and out. In a class setting, the teacher may encourage students to notice when their mind wanders and gently remind them to bring their thoughts back to the sensations of their breath. Younger kids may be given a stuffed animal to place on their belly. Watching it rise and fall makes focusing on breathing more concrete. This strategy of "breathing buddies" will be further described later. Remember that focusing on your breath can be harder than it sounds—especially for kids who struggle with attention. The purpose of mindful breathing is to anchor yourself in the present moment, so that you can let go of worrying about the past or the future.

Breathing is something the body does automatically. We rarely stop to think about it, but we should. Conscious breathing is simple to learn; we just need to be willing to take the time during our busy instructional day to do it. Start integrating mindful breathing during circle time, morning meeting, or transition time. Encourage students to notice and name how the different breathing exercises affect how they feel and think and behave.

Breathing Tips for Kids   Our students' brains are tired, and children of all ages really need opportunities where they can take time out of each day to relax and focus. Mindfulness and breathing exercises offer this break and help kids function more effectively and clearly.

1-2-3-4   Instruct your students to use this simple technique that reminds them of the power and sequence of breathing mindfully. It combines a rhyming activity with a procedure to focus on their breath.

1. On the first breath, look up to the *sky* (or ceiling). This movement opens our body and chest.

2. On the second breath, bring your breath to your *shoe!* Focusing on bringing the breath to another part of the body *literally gets us out of our heads.*

3. On the third breath, breathe through your whole body (*me*). Can you bring your breath all the way from your feet to your head?

4. Do *one more* for good measure!

SCAN Breathing   With older kids, you can use the acronym SCAN. As in the 1–2–3–4 exercise, it teaches students to bring their attention to their breath in different parts of the body. It helps them focus on the present and gives them a sequenced task to think of instead of just "breathe!"

When you need to stop and take a breath, do a quick SCAN and consider, "How does your breath feel..."

- In your *S*tomach?

- In your *C*hest?

- *A*ll over?

- In your *N*ose?

Breathing and Movement   Engaging children in breathing activities helps them become more aware of their bodies and the stressors within their bodies. It teaches them how to use breath to focus their attention and calm themselves. The goal is for students to learn techniques that they can later use when they need help regulating their emotions or behaviors. Remember, the more children practice—whether in school or at home—the easier it will be for them to call on these simple techniques during uncomfortable or overwhelming situations.

Breathe Like a Bear by Kira Wiley is an excellent book that teaches kids how to flex their mindfulness muscles and be calm, focused, imaginative, energized, and relaxed. Wiley provides many fun activities that are sure to captivate children and start them on their path to developing positive mindfulness habits for their physical and mental well-being.

Balloon Breathing   Here is a FUN way to teach your kids about deep breathing.

The type of breathing we want students to do during these exercises is deep belly breaths, not shallow chest breaths. When they breathe in, their belly should expand, and when they breathe out, their belly should contract.

Balloon breathing (see Figure 5.3) is a simple breathing exercise that you can do anywhere. Slow, deep breaths are one of the best ways to calm an anxious child. Have them pretend to blow up a balloon by holding their hands together in front of their mouths. Count to five slowly as they blow all the air out. While they do this, their hands expand outward as they begin to blow up their imaginary balloons. Count to five again as students inhale. Hold their breath for a count of two. Then they should begin again to blow up another imaginary balloon.

Here is an exercise to help you relearn abdominal breathing. You can complete the exercise lying down or sitting.

- Place your hands just below your belly button.

- Close your eyes and imagine a balloon inside your abdomen.

- Each time you breathe in, imagine the balloon filling with air. Feel your abdomen expand as the balloon fills.

- Each time you breathe out, imagine the balloon collapsing. Feel your abdomen contract as the balloon shrinks.

We are born to move as human beings and movement is a natural part of our life. Introducing movement with mindfulness into your classroom allows your students to tap into their natural way of learning.

Practice With a "Breathing Buddy"

For younger children, telling them to simply "pay attention to the breath" can be difficult to understand. You can invite your students to relax, and have each student grab a stuffed animal. The child then lies down on their back with their "buddy" on their belly. They focus

Balloon Breathing

Breathe in . . .

Place your hands on your belly and breathe in slowly to fill your lungs. Feel your belly and chest expand out like *a* big balloon. Count to 5.

Breathe out . . .

Now open your mouth and SLOOOWLY blow all the air out of your lungs, like you are deflating an imaginary balloon. Repeat. This time, breathe in and out through your nose. How does it feel?

Figure 5.3. Balloon breathing worksheet.

Figure 5.4. Breathing ball example.

their attention on the rise and fall of the stuffed animal as they breathe in and out. It really is fun to watch and helps the child to relax and learn about their breath and the movement it creates in their body.

Breathing Rings Many teachers who integrate mindfulness into their school day use a breathing ball (like the one shown in Figure 5.4). Expand and contract the ball slowly as you breathe in and out. Kids like to play with these and find them very calming.

Try a SELF Breath Together Take *S*low, *E*ven, *L*ong, *F*ull breaths to a count of four on the inhale and four on the exhale. With practice, the class will master the four-count breaths. Then challenge them to make their breaths six or even eight counts. Breathing together builds unity.

Pretzel Breathing This type of twisted-up breathing is powerfully soothing. It's basically giving yourself a big hug! Have the kids wrap their arms around their body like a pretzel and then slowly breathe. This can help students soothe themselves when they are angry or scared.

Mindfulness Mantra

This is a very simple exercise and involves the practice of directing positive thoughts and well wishes to ourselves and others. It is easy to do and easy to learn. You should model it first and then have the children repeat and chant after you. Ask the children to sit comfortably with their eyes closed. Ask them to imagine what they wish for in their life. They can use the following four phrases:

- May I/you be happy.
- May I/you be safe.
- May I/you be healthy and strong.
- May I/you be peaceful and at ease.

Guided Meditations for Mindfulness

Younger children might benefit from guided meditations when they first begin learning about mindfulness. It can be easy for their minds to wander, so consider using the following guided meditations where students are being gently instructed during their mindfulness practice.

The Balloon   This is a simple guided meditation to help your children bring visualization to a deep breathing exercise. You can ask them to do this standing or seated. Here are the steps:

- Relax your body and begin to take deep breaths inhaling and slow breaths exhaling through the nose.

- Start to take a slow, deep breath to fill your tummy up with air, as if you're blowing up a big balloon. Expand your belly as much as you can.

- Slowly let the air out of the balloon (through the nose) as you release the breath from your tummy.

- Encourage your kids to feel their entire body relax each time they exhale, or every time air is slowly released from the balloon. You can even make a soft "hissing" noise to encourage them to slow down the exhale even more, "Like letting air out of the balloon."

- Continue for several minutes.

- Ask them to think of their favorite color and picture a giant balloon of that color in their mind.

Follow the Leader   Ask your students to picture or imagine a friend or a sibling—someone they spend a lot of time with. Then ask them which one (the sibling or their friend) usually takes the lead or gives directions. If they are the leader, have them imagine that they are the "breath." If they are the follower, ask them to picture themselves as the "brain." You can modify the directions to suit the age of your students. Here are some suggestions: "You and your friend do everything together. Let's pretend that your breath and your brain are friends, too. And you are the brain—the follower, and your friend is like the breath—the leader." Then follow the steps below to guide them through this mindful breathing exercise:

- Sit down and close your eyes.

- Bring your attention to your breath and slow it down, taking deep breaths in and out.

- Let's have the brain follow the breath—no matter what. Picture yourself as your brain, the one that's following your friend, your breath. Try to focus your brain on the breath and follow as you inhale and exhale.

- Count your breaths at the end of every exhale. Don't let your brain count before the end of the exhaled breath. The brain always wants to jump ahead, but don't let it. Allow it to remain focused on being the follower.

- Count up to 10 breaths slowly, always at the end of each exhaled breath, continuing to let the brain follow the breath.

Other Mindfulness Activities

Though breathing exercises are inextricably linked with mindfulness, there are many other activities that you can use to teach mindfulness practices to your students.

Try "Brain Massage" With Your Students   Begin with feet flat on the floor and have students stand up straight and tall. I would recommend modeling this with your students. Tap fingers gently on the forehead, temples, under the eyes, bridge of the nose, jawline, and chin.

Use all the fingertips simultaneously to gently knead the scalp. Use a bit more strength in the fingertips to pull the skin on the back of the neck forward a few times. Roll the shoulders back. In just a few moments you will feel better, the students will feel better, and you'll all be ready to focus on the lesson.

Tuning In to the Heart Have your students jump up and down or do jumping jacks for 1 minute. Then have them sit down and put their hand over their heart, closing their eyes and paying attention to their heartbeat. Discuss how they feel or encourage students to write about it in a mindfulness journal.

Open Your Heart Instruct students to raise their arms above their heads and gently stretch them out and bring them down to their sides very slowly while breathing deeply. Tell them that they are "opening their hearts" by doing this. It is important that our hearts are open to the feelings of others.

Dance Party! Crank up the music and dance! Get out of your head and into your body. Take a much-needed "brain break" with your students and allow some free-dance movement time. I love dancing with kids—there's no self-consciousness. It's just pure movement and joy and self-expression. This is a very positive way to "shake it out" and release the stress and uncomfortable emotions that you and your students may be experiencing.

Guided Imagery Guided visualizations are an excellent way to help students clear their minds of worries or stressors. This script can be recorded or read aloud slowly in a quiet place, free from interruptions. You may want to have soft, relaxing music playing in the background while you read the script. There are many guided visualizations available for educators to use (see the Appendix of this book) or use a suggested read-aloud story to guide their imagination and breathing.

While your students are quietly listening to the visualization, have them sit quietly and comfortably in their chairs or on the floor. Tell them to close their eyes and listen to the rhythm of their breathing as they follow the directions, and focus their attention on relaxing one part of their body at a time. Afterward, help them remember what this relaxed state feels like whenever they feel tension or when they are worried, afraid, or angry.

The use of guided imagery and visualization develops children's imaginations. It also helps them to connect learning with prior knowledge. When you start a new topic in your classroom, have your students close their eyes and gently take them through a pretend "journey of the mind" through the images you stir up with your words. For example, if you're beginning a unit in science on the ocean, have them imagine getting into a submarine and cruising through the ocean waters, looking for fish, animals, and seaweed. End the guided imagery session with a few deep breaths, and then students can draw what they imagined and discuss their ideas as a class. You could also take them on similar pretend journeys into the solar system, to the jungle, to the desert, on a safari, or up a volcano, depending on your curriculum topics. This helps them to calm down and to focus on images of the topic you are studying.

Stretch to the Sky! Ask your children to stretch toward the sky and reach upward on their toes, stretching their entire body. Have them hold their breath for at least 5 seconds while doing deep breathing, and then release. Ask them to shake their body out and then do it again.

Five-Finger Gratitude Ask the children to close their eyes, get in a mindful position, and spread out one hand like a starfish. With their other hand, they gently trace each finger and, while they do so, ask them to think of one thing or person they are grateful for. This could be a special friend, their family, or a pet. Invite the children to spend a few seconds with each thought, really appreciating the person or thing that they are thankful for. While they are tracing over each finger with the opposite hand, ask them to inhale through their nose on the outside of the finger or thumb and then exhale through their mouth as they trace over the outside of their finger or thumb. This breathing and tracing process continues until all fingers have been traced. As they trace their fingers, have them focus on their breath and how their fingers feel. Now that they are more relaxed, they can draw the images of what they are grateful for inside the "Take 5" gratitude hand activity sheet in Figure 5.5.

Clench and Calm   While they are in their seats, instruct the students to raise their shoulders up and clench both of their fists, holding this tension for at least 5 to 10 seconds. Then ask them to release their fists and shake them out.

Doodling or Drawing   Drawing, doodling, and coloring can be wonderful mind–body exercises to calm and focus your students. Why not take a break from your hectic schedule and put on soft music, dim the lights, and let your students enjoy creating something unique? You may even want to join in! Being willing to press the "pause button" and to foster quiet concentration will help increase your students' capacity for a soothing strategy to use in upsetting situations, such as when they are in a fight with a friend or are worrying about not finishing homework.

You might want to try to give them a drawing prompt such as one of the following:

- Draw a picture of one of your friends.

- Draw a favorite pet or animal.

- Draw your favorite place.

- Draw a picture of what you like to do for fun.

Journaling and Free-Writes for Mind-Body Connections   Journaling or free-writes can be a positive and relaxing mind–body exercise for your students. It can be as simple as adding words to their mindfulness drawings. Putting their thoughts and feelings on paper has the benefit of giving children an opportunity to work out problems or stressors they are experiencing—sadness, loss, worries, anger, challenges—as well as the chance to remember fun experiences. Try not to prescribe the content or format of their writing. The goal is to get them comfortable expressing their feelings in words . . . in any way they choose. The format might be as diverse as a list, poem, essay, letter, or random words and letters.

Sometimes students may need an open-ended prompt to get them started at the beginning. You might want to suggest that they write something from the following list:

- "Things that make you glad (or sad or mad) are . . ."

- "One of my favorite stories I've ever heard or read is . . ."

- "My favorite place to be is . . ."

- "One of my favorite foods is . . ."

Be the Sky   Ask the children to close their eyes, and imagine that their thoughts are as big as the sky. As thoughts pop up (which they will do), just notice them. Prompt students

"Take 5" Finger Gratitude

I am thankful for . . .

Figure 5.5. Take 5 worksheet.

with the following questions: Can you see each thought as a bird flying through the huge sky of awareness? Can you watch the thought as you would a bird, with wonder, and without knowing what will happen next? Is the bird (your thought) fast or slow, loud or quiet, calm or scary? Can you just be aware of it, or does it need your immediate attention?

Walking Meditation   I use this technique to help students with mindfulness and self-regulation.

- Practice mindfully walking with students by having them walk in a circle.

- Tell them to take one step, think about feeling their heels on the floor, then their toes. What else are they feeling? Tell them to notice how they breathe—are they breathing fast or slow?

- After the students have practiced, give them an idea to think about as they walk from one place to another. I have also practiced this with complete attention to the walk and the bodily sensations and awareness of the physical space we are walking through.

Make "Mind Jiggle Jars"   This is one of my favorite mindfulness activities for my students. Using glitter and water, you can make a "Mind Jiggle Jar" (see Figure 5.6)—the glitter represents all the thoughts and emotions in their minds. Recycled baby food jars can also work well for this strategy. Ask the child to gently jiggle the jar to represent how their brain goes "crazy" sometimes with emotions and feelings. Invite them to stare at the jar to watch the glitter gently fall to the bottom of the jar. Encourage children to take deep breaths in and out as they watch it float down. When the glitter settles, the water becomes clear, and so does our mind when our emotions have settled down.

This is a great way to practice deep, calming breathing with your students; as a group, shake the jars, and then breathe calmly while watching the glitter settle. I kept the glitter jars in our "Peace Place" or "Quiet Corner" where the kids could reach them and access them if they needed to use them during the day to calm down.

Mindful Eating Practice   This exercise of mindfully eating a raisin or a slice of apple is a favorite activity of mindfulness education with children. This is a fun and easy way to teach children to pay attention to and savor their food, and by doing so, also savor the present moment.

Figure 5.6.   Mind jiggle jar example.

Place the selected food on a napkin in front of each child (a raisin works well for this). You can use the following script (adapted from Christopher Willard's *Child's Mind* [2006]) as your guide to help your students be more mindful of their eating:

> Look at the [food's name]. What is its shape? What size is it? What color is the [food]? What smell do you notice? What do you notice as you look at the [food]? What's the feeling in your stomach? Pick up the [food] slowly. Hold the [food] and look at it in your fingers. What does the [food] feel like in your hand?
>
> Bring the [food] slowly to your lips. Before putting the [food] to your mouth, pause and be aware of what you are experiencing in your mouth. Slowly open and place the [food] on your tongue for a moment without biting into it. Feel what your mouth wants to do with this [food]. Take a few moments before you bite into it. Feel its texture on your tongue and in your mouth. What do you taste?
>
> Now bite into it noticing what you taste and what it feels like. As you continue to taste, try not to swallow the [food] right away. Does the taste and feeling change as you are chewing it? Feel the [food] going down your throat as you swallow. Notice your stomach and what it may be feeling. What are you feeling?

SUMMARY

The benefits of mindfulness in school settings have been proven through an extensive body of research over the last 30+ years. This research demonstrates just how powerful the practice of mindfulness is in helping students regulate their emotions and refocus their energy on learning and the tasks in front of them. Mindfulness has been shown to:

- Decrease stress
- Improve sleep
- Improve concentration and memory
- Enhance relationships and compassionate behavior
- Improve attention span and ability to focus
- Promote emotional awareness and regulation
- Enhance resiliency and frustration tolerance
- Promote flexibility and creativity

Choosing Your Own Path to Mindfulness

I encourage you, fellow educator, to find your own path to mindfulness and how to integrate this practice into your classroom to share with your students. In your journey, uncover the unique steps toward mindfulness that work best for you and your students. Choose any life-giving sensation or activity—from mindful eating to dancing to breathing deeply—to bring you back to the moment and out of any thoughts of stress or worry. We can harness the power of personalization to become more mindful and help our students to do so as well. With students, the goal of mindfulness is to help them move beyond their thoughts of the past or future that may be draining, negative, or worrisome. Instead, it is about using different methods to lessen their stress and to relax, empowering them to accept their unique thoughts and feelings and giving them the tools that they need to connect with what's going on in their world at the present moment.

As a result, we just might begin to practice mindfulness not because we have to, but because we want to.

Now more than ever, teaching mindfulness in the classroom is a valuable part of the school day. Our children are stressed and anxious. Teachers and parents are stressed and anxious, too. Our lives are so busy that we often find our thoughts fretting over the past or worrying about the future. Mindfulness teaches us all to live in the present moment—the here and now—enjoying and experiencing what's in front of us.

Educators know that children learn best when they are comfortable, safe, and relaxed. Imagine if, along with giving our children the gift of lifelong learning and the tools to become kind and productive adults, we could also give them the gift of mindfulness—using their breath and mind to lead a happy and healthy life today and tomorrow.

Where do you begin? Try picking one mindfulness practice to start for yourself. Then introduce it to your students, adapting the experience to cater to their needs—even if it's for only 2 to 5 minutes per day during transitions or for brain breaks. Take it slowly and build it into your classroom gradually; you might try introducing a new mindfulness practice every week or every month. Or you could choose just one idea (e.g., mindful breathing) and practice that throughout the year. The primary objective is to plant the seed of mindfulness with your students now, and it will stay with them for their entire lives.

Mindfulness allows students the opportunity to be fully present in the moment and restores a sense of calm in the classroom by helping students develop inner peace. Being mindful and focused on a task can provide relief from revisiting past stress and trauma or from worrying about the future. The time is now for that mindful moment.

CHAPTER 6

Supporting a Growth Mindset

> "A growth mindset is not a declaration, it's a journey."
>
> –Carol Dweck, Mindset

When I was a first-grade teacher, I had a student who was convinced he could not succeed at school tasks. He would come up to me, with tears in his eyes, and say, "I can't do it!" He would throw down his paper abruptly, and I realized that even the simplest task of writing his first name (using a model) was his roadblock. This is evidence of a **fixed mindset**— a belief that our abilities are innate and unchangeable. It is the reason so many students just give up in the spirit of **learned helplessness.** They have met failure along the way, so what's the point in trying?

KEY CONCEPTS

- How do you create a growth mindset learning environment?
- What are some ways of designing learning experiences for success?
- How do you reframe praise statements for growth?
- What are some strategies for giving better student feedback?
- What are ways to help students see challenges as opportunities?
- How can teachers use techniques for modeling growth mindset in the classroom?
- What are some communication strategies to support student achievement?

INTRODUCTION

The contrast between a *growth mindset* and a *fixed mindset* is quite clear: with a **growth mindset,** students believe that they can improve their performance through effort and perseverance. But why is this so important? What are the implications for the classroom? There is an increasing body of research that demonstrates the importance of having a growth mindset to student success.

Table 6.1. Fixed mindset vs. growth mindset

Fixed mindset	Growth mindset
Sees failure as a lack of talent—often leads to giving up early	Views mistakes as a need for more effort or different strategies
Tries to appear as capable as possible	Tries to learn and improve as much as possible
Sees capabilities as inborn and unchangeable	Sees that capabilities can be changed by effort and learning strategies
Views success of others as a threat	Views success of others as motivation for further learning
Avoids challenges—fear of failure	Embraces challenges to learn from them, leading to greater growth
Ignores negative feedback	Learns from constructive criticism
Sees people as being born with a set of talents and abilities	Understands that talents and abilities are flexible and not set in stone
Feels that it is better to look smart than to take risks and fail	Feels that it is better to learn by working to fix mistakes than to hide behind them
Sees failure as permanent	Sees failure as temporary

Let's take a quick look at the contrasts between a growth mindset and a fixed mindset and the implications and applications for the classroom. Fostering a growth mindset is critical to creating a healthy, caring learning community. Students who embrace a growth mindset tend to act in ways that promote their learning and growth, even if that means taking risks. See Table 6.1.

The good news for you and your students is that a growth mindset can be taught and can develop over time. As educators, we need to pay careful attention to what our students say as they are learning, studying, or interacting with each other. Encourage students to try some of the statements in Table 6.2 while they are learning and notice the difference in their attitude and the effort they bring to the work.

Behavioral patterns and predictors for success are affected by our beliefs about our abilities, skills, and potential. As evidenced in the statements from Table 6.2, a student with a fixed mindset believes that their intelligence is static, whereas a student with a growth mindset believes that their intelligence can be developed. For these students, effort is a natural path to mastery instead of giving up. Therefore, the distinction between these two extremes has significant implications for student motivation, productivity, and confidence in the pursuit of success and learning.

Table 6.2. Fixed mindset vs. growth mindset statements

Fixed mindset	Growth mindset
This is too hard. I'm not going to do it.	This is hard and it means that I am learning.
I'm not good at this!	I can't do this yet!
I can't make this any better.	I can always improve on this.
I'm not really good at this subject.	I am beginning to understand this because I have been practicing.
This is good enough. I am done.	Is this the best I can do?
I made a mistake. There's no use going on.	This is my first attempt. Mistakes help me learn.
I will never be as smart as they are.	I will find out how to do it better.
I give up!	I will try some of my other strategies that I have been taught.

What Does the Research Say?

Researcher Dr. Carol Dweck (2008) studied this phenomenon of mindset and the effect it has on teaching and learning. She was interested in students' attitudes about failure. Dr. Dweck designated the terms *fixed* mindset and *growth* mindset to describe the pervasive beliefs people have about how they approach learning and consider intelligence. When students believe they can become smarter and do better if they work harder, they understand that effort does make them stronger. Therefore, they put in extra time and effort, and that leads to higher achievement and more positive attitudes toward learning.

Furthermore, recent advances in neuroscience have demonstrated that the brain is very malleable. Research on *brain plasticity* has shown how our neurons can change with experience and that new connections can be made. With practice, neural networks grow through these new connections, as well as strengthen existing neural networks. This ongoing research has demonstrated that we can increase the growth of our neurons—and therefore our ability to learn and face challenges—by the actions we take, such as using positive strategies and self-talk, asking deeper questions, and paying attention to good nutrition, exercise, and proper sleep habits.

Concurrently, researchers began to understand the link between mindsets and achievement. It turns out, if you believe your brain can grow, you behave differently. So, the researchers asked themselves this: If mindsets can be changed, how does it happen? This prompted a series of studies that revealed a change in students' mindsets from fixed to growth leads to increased motivation and achievement (Blackwell et al., 2007; see Figure 6.1).

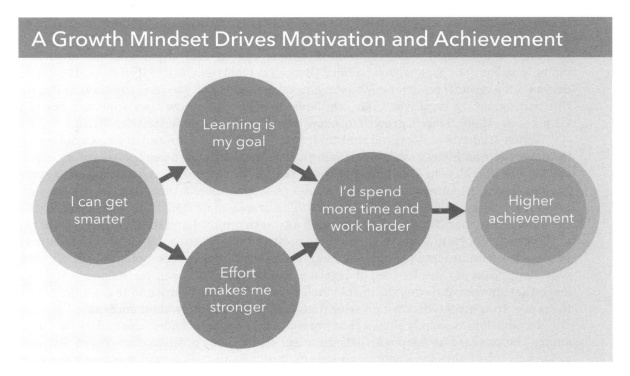

Figure 6.1. A growth mindset drives motivation and achievement. (*Source:* Blackwell et al., 2007.)

In addition to teaching kids about how their brains can grow (malleable intelligence), researchers noticed that teacher response has an impact on student mindset, and teacher feedback can either encourage a student to pursue a challenge and increase achievement or look for an easy way out and shut down. For example, studies on different kinds of praise have shown that simply telling children they are smart encourages a fixed mindset, whereas praising their hard work and effort with specifics cultivates a growth mindset. When students have a growth mindset, they tend to take on more challenges and learn from them, therefore increasing their abilities and achievement. Even our youngest learners can understand that a challenging goal is just an area of weakness that we need to strengthen and to celebrate improvement as we work to overcome obstacles in our way.

The topic of fixed versus growth mindset has received much attention in the press recently, including a summary of research articles from the *Harvard Business Review* (2016), *Huffington Post* (2015), EdSurge (2017), and *Educational Psychology* (2018), among others. As a result, growth mindset interventions are increasingly being implemented to improve student educational outcomes. There is strong evidence to suggest that adopting a growth mindset can have positive implications for students' academic achievement, emotional adjustment, and motivation (Blackwell et al., 2007). Furthermore, other studies have found that students with a fixed mindset exhibit negative academic emotions such as anger, anxiety, shame, boredom, and hopelessness (King et al., 2012). Conversely, interventions that are aimed at developing students' growth mindset are effective in improving academic achievement for all students and are especially effective for underachieving students (Paunesku et al., 2015; Yeager et al., 2016). In addition, students with a growth mindset manifest better adjustment outcomes, such as higher levels of self-esteem and more positive relationships with peers (King et al., 2012). It is interesting to note that students with a fixed mindset are less likely to persevere when faced with a challenge (Dweck et al., 1995; Dweck & Master, 2009), whereas students with a growth mindset exhibit sustained motivation and higher achievement in the face of challenges (Grant & Dweck, 2003).

A growth mindset is also related to students' **resilience,** which is defined as an individual's capacity to cope with adversity (Brooks & Goldstein, 2001; Ryff et al., 1998). Students with a growth mindset view setbacks as an opportunity to improve their skills, and this, subsequently, improves their resilience in school and how they approach learning (Hong et al., 1999). Thus, a growth mindset is positively correlated with resilience.

When students understand that their intelligence is not limited or fixed, goal setting becomes their pathway to success! Having a growth mindset as a teacher, therefore, means you believe that all your students have the potential to grow, learn, and develop if they work hard and apply themselves. For your students, it also means that *they* believe they can grow, learn, and develop if they work hard. The more *you* demonstrate a growth mindset, the more likely your students are to develop a growth mindset and that "can-do" spirit! One of the most important ways to spread that positive belief is through the specific language you use to communicate to students about their progress and accomplishments. By using growth mindset phrases instead of negative, fixed mindset phrases, you help your students learn that success and overcoming obstacles come from hard work and that students have the power to control their own positive thoughts and, ultimately, their success.

In addition, research shows that praising kids for *their effort,* instead of for "being smart," helps them develop a growth mindset and a more positive disposition. By using growth mindset phrases that encourage effort (not just intelligence), you teach your students to value their effort and hard work.

Phrases to Encourage a Growth Mindset

- "You learn from your mistakes."

- When a child says they can't do something or don't know something, reply, "Maybe you can't do it *yet.*" Or, "You may not know it *yet.*"

- "Great effort!"

- "Hard work leads to success."

- "Putting in effort is exercise for your brain."

- "Failure equals learning"

- "Build your brain's muscles by working hard!"

- "Thinking is like giving your brain a workout at the gym."

- "Never give up!"

- "Everyone makes mistakes."

- "I applaud how hard you're working!"

- "I can tell you tried your best on this."

- "When the work gets hard, you start learning."

- "Great job of hanging in there!"

- "When the work gets hard, your brain tries harder, and you get smarter."

- "If it's not hard, it's not helping you learn."

- "Work hard in order to be successful."

- "You did such a good job on this [project/worksheet/test/quiz/etc.] and it shows, because you worked so hard on it."

- "I love how you didn't give up, even when the work was hard."

- "I'm so proud of how you worked through that difficult challenge!"

- "You can learn almost anything as long as you put in the effort."

- "You are so hard working!" (Say this instead of, "You are so smart!")

Using these growth mindset phrases with your students will teach them the value of hard work and encourage them to put in the effort needed to succeed in school and beyond. Furthermore, using the phrases in Figure 6.2 helps you stay positive while teaching and builds positive relationships with your students to create a more caring classroom community.

Figure 6.3 is a worksheet designed to practice reframing statements to students to foster a growth mindset. These are best done with a learning partner or a teacher colleague so that you can better collaborate on positive and specific praise of effort versus intelligence. Figure 6.4 provides a checklist for teachers to better integrate growth mindset teaching into everyday practice.

Growth Mindset: Communication Matters!

How would you transform the statements below to promote a growth mindset?

NOTE: Keep in mind that it's natural to say general things like "good job" or "nice work." These phrases are too general because they do not identify a specific action that you are commenting on.

Instead of . . .	I would say . . .	Why would this be better?
Good job! You must be really smart at this!	Good job! Working hard and trying new strategies is really showing how much you know.	Praising the process instead of ability implies that hard work and trying new strategies is what leads to success.
Some of these problems are tough. Just do what you can.	Some of these problems are tough. Try them even if you think you'll get them wrong because mistakes are what help you learn. Sometimes you learn the most when you think hard.	Just telling students to try hard doesn't help them understand *why* they should try hard. This reframe helps explain that making mistakes is what will help them grow.

Figure 6.2.   Growth mindset phrases for positive communication.

Unpacking Some Myths About Mindsets

Before diving into strategies you can use to teach growth mindset to your students, let's discuss some of the common myths and misconceptions about mindsets.

- *MYTH: Self-affirmations are the same as a growth mindset.* A child's self-esteem is distinct and different from a growth mindset. Growth mindset is focused instead on understanding how the right kind of effort leads to real growth of a child's abilities.

- *MYTH: Your mindset is global and the same as you approach different tasks.* Even though we may have an overall tendency toward a growth or fixed mindset approach to learning, we often approach different tasks and abilities with different mindset orientations.

Rephrasing for a Growth Mindset

Instead of . . .	I would say . . .	Why would this be better?
You are such a good reader!		
This isn't really your strongest subject, is it?		
You made a lot of mistakes on this paper. Now what?		
You don't know how to do this problem, do you?		
I'm so proud of you for getting a good grade!		
Please redo this.		

Figure 6.3. Growth mindset phrases communication worksheet.

Checklist of Growth Mindset Teaching Practices

Avoid Sorting Students

Sorting students into ability groups (high performers together and low performers together) can reinforce a fixed mindset and demonstrate to your students that you have different expectations of them based on their past performance. Instead, try to:

- Use flexible grouping.
- Emphasize high expectations for *all* students.
- Avoid use of labels, such as "smart."
- Acknowledge different students publicly for positive work habits (much easier when focus is on learning strategies and process rather than academic performance).

Set Growth Mindset Norms

Teaching students about how the human brain is malleable helps them understand why it is true that we can all grow our abilities. It is especially important to:

- Teach students that our brains get stronger when we are challenged.
- Emphasize that the goal is learning, above specific outcomes or products.
- Create classroom environments where intellectual challenges are reinforced.
- Teach students to see mistakes as opportunities for growth.

Feedback & Assessment

Opportunities to receive performance feedback are part of improving our abilities and reinforcing a growth mindset. Try to use these strategies:

- Provide praise that focuses on the process rather than the product.
- Ensure praise for effort is authentic and justified.
- When students are challenged, affirm high standards and reassure them that you believe in their ability to succeed.
- Provide specific feedback that focuses on how to improve.
- Structure assignments so that revisions are allowed and "do-overs" are acceptable
- Encourage collaboration and seeking help, but not as a shortcut around meeting a challenge.

Figure 6.4. Checklist of growth mindset teaching practices. (*Source:* Sun, 2015.)

- *MYTH: Your* mindset *is a "golden ticket" for self-motivation.* Knowing that you can extend your abilities through a growth mindset is not enough. You need to perceive those abilities as particularly relevant to achieving your goals to develop them.

- *MYTH: M*indset *is an "either/or" condition.* No one has a completely fixed or growth mindset. We all have a "mixed mindset," depending on the situation. It is more accurate to talk about the degree to which a student holds a fixed or growth mindset about their abilities.

- *MYTH: Mindset is a shortcut to success.* Developing a growth mindset takes time and involves engaging in effective instructional practices. Having a growth mindset does not make you smarter . . . it just opens the door and provides an opportunity to becoming smarter by being more positive and proactive.

- *MYTH: Mindsets are unchanging.* Mindsets in our classrooms can be changed and can evolve over time. As teachers, we must focus on the conditions for learning we establish in our classrooms as well as expectations and the messages we convey in our feedback to students.

- *MYTH: Mindsets are innate.* Mindsets do not define us, nor are they an innate part of who we are. We are not born with a certain mindset. Mindsets are developed through our experiences and the messages we receive from others.

- *MYTH: Offering students generic praise is enough to encourage them.* Research has shown that just telling children that they're smart and implying that their success depends on it fosters a fixed mindset, not a growth mindset. As a consequence, when these children later experience a roadblock or challenge and they struggle, they might conclude that they aren't "smart" after all, and they lose confidence. Therefore, our generic praise has the opposite effect of what we intended. However, being more specific about praising hard work or strategies used (things that children control) has been shown to support a growth mindset.

- *MYTH: All that matters is what's in the mind.* Another confusion about mindset is that the only determining factor for success is our mindset. However, other factors matter as well. For instance, context, culture, environment, and systems play a role in success. Furthermore, students' mindsets (as well as other beliefs and behaviors) are strongly shaped and influenced by the people around them.

STRATEGIES FOR YOUR CLASSROOM

Helping Students Develop a Growth Mindset: Focus on the Positive

In fostering a growth mindset, it is important to be a cheerleader instead of a critic. Try to focus on positive behavior. For instance, you watch students to determine what motivates them and get to know what they enjoy outside of school. Students who struggle with academics are often very talented in other areas. Therefore, ask yourself, "What motivates this student?" and "What special talents does this student have?" I discovered that once I made this change in *my* attitude, I started to see the students differently and embraced the concept of growth mindset.

It is important to do some specific, positive mindset prep with your students. Here are some strategies that are easily implemented in your classroom:

- *Help your students make achievable, believable, and doable progress step-by-step by being "goal getters."* After your morning meeting, have students think about setting their own personal goal for the day. Be sure to model this activity with them so their goals are indeed specific, achievable, and measurable. Encourage students to jot this personal goal down on a sticky note. For the younger students, provide a sentence stem: "This day would be a success for me if . . ." Then have them share their goals verbally with a learning partner. In conclusion, they place their sticky note on their desk or table so they can focus on it all day. At the end of the school day, give students a few minutes to revisit their goal and share with a learning partner whether they achieved it.

Accordingly, praise their efforts and strategies as opposed to their intelligence. Why? Because children praised for their intelligence tend to view their intelligence as a fixed trait and don't put effort into their learning.

- *Develop classroom activities that foster cooperative—rather than individualistic or competitive—work.* Research supports that children are more motivated and successful when working in groups (Veldman et al., 2020). Why? Students feel a sense of responsibility to their group to try their best and receive positive feedback from their peers for both effort and success and encourage the development of a growth mindset.

- *Help students focus on the value of the learning process.* Without this emphasis on *learning outcomes,* students might often base their perceptions of their own intelligence on a singular test score or grade received, promoting a fixed mindset. While grades may be important, the *value of learning* needs to be prioritized.

- *Like muscles in your body, your brain can be strengthened with exercise.* Be sure to remind your students that they have the ability to strengthen their brains. Relate it to playing sports or their time at recess on the playground. How do you get better on the monkey bars? By practice and using the right muscles. The same thing can apply to their brains.

- *Hand out "Goodness" awards.* Be sure to explain *why* that student has demonstrated a specific positive quality, gesture of kindness, and/or goodness. Celebrate their accomplishments at the morning meeting or closing community circle.

- *Create a caring classroom community in which students feel comfortable making mistakes.* Mistakes need to be viewed as learning opportunities, not roadblocks. Teachers need to respond to mistakes as teachable moments, not as an excuse to point out impairments. It is important to have students learn to work through challenges to build confidence and a growth mindset. For instance, if one of your students misreads a word problem in math, use it as an opportunity to teach the "language" of math, help them to reread, or highlight key words, rather than attacking it with a red pen, which signals failure to many students.

- *Use the windowpane strategy to highlight role models.* It's important to post pictures and stories of positive role models in your classroom. Ask your students who their role models are (a caretaker, a friend, a celebrity, etc.). Your students can also be role models for each other. Create a "windowpane" poster, as in Figure 6.5, and post around your room. You can use other prompts appropriate for the age level of your students.

- *Be careful not to nurture a sense of "learned helplessness" in class.* Model a growth mindset in the language you use and how you respond to your own challenges. Show them what a growth mindset looks like in action. For instance, if you are having difficulty with projecting and interacting with your lesson on the Smart Board, you could say, "I am facing some hurdles with this new technology, and I haven't figured out how to project it clearly *yet,* but when I do, I know it will be a valuable tool for our classroom." This is much more positive than saying to the class, "I am not good at technology, so I won't use this."

Name	
Picture of student	Interests
Goals	Favorite subject (and why)

Figure 6.5. Windowpane poster worksheet.

- *Practice managing mistakes.* This activity helps your students understand how to manage mistakes and use failure as an opportunity rather than getting stuck and discouraged. Here are some steps to take in implementing this activity:

  - Ask students to write down a mistake that they made this week and how it made them feel.

  - Next, instruct students to crumple up the paper in a tight little ball and toss it away with the same feeling they experienced when they made their mistake.

Scaffold Instruction to Support *All* Learners to Succeed

Look for signs with your students of undue frustration and support those students, not by making the task easier but by helping them find another way to complete the task. Unproductive struggle can lead the students to embrace a fixed mindset. In contrast, productive struggle can be a positive process as you scaffold instruction for students to be successful with rigorous tasks. Scaffolding is breaking up the learning into chunks and providing a tool, or structure, with each chunk. When scaffolding reading, for example, you might preview the text and discuss key vocabulary, or chunk the text and then read and discuss as you go. For my student who was struggling to write his name, I perceived he might have been overwhelmed by how many letters in his name he saw at once. I modified the task by cutting up the letters and allowing him to succeed by manipulating the letters one at a time. This hands-on approach supported him in the writing of his complete name with all the letters included.

"Make the Lightbulb Go Off!"   This activity sheet in Figure 6.6 gives the students a time to reflect on learning something new as well as their reactions to failure.

Meet to Discuss Mistakes   During your morning meeting, discuss how mistakes are actually good and how we learn from them. Here are some questions to get you started:

1. How do you feel when you make a mistake? Why?

2. Have you ever discovered something new after making a mistake? Did you learn from this mistake? How?

3. How do you think other kids see you when you make a mistake? Why?

4. Have you ever felt proud after making a mistake? Why?

5. Has a mistake ever shifted your response to a problem? How?

Reflect on Mistakes   This is a positive strategy to use with individual students who seem particularly bothered by a mistake they made. First, remind them that mistakes are a necessary part of life. They can use a mistake as an opportunity to grow. Encourage them to reflect and/or write in their journal first, responding to the following questions:

1. What did you do when you made the mistake?

2. How did you realize you were wrong?

3. How did you think about the problem?

4. How did you feel when you made the mistake?

5. How did you respond at the time?

6. What did you learn from this mistake?

Lightbulb Worksheet

Name: _____

Draw or write your reflections

Think of a time you learned something new.

What steps did you take?

Think of a time that you failed at something.

How did you feel?

What happened?

Figure 6.6. Lightbulb worksheet.

Take some time to discuss their responses with them. Praise them for their effort and be specific about the praise you give. Encourage them to try new strategies in the future.

Talk About How to "Own Your Learning" During Morning Meeting   Create an anchor chart by the same name and have the students share their own ideas before you record them on the chart. Empower the students to be more in control of their own reactions based on certain circumstances. Figure 6.7 includes some suggestions to get the brainstorming started.

Techniques for Teaching Students About Growth Mindset

The following is a list of easy-to-implement teaching strategies that can be included in any curriculum to encourage students to use effective learning strategies, demonstrate effort, embrace challenges, and persist through challenges.

- *It is important to focus on process over product.* You can do this by posting students' works in progress, instead of only what they've finished, so that students can see how their work develops over time with effort.

- *Nurture a caring classroom culture that allows risk taking and mistakes to be seen as learning opportunities.* When students do make a mistake, show them how to try different strategies if the first ones don't work. In other words, teach them how to think about what to try next, like a detective solving a mystery.

- *Embrace mistakes as part of the learning process.* Communicate your own growth mindset goals by writing your students a letter about how mistakes are opportunities to learn.

- *Use targeted language that focuses attention on the strategies students can use and the importance of efforts, rather than results.* Doing so encourages students to "hang in there" and attempt greater challenges.

- *Teach them that "the struggle is good" and is part of the learning process, and emphasize reflection by modeling and guiding student learning through think-aloud strategies.* See Table 6.3 for examples of a fixed mindset versus a growth mindset when it comes to facing a challenging situation.

Being a Growth Mindset Teacher

With some practice, teaching through a growth mindset lens will become second nature. The following strategies will help you on your journey to becoming a growth mindset teacher.

Communicate Consistently With Students   It is important to value a student's persistence and effort, not just the grade that they earned. Base your feedback on the *process* of learning and be specific in your praise. Assessment should be formative and ongoing so that the student clearly understands their own progress.

Pay particular attention to the kind of praise used to recognize a student's accomplishments. Remember that the vague statement of "Good job" goes in one ear and out the other. That phrase tells them nothing. How could you reframe it to be more specific? See the Resources section (Appendix A) of this book for activities you can complete to help you with reframing statements to promote a growth mindset.

Teach the Process of Learning   Spend time teaching and modeling specific tools, strategies, and techniques that help the students succeed so that they feel empowered to move ahead.

Own Your Learning

Before you say, "I'm done," ask yourself . . .

- Did I do my best?

- Did I ask for help?

- Did I include everything I was supposed to?

- Did I double-check my work?

- Did I ask for teacher feedback?

- Is there anything I can do to make it better?

- How can I improve?

- Am I satisfied that this is the best I can do?

- What else can I do?

Figure 6.7. Own your learning poster.

Table 6.3. Differences between mindsets, based on specific reactions to certain issues

Fixed mindset	Growth mindset
Challenges are avoided–Lead to failure.	*Challenges* are embraced–Lead to growth.
Success of others–Seen as a threat; perceive others as more talented.	*Success of others*–Seen as inspirational and something for which to strive.
Tendency–Tries to appear to others as capable as possible.	*Tendency*–Tries to learn and improve as much as possible.
Effort–Seen as an indication of lack of talent.	*Effort*–Views success of others as motivation for further learning.
Response to failure–Seen as an indicator of lack of talent and gives up easily.	*Response to failure*–Seen as indicator that more effort needed or to try different strategies.
Impact on development–Potential is underutilized.	*Impact on development*–Potential is ever-involving.
Response to criticism–Self-defeating defensiveness.	*Response to criticism*–Eager to learn; inquisitive and interested.
Effect on other people–Can impede feedback and growth.	*Effect on other people*–Can impact cooperation and stimulate growth.

Understand Mindsets   When you hear fixed mindset statements from your students, take time to reframe the language through a growth mindset lens. Help your students discover the power of the word *yet*. ("I haven't figured this out, yet!") Teach your students the basics about growth and fixed mindsets—both facts and myths.

Design Learning Experiences   Provide clear objectives, expectations, and outcomes in advance of the lesson. It is important to emphasize and value individual growth instead of ranking among their peers. Frame your feedback to students using growth mindset language and messaging.

Model Growth Mindset   Embrace your own mistakes as learning opportunities and, when appropriate, share these when they happen with your students. Share your learning goals with the students as well as your progress in attaining them so that they see that learning is a journey.

Create a Growth Learning Environment   Let the students know that you value mistakes as part of the learning process. Encourage students to take responsible risks. Provide students with formative assessment techniques that are ongoing and shift to assessment for learning.

Embrace Parents as Partners   Connect and collaborate with parents and other caretakers on an ongoing basis. Report on student progress and growth throughout the semester, not just on report cards or for parent conferences. Discuss establishing shared values with families for growth.

Focus on Growth Assessments   *Growth assessments* are formative assessments that help guide student learning and monitor progress and successes. Students with learning challenges can especially benefit when teachers check in often and provide additional instruction and positive feedback. Growth assessments also help students identify their areas of strengths and learning opportunities that need further practice and reinforcement. Some examples of growth assessments may include individual conferences, class discussions, interviews, and informal observations of how students are applying what they've learned. Children can also contribute to their growth assessments—depending on the age and ability level of the students—and use self-assessments such as journal entries and personal checklists to monitor their own progress. Keeping track of students' growth, including learning challenges they have overcome, helps to develop a growth mindset.

Design an "I Am" Mirror Wall   This is such a positive way for children and staff to reflect on what makes them special. A section of a hallway in the school is lined with mirrors of various shapes and sizes and varying styles and frames, all with dozens of statements beneath them written neatly by kids on multicolored paper: "I am kind," "I am a mathematician," "I am my own work of art." It helps kids envision what they can become and gives them a confidence boost while they're passing by the mirrors in the hall.

Complete the How to Grow a Growth Mindset Worksheet   Instruct students to use the "Growth Mindset" growing plant activity sheet to complete and fill out the blank speech bubbles with positive language (Figure 6.8).

Read Stories With Characters Who Face Roadblocks and Overcome Them   Take time during your teacher read-alouds to feature books with resilient main characters to model growth mindset to your students. Teaching growth mindset using picture books in your classroom community is so important! Students connect with the characters and are transported on a journey of growth and change. This is also an excellent way to start a discussion about growth mindset or to introduce the concept to your students. Here are some sample titles with which to start:

1. *Your Fantastic Elastic Brain: Stretch It, Shape It,* by JoAnn Deak, PhD: This picture book will show your students how to make themselves smarter, better, and faster! It's a story about being brave, trying new things … and why you can't give up on learning. It teaches growth mindset in kid-friendly phrases such as "Reaching for the Stars!"

2. *The Most Magnificent Thing,* by Ashley Spires: The main character of this story has the vision to create something amazing and magnificent. But after many failures, she realizes that creating it is not as easy as she thought, and she gets mad and gives up. With a little nudging from her best dog friend, she decides to look at things differently and try again.

3. *Beautiful Oops,* by Barney Saltzberg: This book is filled with many inspirational ideas of how to turn mistakes into something beautiful!

4. *The Girl Who Never Made Mistakes,* by Mark Pett: This story is about a girl who loves to be perfect and who is afraid to make a mistake. She learns that she can't control everything and that mistakes do happen. Eventually, she begins to embrace making mistakes and doesn't give up.

In these stories, students will meet characters who are faced with problems and learn how they handle mistakes. When they encounter similar challenges in class, refer them to these stories so they can apply one or more of them to their situation.

Use Music to Set a Positive Mood   Music can be a powerful instructional tool. Set the stage for movement to make your lessons livelier and more meaningful. Here are examples of a few songs that focus on that "can-do" spirit of determination and courage:

- "It's Not Over Yet," by for KING & COUNTRY (an inspiring song about not giving up)

- "Celebration," by Kool and the Gang (a lively, fun song that will get them up and moving and feeling joyful)

- "Rise Up," by Andra Day (a motivational song about staying strong)

- "Eye of the Tiger," by Survivor (a song about fighting through challenges)

Growth Mindset

Having a **growth mindset** means that when you make mistakes you can stay positive and remind yourself to keep going and try to improve. A **fixed mindset** means you are "stuck" and think you can't get better – even if you try. You might say, "I can't do this," or "I give up."

Read the samples below and color in the ones that you think will help you grow when things get tough for you and cross out the ones that show you are giving up. What other "can do" statements do you think of? Write them in the blank bubbles.

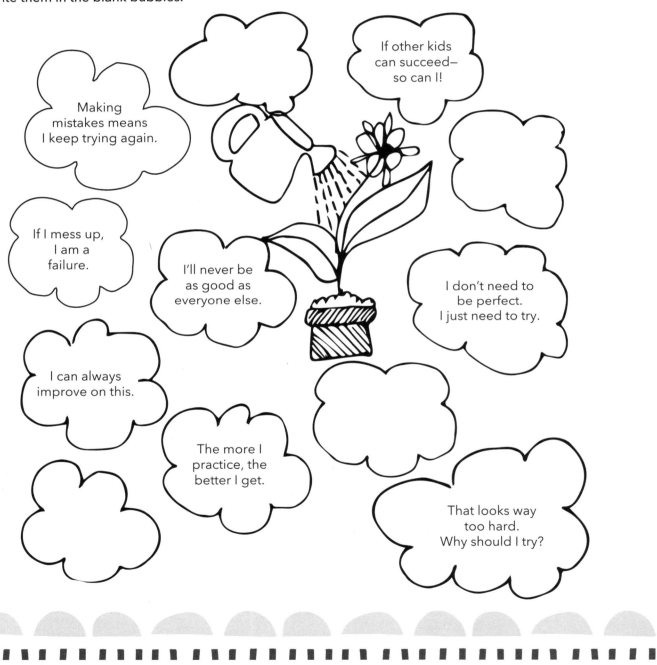

Figure 6.8. Growth mindset worksheet. (From MyleMarks. [n.d.]; adapted by permission.)

In *The Social-Emotional Learning Toolbox* by Kathy Perez (2022, Paul H. Brookes Publishing Co., Inc.)

After playing the songs in the classroom, you can extend the learning and help the kids apply the lessons from the lyrics with the following activities:

1. Duplicate and pass out the lyrics of the songs. Ask the children to choose their favorite line from the song and then answer the question, "How does this describe a growth mindset?" Consider putting this message from the music on a sentence strip and posting it on the classroom wall to reinforce the positive pointer.

2. Ask your students to find their own growth mindset song and bring it into the class to share.

3. Have the class vote on a growth mindset theme song. After several songs have been shared that demonstrate a growth mindset theme, ask the class to select one of the songs to be the class's "anthem" or theme song. This song can be a unifying and bonding theme song that your students identify with and use throughout the year to inspire them.

Mindset Reflection Is the Key to Success!   After you have discussed growth mindset and fixed mindsets with your students and you think they understand it, press the "pause button" and let them reflect on times when they have demonstrated a growth mindset in their own lives. I like to use the analogy of a lock and key when discussing the difference. A lock represents a fixed mindset or a challenge they are facing. The key represents a growth mindset. When students have a growth mindset, they can unlock their challenges. All you need is an open lock and key graphic such as the one in Figure 6.9. Have students write a challenge that they have faced inside the image of the lock. Then, discuss how having a growth mindset can help them overcome the challenge. Next, ask students to write about their own growth mindset messages inside the key.

Try a Different Way   When students initially struggle or make mistakes, use that as an opportunity to teach students how to try different strategies if at first they don't succeed. Invite them to think about what to try next.

Complete Growth Mindset Exit Tickets   Instruct students to reflect on their day and their successes. Use reflective question prompts to have the students write about their daily accomplishments before they leave for home—even if they struggled during the lesson. Meet them at the door and have each student submit an "exit ticket" when they leave. These tickets can be used as a formative assessment tool so that you can identify the emotional states of your individual students and who might need more support.

Act Out Growth Mindset Skits   Have pairs of students or small groups act out a short skit that demonstrates growth mindset in action! Set the stage by sharing with the class a pretend challenge. Then, have groups or partners discuss how they would respond to the challenge with a fixed mindset. Older students can write out their responses. Then ask them to take the same situation, but this time, they should respond with a growth mindset. This makes for fun discussions and lots of learning!

Say, "I Believe You Can"   Use thoughtful comments when providing feedback to your students that nudge them to achieve their goals and show your confidence in them. For example,

Figure 6.9. Lock and key image.

"I'm giving you these comments because I have high expectations and I know that you can reach them."

Utilize "Doodle and Do" Mindset Messages   Use simple drawings as a way for your students to playfully express themselves and get excited about growth mindset messages. When students create a quick sketch or doodle of something, they engage their body and their brains in the process. Doodling also helps them make connections to their learning. Here are a few ways to share with your students:

1. *Doodle desk cards*—Have kids combine growth mindset quotes or messages with colors and designs to serve as a daily desk reminder.

2. *Doodle* mindset *makeovers*—When discussing the difference between growth mindset and fixed mindset, challenge students to doodle what they would look and feel like with a *fixed* mindset. Then, have them give those doodles a makeover to switch the drawing to what they would look and feel like with a *growth* mindset.

Create "Celebrating Success" Files   Consider keeping track of students' successes. Encourage your class create their own "Celebrate Success" file by transforming a simple manila folder into a colorful collection of evidence and artifacts of even their smallest successes. The file is continuously updated and provides evidence to help students remember their learning successes. Here are the step-by-step directions:

1. Give every student a folder to use as a success file.

2. Ask students to write the word *success* on their file and/or draw a picture that represents success for them.

3. As a daily routine, ask students to add to their folders examples of their own successful learning.

4. As part of your morning meeting routine, have students review their Success File to reinforce the accomplishments they have made and to set the stage for a positive start to the day.

Use "Fresh-Start Reframing" for Your Own Mindsets   Don't get caught up about what last year's teacher told you about your students. Start fresh with your students and have high expectations to instill in them that "can-do" spirit. Let them know that you want them *all* to reach for the stars and that you will help them succeed. Then, follow through with your promise—*every day*. Learn one new thing about each student each week. Maybe eat lunch with your students or connect more deeply with students who are not connecting with others or with you.

Share and Discuss Mindset Heroes   Read biographies about famous people who have a growth mindset. Discuss how the person demonstrated a growth mindset in their lifetime. What challenges did they overcome?

Consider setting up a Growth Mindset Person of the Week. Each week, discuss a famous person and his or her growth mindset. Some examples include Michael Jordan, Malala Yousafzai, Dr. Martin Luther King Jr., and Albert Einstein.

Allow for Student Choice and Voice   When students can choose topics to study that tap into their own personal interests, they are more likely to maintain interest and motivation. Giving students choices also emphasizes that they are in charge of their own learning. It is so exciting to see the "lightbulb go off" with even my students who are struggling as they are allowed to follow their passion projects.

Growth-Mindset Quotes for Kids

I like to share growth mindset quotes during morning meetings as a time to discuss important concepts and ideas. The students are fresh and focused, and they enjoy gathering as a classroom community. This is a time when we explore feelings and students feel empowered and know that their voices are heard when we are all together during this time. This special time starts our day off on the right note. That is why this time to come together is the perfect time to share favorite quotes for growth mindset. Instead of sharing quote after quote, we spend a great deal of time each week focusing on just one quote. Here is an overview of how we "unpack" a quote and develop it one day at a time:

- *Monday:* Share the quote, hang it up, and let it sink in.

- *Tuesday:* Revisit the quote and have a few students share what they think it means.

- *Wednesday:* Instruct students to discuss with learning partners what they think it means.

- *Thursday:* Have students share how they might apply the quote to their own lives.

- *Friday:* Have students do a quick-write about the quote or draw a sketch of what the quote means and how they can put it into practice.

Teaching Practices to Promote a Growth Mindset Classroom

By making simple changes in the classroom, we as educators can begin to foster an environment in which students are not only aware of growth mindset but can also actively take part in creating such a caring classroom community.

Avoid Fixed-Ability Grouping   Sorting students in homogeneous, fixed-ability groups can reinforce a fixed mindset with students as they begin to exhibit a sense of "learned helplessness" and an attitude of "Why try?" This reinforces to the students that you have different expectations of them based on past performance. However, using heterogeneous grouping of mixed-ability students emphasizes high expectations for all students. It is important not to use labels such as "smart" or "gifted" because that acknowledges different students publicly, instead of encouraging students about their effort or learning strategies used.

Keep Growth Mindset Standards High for All Students   Reinforce the concept of flexible mindsets with students to show how our brains are malleable and can grow and change over time and that we can grow our abilities. The depth to which you may go in this concept and in brain plasticity will change depending on the age and ability level of your students. However, for all students, emphasize how our brain becomes stronger when it is challenged. Focus on the goal of learning instead of the grade obtained. Create opportunities to see mistakes as opportunities for learning and explain why.

Formative Assessment and Feedback   Providing performance feedback that is ongoing over time is an essential part of improving our abilities and fostering a growth mindset. Take time to praise the process, not just the product. Ensure that praise is authentic and specific. Design assignments that allow for "re-dos" and revisions. Provide reassurance that you believe in students' ability to succeed.

SUMMARY

It is important to be aware that developing a growth mindset needs to be infused into our entire curriculum and classroom procedures and routines. It is a powerful concept that can truly change a child's life! Be patient, because this process can take time throughout the school year, but it is a process that is worth the time and attention required to make a difference with all of your learners. Through the use of these strategies, tools, and resources, your students will begin to exhibit a growth mindset, show effort, and enjoy working hard. Be sure to celebrate the *process* of their work and not just the *product*.

Finally, remember to model growth mindset in the classroom. You're one of the most influential people in your students' lives, so be sure to use growth mindset statements throughout your day. As you face challenges, point them out to the students and clearly state what you do to respond to these adversities. The more you celebrate students' successes, the more they will celebrate each other—and then you are on your way to an even more creative, caring classroom!

CHAPTER 7

Social-Emotional Learning and Relationships

How to Create a Caring, Positive Classroom Environment

Building a strong, caring, collaborative classroom environment is of paramount importance for your students' well-being. And yet, educators tend to become preoccupied with teaching lessons, prepping for tests, making sure students hit certain benchmarks, and worrying over principals' observations. Creating a caring classroom starts on the very first day of school. One of the most important steps a teacher can take that first week of a new school year is to establish a warm and caring atmosphere in their classroom. This includes building an environment of trust, where students can feel free to be themselves without worrying that their classmates will make fun of them. Similarly, and at the same time, you'll want to establish clear expectations for acceptable behavior that first day.

KEY CONCEPTS

- Why is a caring classroom environment so important?

- What are some classroom routines that build community?

- What are some strategies to support the whole child?

- How do you provide voice and choice in the classroom?

- What are some flexible grouping strategies to ensure collaborative and cooperative learning?

INTRODUCTION

How can a teacher build a strong classroom community with so little time in the day? This chapter shares some of my favorite ways to build that caring classroom community. It is important to ensure that your classroom is an emotionally safe place for *all* students. The good news? The strategies in this chapter require little prep work and may just be the highlight of your school day! The key factors to creating a welcoming environment include cultivating relationships, creating positive classroom procedures and routines, and investigating innovative ways to create collaborative communities. Using these techniques, we enhance our students' ability to learn and succeed throughout the school year.

Creating a caring classroom community involves providing a warm, safe environment in which children can learn and grow. Abraham Maslow's "Hierarchy of Needs" (1943) states that having one's basic needs met is the foundation for building "higher levels" of understanding. For children to become successful learners, their basic needs for safety and belonging must first be met.

In a caring classroom setting, children will be able to experience and celebrate a positive sense of their own power, strengths, and abilities. When students are able to experience a productive sense of their ability to learn, grow, and contribute to the lives of others, they are also able to maintain positive interactions, which promotes their resilience as well as academic achievement.

What Does the Research Say?

The phrase "a caring community of learners" has occurred with increasing frequency in the literature (Wisneski & Goldstein, 2004). Research indicates that student achievement increases when students feel comfortable in their learning environment. A caring classroom is not only comfortable, it also allows the teacher to spend more time teaching and less time handling student conflicts and behavior issues.

From a historical perspective, almost a century has passed since John Dewey pondered and published his findings on the meaning and practice of education, and yet his writings still hold truth today. His writings presented a new perspective on viewing education as a process (Dewey, 1938). In other words, Dewey promoted learning by doing, rather than learning by passively receiving. He believed that students learn through experience, are naturally inquisitive, and need to explore. This chapter presents a robust collection of many strategies built on the theories, philosophies, and models of Dewey and others that embrace experiential learning to create a positive classroom community. For instance, Howard Gardner (1993), Daniel Goleman (1995), and Susan Kovalik (1998) present compelling evidence in their research that a classroom needs to consider the whole child, rather than just focusing on cognitive skills and academic achievement. Their theories of multiple intelligences, emotional intelligence, and brain-based learning are all essential ingredients of a total classroom experience. Addressing the multiple needs of all learners can be accomplished through creating a safe, caring classroom that offers student voice and choice.

Furthermore, Alfie Kohn (1996), William Glasser (1988), and Jeanne Gibbs's TRIBES Program (1995) all extend the vision on how this can be accomplished. Glasser asserts that the majority of the student's day is unsatisfactory if it does not develop essential human needs of belonging, freedom, fun, survival, and power (Glasser, 1988). He further contends that someone who does not feel a sense of belonging may seek it in ways that are less socially acceptable in school. Similarly, Purkey and Novak (1996), in their invitational education approach, promote the concept that there is one overarching theme to creating an inclusive classroom community in summing up the axiom "I teach people, not subjects." Their approach to invitational education is based on how students perceive themselves and classrooms' ability to be a welcome place for all students to enter. If education is to be truly inviting, then it must be intentionally so. Creating community in the classroom takes more than just an attitudinal shift. It takes perseverance, empathy, and commitment to properly use the tools and techniques that are shared in this chapter based on the research of what really makes a difference in educating the whole child.

Focusing on schools as communities is becoming quite common in the literature on effective schools (e.g., Brandt, 1992; Carnegie Council on Adolescent Development, 1989; Hallinger & Murphy, 1986; Lightfoot, 1984; Schaps & Solomon, 1990; Sizer, 1984). However, there is not a general agreement about the definition of what a school community is, nor has there been much research on the effects of school communities on teachers and students. There are, however, common elements in descriptions of classroom communities. In general, communities are defined as places where members care about and support one another; actively participate in and have influence on the group's activities and decisions; feel a sense of belonging and identification with the group; and have common norms, goals, and values (Bryk & Driscoll, 1988; Goodenow, 1993; Higgins et al., 1984; McMillan & Chavis, 1986; Wehlage et al., 1992).

Furthermore, research has proven that positive, caring interpersonal classroom relationships can actually increase student motivation and academic achievement (Furrer & Skinner, 2003; Pianta & Stuhlman, 2004; Wentzel, 1999). Teachers realize that this collaborative approach, when modeled and practiced properly, is positively infused in all lessons throughout the day. In fact, the impact of caring classroom relationships is so powerful that studies have found a connection between students' relationships with their kindergarten teachers and their achievement scores all the way through middle school (Hamre & Pianta, 2001).

It's important to recognize that teaching can be stressful for any educator. Creating and modeling caring relationships in the classroom make empathy and compassion more likely in students, thereby reducing teachers' stress (Mikulincer et al., 2005). Therefore, fostering teacher–student relationships helps to prevent some behavioral problems from happening and makes it easier to deal with those that do arise.

It has been a unique decade for school climate. Growing numbers of schools, nationally and internationally, have given increased focus to students' SEL. There is a call to action for the general educational community to understand how integrating SEL can improve students' well-being, academic achievement, and the overall school climate. In the current educational climate, and with the increased demands that parents have in balancing caregiving with their careers, our times demand more intentionality for the community as a whole in building relationships with others (Putnam & Feldstein, 2009). That's why having students participate in building the classroom community where everyone feels valued, connected, and responsible is so important.

It is also important to develop positive relationships among students to make for a more peaceful, caring classroom environment. In fact, positive relationships with peers are an essential factor that helps build children's resilience, and mutual friendships can reduce the probability of maladjustment (Ladd & Burgess, 2001; Sroufe et al., 2005). When our students get along with one another and feel as if they are an important part of the classroom community, they are more likely to perform better academically (Gifford-Smith & Brownell, 2003; Wentzel, 1999). In fact, in *Understanding by Design*, Wiggins and McTighe (2005) identify understanding another's perspective and responding empathetically as a central component to promoting achievement.

Although we may be looking for a quick fix for making our classrooms caring communities, Gibbs (1995) reminds us that the process takes time and requires that we make the classroom more student centered. This involves creating community agreements, convening morning meetings and community circles for sharing feelings, and the teaching of collaborative skills. Kohn (1996) also supports the need to adopt this community approach in the classroom and changing from the notion of "doing to" students to "working with" them. This involves seeing students as partners in the educational process.

STRATEGIES FOR YOUR CLASSROOM

Importance of Procedures and Routines

According to Howell and Reinhard (2015), "Rituals and traditions have the power to shape classroom routines into times that build meaningful connections and bonds among children, families, and teachers, creating and strengthening a sense of community" (p. 6) in the classroom setting.

What are some of those positive, classroom routines? Gather the students together as part of your morning meeting, early in the school year, to discuss the "conditions needed to work together." Notice, that I did *not* say, "Classroom Rules." Why? I do not suggest that teachers create a list of punitive rules that start with negative phrases such as "No _____" or "Don't do this or that." Instead, you want to involve all the students to discuss what everyone *should* do as part of the classroom community. Together, create an anchor chart that will remain posted in a prominent location in the classroom so that these conditions are clearly visible to all, all day long and all year long. Some sample "conditions" or "norms" might include those listed in Figures 7.1 and 7.2. It is important to practice, model, and review important classroom procedures and routines to ensure smooth implementation throughout the day and throughout the school year.

Routines are helpful procedures that assist memory, and rituals are repeated events that elicit feelings and provide a feeling of belonging. Consider setting up several procedures that support a positive feeling.

At the beginning of class:

- Play the same music.

- Instruct students to meet in the circle or in small groups to check in with each other.

- Complete quick-write activities.

- Integrate movement activities.

- Teach a clapping ritual to get students' attention.

    At the end of class:

- Play familiar music.

- Instruct students to complete exit tickets.

- Complete a quick recap of important points.

- Gather for Closing Community Circle time.

Working Together

- Work as a team

- Be responsible

- Listen to others

- Be respectful to everyone

- Be kind and helpful

- Do your best

- Take turns

- Pause before reacting

Figure 7.1. Working together poster.

Procedures and Routines
Review, Model, and Practice How To . . .

- Enter the room in the morning

- Put away your belongings

- Gather for morning meeting or mini-lesson

- Respond to teacher's signals (for quiet, attention, transitions)

- Get the teacher's attention

- Complete "classroom helper" jobs

- Clean up at the end of day

- Distribute paper, materials to your table group

- Collect materials, papers from your table group

- Sign and date your papers

- Line up for recess

- Walk in the halls

- Select books for your "book basket"

- Play at recess

- Use play equipment safely

- Read with a partner

- Work with a partner/small group

- Turn in homework

- Signals for talk time/quiet time

- Use and care for classroom computers and technology

- Keep papers and notebooks organized

- Throw away and recycle trash

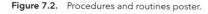

Figure 7.2. Procedures and routines poster.

Conditions Needed to Work Together

Here are some things you would see in a caring, collaborative classroom community that embraces social-emotional learning:

- Student work posted around the classroom walls

- Students learning one another's names

- Students being grouped with peers randomly and flexibly in new and different groupings and not in fixed-ability groups

- Photographs of students used to organize them into groups

- A class "Welcome" sign on the front door

- Teacher's desk in the back of the classroom

- Students' desks grouped together in "pods" of four or five desks as a workspace cluster

- Use of "we" more than "me" or "you"

- A class poem written together in the first week of school

- Classroom "norms" or "conditions needed to work together" that are posted, based on student contributions and voting agreements

- Talk of *learning* more than worksheets or grades

- A "know it when you see it" culture (attempt to categorize an observable event)

- A "love it when you live it" (being true to yourself) community

Integrating Cooperative Learning

Cooperative learning is particularly valuable in helping to teach and model SEL skills such as listening, teamwork, and relationship building. Cooperative learning happens when students work collectively to complete learning tasks. This approach provides students with opportunities to practice and reflect on their social and emotional skills as they also develop academic ones, whether they are working on solving a math problem or discussing a story they read. Through the use of these structures, students learn to support and challenge one another using their relationship skills and decision-making strategies for the collective good. These structures also provide students with a voice to share their ideas with their peers and reflect on their own thinking as well as learning from their peers' perspectives.

To ensure that students collaborate, contribute equitably, and resolve possible conflicts effectively, you need to be clear about certain principles and procedures:

- All team members have roles and responsibilities to the group (summarizer, reporter, recorder, timekeeper, questioner, etc.).

- Decide on the sequence and order of tasks to be accomplished.

- Agree on communication signals to use when the group completes a task or needs assistance.

- Collaborate on establishing norms for using materials and equipment.

This process requires a great deal of social and self-awareness. Cooperative learning structures and procedures also reinforce positive mindsets for students by asking them to take on challenging material in a supportive and social setting (Marzano et al., 2001).

Key Elements of Cooperative Learning   There are certain central ingredients in any cooperative learning structure, according to Johnson et al. (1989):

- *Positive interdependence.* Students need to understand that their personal success depends on the overall success of the group as a whole. This fosters social awareness and tends to motivate students who easily give up when working independently.

- *Clear intentions.* The purpose and outcomes of group work not only need to be clear to the students, but also to the teacher.

- *Individual and group accountability.* Students need to acknowledge that they are responsible for both their own learning and the learning of the group, which promotes the skills of self-management, social awareness, and responsible decision making. Structured collaboration is the key. This means that carefully developed procedures and routines need to be in place.

- *Promotion of others' success.* Relationship skills are developed when teachers encourage students to celebrate their team's efforts and to support their peers who may be struggling. Role-playing and modeling of specific behaviors and reactions can also be helpful for students so they know how to appropriately respond to a teammate who may be getting off task, for instance.

- *Group processing.* As students become more involved with cooperative learning, active listening, turn taking, and shared decision making, they also learn important skills for being more responsible for their own learning. Have the students discuss and reflect on how they are working as a group and how this guides their individual participation.

Strategies to Support the Whole Child

All children deserve a school where they experience a sense of belonging. The need for belonging and a feeling of being respected and accepted is deeply human. Start small and gradually increase the implementation of structures and strategies to foster a caring classroom community. Many of these activities can easily be integrated into the routine of your "Morning Meeting" time. Here are some ideas to create smiles and spread kindness . . . one student at a time.

Morning Greetings   Start your students' day out right! Greet every child at the door with a smile and say their name. For example, I stand in the doorway, awaiting students' arrival each morning. I greet them with a handshake, fist bump, or "high 5," teaching them the value of looking someone in the eye and making connections. I also call each student by name and ask how they are doing. If I am absent, I leave a note for my guest teacher to do the same routine.

Welcome Doors   Another way to welcome students to your classroom is to decorate your door. You can use a theme, or just words, but the message must be clear: *I want you here to learn!*

Ideas for Door Themes.   Welcome the New Bunch!—Use student photos to display students' faces on apples that are all on a large apple tree.

- Oh, the Places You Will Go—Use student photos to display students' faces on balloons with a welcome message.

- Celebrate Our Differences—Create a large rainbow fish with students' faces as the scales. The message encourages diversity (the rainbow fish has many colors).

- Winners Enter Here: Success in Progress!—Create an Olympics-themed door with students' names written on Olympic medals.

- What I Am Taco'n About...—Display many small tacos with students' names and their favorite hobbies listed.

- Welcome to Ms./Mr. _____'s Nest—Create an image of a large tree on the door with tiny birds on the branches with students' names on them.

Ask a Question of the Day   To begin the morning meeting, students answer a random question of the day (see list in the Resources [Appendix A] section of this book). These questions could be anything from "What makes you happy? Sad? Angry?" to "If you could change a color in the crayon box, what would it be and why?" Students' answers allow the entire classroom community to get to know each other and have a brief conversation before the day gets started.

Celebrate Student Success   Plan a success party every year. Students and their parents are invited to celebrate individual and group successes. Parents who cannot attend are invited to participate by creating a paper heart at home and inscribing it with the success they have seen from their child at home. At school, students make their own heart and reflect on their own success. They write about where and how they have grown and developed. When I have done this in the past, I put these hearts on our door frame to greet the children as they enter the classroom.

Letter to Self   At the end of our school year, students write a letter to their future self to be opened when they graduate from high school. These are sent home as keepsakes to their parents with instructions about creating a time capsule of various artifacts from the school year to revisit upon graduation. Just the other day, a student wrote to me on Instagram that a project we did in third grade had him reflecting on his own life several years later. Isn't that the impact we want to create now for all of our students?

Friendly Fridays   It is only one day a week, but my students really look forward to this activity to end the week. Put together a jar of popsicle sticks with each student's name on them. One at a time, call the students up to pick a stick and keep the name a secret, which they love to do. They return to their desk and create a unique and friendly fun note or card to give to their classmate. Students look forward to this every week and are motivated to do quality work in this positive activity.

"Me Posters"   In order to get to know your students better, instruct them to create a "Me Poster" at the start of the year. Provide some starting points using basic pictures or shapes and then students customize the posters. When I did this as a teacher, the activity gave me valuable information about who my students were and their interests and goals—probably much more than I would have known if I had merely talked with them.

Helping Hands   Children create this collaborative class project one hand at a time by tracing the shape of their hand on construction paper. They create their own unique design on their hand and write a friendly message on it about kindness or patience. As an extension of the activity, you can pair students up and have them share their hands and the positive message with each other before creating a "Helpful Hand Collage" to display in the class. This creates a beautiful reminder of how to be friendly to each other. Some examples of the positive phrases include "Say hi to someone in the lunchroom" and "Let a classmate borrow a pencil."

Sticky Note Brainstorming   This is an excellent way to promote relationship building. Students must learn to listen, take turns speaking, prioritize ideas, and communicate in a respectful way with one another. The goal of this activity is to brainstorm, review, and think outside the box. It can be used as an "activator" at the beginning of a lesson to harvest their background knowledge about a topic, or as a "summarizer" at the end of a lesson so that students can share what they found memorable. It's also a great way for students to teach and learn from one another. It works best when kids are seated in small table groups. First, provide each table with a supply of sticky notes. Then, pose an open-ended question with multiple responses, set a time limit, and give students a moment to think before writing. At your cue to start writing, each student writes down as many answers as they can think of—one idea per sticky note—and sticks it to the center of the table. The goal is to generate as many ideas as possible and cover the table with sticky notes! At the end of each round, students review one another's ideas. Students can then select four to six of their favorite responses that they agreed on and add it to the class "Graffiti Board" (a poster placed prominently with the topic written at the top). Teams can also then discuss what common themes emerged.

Reporter and Recorder   In this activity, one student plays the role of teacher (Reporter) and the other plays the role of a student (Recorder). Explaining ideas clearly is a challenging skill that requires a lot of practice, and recording information helps students increase their note-taking skills. Pose a question and allow a few moments for Reporters to think. When the teacher says, "Go," the Reporter explains the topic clearly to the Recorder. The Recorder summarizes the key ideas from the Reporter on paper. When time is up, the Reporter and Recorder switch roles with a new question or subject matter.

Strategies to Give Your Students a Voice

Providing students with opportunities to share their opinions is an essential part of building SEL skills that will last beyond the classroom. Give your students a voice to share their opinions and beliefs via notes. For example, create different fill-in-the-blank sheets with ideas and themes that work well with the age and ability levels of your students. Some examples include "I wish my teacher knew _____," "I wish my classmates knew _____."

Positive Self-Talk   It is good to remind our students that we all need to pause and be friendly to ourselves. Start this with a discussion about how the words we use to talk or think about ourselves affect our moods and dispositions. Make an interactive bulletin board of speech bubbles with these "positive pitches" that the kids generate. Then have the students create cartoon heads of themselves or use digital headshots to attach to their speech bubble. The message is simple, but very important: be friendly and kind to yourself.

The Importance of Compliments   Researchers suggest that the use of effective compliments and appropriate praise can condition students to respond positively to tasks. Compliments provide students with the kind of positive reinforcement that builds on success, motivates them to focus and learn, and increases their participation in class. However, research also suggests that praise and compliments in the classroom are surprisingly underused (Brophy, 1981; Hawkins & Hefflin, 2011; Kern & Clemens, 2007). These strategies offer techniques for using meaningful praise and compliments to maximize positive impact on students.

Create a Compliment Chain   Take time during your morning meeting to start a tradition of giving a student in your class a genuine compliment. Then it's that student's turn to, at some point in the day, give a compliment to a classmate. It is important that you keep track of who receives your morning compliment each day so that everyone gets a chance to be part of the chain.

Compliment Circle Time   Have students form a circle and, one at a time, share a kind comment and/or a compliment about one of their classmates. The rest of the class affirms this response with a clap, clap or a snap, snap of their fingers.

Compliment Cards   Create and cut out compliment cards for students to hide around the school or classroom. Have them look for these as they go on a "treasure hunt" throughout the day. Keep them to share at the closing community circle at the end of the school day. Keep the cards simple. Depending on the age and ability level of the students, they can also create their own cards and hide them as well.

Compliment Quick Starters   Share these sentence stems with your students and ask them to choose one to complete and share with a partner next to them:

- My favorite thing about you is . . .

- I like you because . . .

- One thing I admire about you is . . .

- Thank you for . . .

- I appreciate the time you . . .

- You are a great friend because . . .

- You are special to this class because . . .

- You make this world a better place because . . .

Strategies to Get to Know Each Other

The key to teaching children social and emotional skills is creating a classroom culture built on community. Nurturing a positive community in your classroom is an ongoing process with significant benefits for students. As they get to know one another, they feel both empowered and invested.

Before discussing strategies that can help teachers build a classroom community, let's understand the importance of creating this type of classroom environment and having the students get to know one another.

Benefits of a Classroom Community   There are many benefits of fostering a caring, collaborative classroom community, including the following:

- Provides a way for all students to feel *included*

- Learns about *similarities* and *differences* between students

- Fosters students' *needs for belonging*
- Allows students to form and maintain *positive relationships* with others
- Teaches students *social skills* and the importance of working with others

Venn Diagram   This is a visual and creative way to celebrate what we have in common with each other and the differences that make us unique. Students pair up and share traits that are unique to them and their partner as well as the intersection of things they share in common.

Group Salutes   A group salute can be a teacher-prompted interaction that is quick, with minimal prep work, to cultivate community in your classroom. This shared gesture can be physical, like a fist bump or a "high 5" or verbal, like "Woo-hoo!"

"Fun Facts" Cards   Have students write a little-known "fun fact" about themselves on an index card. The teacher will select a card at random, and the rest of the class guesses who they think this fact is about. After the guessing is over, the student who wrote the fact stands up and is recognized by their classmates.

Snowball Toss   There are many ways to do this quick "summarizer" activity. For younger students, you can have them jot down three new words they learned in class that day, three new ideas, and so forth on a blank sheet of paper. Older students can write down three successes they had in class that day or three stressors/challenges they are feeling. These are anonymous, which adds to the excitement and mystery of this strategy. They crumple up their paper into a small ball (resembling a snowball). Instruct the students to gather in a circle and give them a signal to gently toss their paper "snowballs" in the air and catch somebody else's "snowball" and read it. This is a very active strategy and tends to excite the students, so it is better to save it until the last 5 minutes of class or right before recess or lunch. It is also a fun way for them to reflect on what they have learned or feel and share that with others.

Sharing "Shout-Outs"   Consider using the classroom door as the backdrop for an interactive bulletin board display that serves as a community builder. Students jot down a "shout-out" (positive comment) about one of their classmates on a sticky note and add it to the "graffiti board" display that grows and grows throughout the school week. This is a quick way for students to celebrate each other for doing something special or for attempting something challenging. Shout-outs can be incorporated at any point in the class day. It's not just the teacher saying, "You're doing well"—it's a way for the students to interact with each other and celebrate positivity.

People Bingo   Provide each student with a "People Bingo Sheet" such as the one in Figure 7.3.

- Instruct students to move around the room finding students who can do the things in each box.

- If a student can perform one of the prompts, they write their name in the box. Students cannot have a classmate sign the sheet more than once.

- Students continue collecting signatures. When a student has five boxes in a row completed, they call, "Bingo!"

Finish with a whole-class sharing. Ask students to introduce others to the class using the information that they collected.

People Bingo

Can whistle loudly	Has curly hair	Has a brother or sister	Has won a contest	Rides a bike
Loves the color blue	Has lived in another state	Plays soccer	Can speak another language	Likes to dance
Can play a musical instrument	Loves peanut butter	Has gone camping	Plays football	Is wearing green
Loves video games	Loves to swim	Has three or more pets	Enjoys math	Enjoys boating
Watches cartoons	Is an only child	Likes to read	Has freckles	Wears glasses

Figure 7.3. People bingo.

Strategies to Cultivate Kindness

Children do not learn about kindness by only thinking about it or talking about it. Kindness is best learned by feeling it so that they can pass that feeling on to others. Kindness is an emotion that students need to feel. Teaching the value of kindness to children is best done with actions, not just words. Scientific studies prove there are many physical, emotional, and mental health benefits associated with kindness.

Make "Kindness Chains"   Hanging on the wall in my classroom is always a "Kindness Chain," and it grows and grows as the children recognize and call out each other for random acts of kindness. This colorful paper chain is a visual reminder of the importance of being aware of the words we use with each other and the positive actions we take.

Play "Kindness Bingo"   Create a "Random Acts of Kindness Bingo" board and duplicate it for the class. Challenge the students to get "bingo" after they accomplish four acts of kindness in one school week. The students can color or mark it on their bingo sheet after the action is completed. Here are some examples to put on the "Bingo" grid:

- Give a compliment to someone.
- Clean up after yourself.
- Let someone go before you in line.
- Make a caring card for your teacher.
- Write a positive note to a classmate.
- Thank someone in the school for the work they do.
- Say "hi" to someone new.
- Clean up after someone else.
- Play with someone new during recess.
- Sharpen someone's pencil.
- Hold a door open for someone.
- Help someone before they ask.

Create "Kindness Rocks"   Ask each student to bring a flat, round rock to school. Instruct them paint their rocks with bright colors and write a positive message on it. The students can then put them at significant places around the school grounds to brighten the days of others when a rock is found.

How to Fill a Bucket   Bucket-filler activities encourage students to be kind in a variety of ways. Use an anchor chart with a bucket placed below it to talk to your students about what a bucket filler is and how they can fill someone's bucket. You can use an actual plastic bucket placed below the chart for them to fill with their kindness comments to each other or even use a shoe organizer to hold "minibuckets" of small plastic cups with students' names on each. Provide a stack of blank "bucket-filler" slips nearby. Kids then can write messages to each other and place them in the cups. Have everyone contribute their ideas of what they could comment to each other, including the following:

- Listen to others.
- Be nice.
- Follow the rules.
- Say "sorry."
- Take care of your own materials.
- Don't forget to smile.
- Say "please" and "thank you."
- Clean up after yourself.
- Follow the rules.
- Help out.
- Sharing is caring.

Pom-Pom Bucket Fillers Make individual "kindness buckets" using large plastic drinking cups with students' names on them. This is a cute and quick way to fill buckets throughout the school day. Recognize bucket-filler acts of kindness and behaviors by tossing a pom-pom into a student's bucket. Students will love watching their buckets fill up!

Caring/Kindness Circle Divide students into small groups of four or five. Give each group a piece of paper and a poker chip or token. Have one student in each group start by writing a way they can show kindness to others. Then pass the paper to the next student in their group. Instruct each student to write a way they can show kindness until the paper makes it around the whole group. Then have students discuss their kindness statements with the class. To indicate that they want a turn to share, students should hold up their poker chip. The poker chip is a visual reminder to show caring by listening to what others have to say and by respecting turn taking.

Random Acts of Kindness Start a discussion among the students on things they can do in class or at home to practice caring and kindness. Write ideas down on the whiteboard and ask students to pick one action to complete that month. Have them write it down on a sheet of paper like a pledge form and decorate the pledge to take home. Here are some ideas:

- Play with someone new at recess.
- Cut out a funny cartoon and give it to a friend who is sad.
- Draw a picture for someone.
- Make a happy card for someone who needs it.
- Say hello to a new friend.
- Create sticky notes with positive messages and kind words and post them around your house.
- Share lunch with someone in the cafeteria.

- Hold the door for someone who needs help.

- Let someone go ahead of you in line for recess.

- Clean up after someone else.

- Thank an adult at school for something they do.

Caring Coupon Books   Make a template in advance and print three to five coupons per student. Have each student come up with ideas of how they can help someone they care about. Instruct them to complete the coupon template and decorate them. They can give these out to family members or friends.

I care for you. I will help you _____.

Love, _____

Share the Joy   This is a fun activity designed to invite students to share happy moments in their life. Give each student a pencil and paper and ask them to remember one of the happiest moments of their lives. A simple, quick sketch is best. Next, in the discussion part of this exercise, each child comes up with a brief description of the story they have sketched, and the others listen and are encouraged to ask questions.

   This activity benefits the students because

- They relive a happy moment of the past and experience the positive emotions related to it.

- They can reflect on their inner feelings and emotions while they retell their stories.

- By listening to others, they gain insight into their own and others' feelings.

Kindness Quick Starters   The following list of quick and easy ways to show kindness will help students realize that even the simplest act of being kind to another can create a ripple effect throughout the school and their home:

- Compliment your students for a specific accomplishment, such as their creative ideas, incredible word choice, or super math skills.

- Post students' work everywhere—even in the school hallway.

- Put up a mailbox for students to deposit "kindness reports" about their classmates.

- Acknowledge each student with a greeting as they enter your room. Let them see how happy you are to see them.

- Publicly acknowledge every kindness you witness in your classroom.

- Ask your students questions about their time away from school and what they did over the weekend.

- Stay with your class during library time and help them pick out books that tap into their interests.

- Give your "grumpy" voice the day off and try to be more cheerful in your interactions.

- Take time to listen to their stories.

- Laugh at your students' jokes.

- Give away free "No homework" passes.

- Try not to rush your students to finish a task.

- Thank your principal for setting a positive tone in the building.

- Have your students decorate and sign a thank you poster for everyone in the front office.

- Invite your principal or assistant principal to a special event in your classroom, such as a readers' theater performance or class party.

- Send your students to the office occasionally for *positive* reasons, such as to share a favorite story or to show a perfect score on a spelling test.

- Email a happy note home to one of your more difficult student's family.

- Forward funny teacher cartoons to the staff . . . share the joy.

- Call a few parents after school just to tell them something wonderful their child did that day.

- Tell your parent volunteers what a difference they make!

- Invite family members to join you in class for special events and have the kids create the invitations.

- Linger at the classroom door at pickup time just to be social.

- Slow down! Don't forget to breathe.

- Make eye contact.

- Offer sincere compliments.

- Be fully present.

- Smile!

- Listen actively.

Strategies to Cultivate Gratitude

Research on gratitude has shown that regularly integrating appreciative practices throughout the school day and having students think about what they are grateful for has numerous benefits to support an SEL classroom (Froh et al., 2008). These benefits include having students feel better about themselves and having more resilience.

As teachers, we sometimes forget that even a small gesture of appreciation can help transform relationships and boost student self-worth. But gratitude is not just about recognition—it's also about supporting and inspiring others. Studies have shown that when children are appreciated, the more inclined they will be to do the same, leading to a more appreciative, supportive, and caring classroom.

Write Thank You Notes   Teach your students the art of writing a simple thank you note. Ask them to think of a family member they can thank for a recent act of kindness. (For a template and steps involved in this procedure, see the Resources [Appendix A] section of this book.)

2-Week Thankful Challenge   For this special thankfulness campaign, each student has their own poster, and every day for 2 weeks, they write down something they are thankful for. Students can also paste an image that represents something they're thankful for, gradually creating a collage of images. At the end of this Thankful Challenge, display the posters in your classroom or the school hallway. You can even challenge another classroom to complete the Thankful Challenge, too!

Play the Gratitude Game   You can use various colored pipe cleaners, toothpicks, different colored pencils, straws, or pick-up sticks for this fun game. Display a color-coded chart using colored dots for various actions. Some sample prompts could include the following:

- Red—Name a person you are thankful for

- Orange—Name a special place you are thankful for

- Green—Name a food you are thankful for

- Blue—Name a thing you are thankful for

- Purple—Name anything of your choice you are thankful for

Students randomly select a colored stick and share their response to the color-coded prompt. This can easily be integrated into a morning meeting or closing community circle time in class. Meeting in small-group contexts enhances students' overall learning experiences in several ways. Students develop skills in communication, interpersonal relations, critical thinking, problem solving, empathy, and collaboration. These meetings can take place at that start of the day (morning meeting) and/or a closing community circle. Taking time to gather the students like this brings a sense of calm, safety, and community (Durlak, 2011; Goldenberg, 1993). These special meetings also provide students with time to practice reflecting on what they know and what's meaningful to them about their schoolwork, their classmates, and themselves and receive feedback from other students and the teacher.

Strategies to Create a Learning Environment for Small Groups

Choice is one of the basic human needs, often mentioned by the experts to boost learners' motivation and engagement. Students need to feel that they have some control in their lives, and that also relates to school, which is a large part of what children do each day. You do not lose any control by offering students choices in the types of projects they create, in the types of assessments they are given, or even in the topics you cover. Within limits, students can make these choices effectively.

Flexible Grouping for Student Success   Student-centered, caring classrooms emphasize collaboration, which means that you do not see rows of fixed chairs lined up and facing a teacher's desk in the front of the room. Instead, desks, tables, and chairs are arranged in moveable "pods" for four to six students to facilitate collaboration and communication and team building.

Fixed-ability groups do not have a place in a classroom that fosters social-emotional growth. Some options for assigning grouping include the following:

- *Rhyming partners:* Distribute pictures of rhyming pairs (e.g., bat/cat, ring/king); students must then find their rhyme partner(s) for the group activity.

- *Animal sounds partners:* Duplicate pictures of animals, then pass out cards. Students make the noise of the animal on the card to find teams (e.g., cats meow, dogs bark, ducks quack).

- *Candy bar wrapper partners:* Collect an assortment of candy bar wrappers. Pass them out randomly to the students. Give them a signal to find their candy bar "teammates" with matching wrappers.

- *Valentine buddies:* After Valentine's Day, purchase leftover boxes of valentines at a discount. After you have determined how many teams you want, sort and divide the matching images of valentines into groups. Then shuffle and distribute these valentines randomly, inviting the students to find their matching "valentine buddies" and form a small team.

- *Pick a pair:* Print pictures of images that have words or pictures of things/people that go together (e.g., spaghetti/meatballs, peanut butter/jelly).

- *Comic strip teams:* Cut up comic strips into individual frames, pass them out, and instruct students to find comic strip matchups and put comic strip frames in order. This can also help teach story sequencing.

- *Opposite partners:* Have words or pictures of antonyms (e.g., happy/mad, day/night) and instruct students to find their opposite.

- *Birthday line-up:* Students form a line around the classroom in order of their birthday month and day. Then the teacher decides where to break it up in groups of three to four.

- *Puzzle pieces:* Cut up greeting cards or postcards into interlocking pieces (depending on how many students you want on each team). Distribute these "postcard puzzle pieces" randomly to the students and invite them to mix and mingle to put their pieces together to form an image. That will be their team.

- *Playing card teams:* Count how many students are in class that day and decide on the size of the teams you want. Then divide a deck of cards into corresponding groups, depending on the numbers. Shuffle the deck and distribute randomly. Students find their playing card partners or teams of four (e.g., all the 2's work together, the 3's, the 4's).

- *Word family teams:* Select frequently used word families that your students are familiar with. Using index cards, decide on the size of the groups you want and then make corresponding cards with words that have the same ending (e.g., *bat, mat, sat,* and *chat,* or *ball, call, stall, tall,* and *small*). Students are given a random card with a word on it and told they need to find their team by reading the word and finding their team members with words that are from the same word family.

In a creative classroom, one size does not fit all. These flexible group settings can provide every learner, including both struggling and advanced students, with opportunities for success.

Foundations It is important to establish expectations for procedures and routines before any kind of grouping can begin. By changing your classroom environment, you can deliver more content in a meaningful way and have your students understand and retain more information. What physical structure will work best for you? Decide on a physical classroom desk and table arrangement. The following are some questions to consider:

- Will one room arrangement work, or will you need to have options for multiple arrangements depending on the group activity required?

- How will the class be rearranged when necessary? What will be required to accomplish rearranging the classroom?

- What routines and skills are necessary for students to learn so the class can run smoothly when you deviate from the traditional arrangement? Work with students to practice moving from one room arrangement to another.

- Is there a signal, either a hand gesture or a sound, you can use to notify students of time remaining until a transition? Can you then use the signal again when the transition needs to occur? Before any transition, remind students of behavioral expectations.

Planning Guide for Instructional Grouping   Before grouping your students for any activities, ensure that you identify the purpose of the group work. What is your purpose/rationale for grouping?

Logistics

- How many groups will you have? How many students in each group?

- How long will students be working in their assigned groups?

- How will groups rotate? How often? What is the schedule?

- How will you set up the group areas in your classroom? What materials do you need?

- Will you keep activities permanent or change them on a regular basis?

Materials and Instruction

- Will you have a teacher-led group? If so, what will be your instructional emphasis for this group? Will all students rotate through your group?

- What materials and resources will you use for each group?

Assessments

- How often will you assess students' progress in groups and adjust groupings? What criteria will you use?

- How do you plan to keep track of student work? Assessment? Record keeping?

Concerns

- Will students have something to do if they finish their group activity early?

Procedures and Management

- How do you plan to introduce grouping to your students?

- If you are working directly with a group, how will you ensure that you are not interrupted?

- How will you facilitate smooth transitions when students rotate?

- How will you assign group activities (menu, contract, checklist, etc.)?

- How will students be asked to keep track of their work (in progress and/or completed)?

SUMMARY

In teaching, every day is an adventure! Reaching and teaching our diverse learners requires a palette of possibilities. Creating a caring classroom community requires conscious planning and intention. In a classroom or school in which SEL is purposefully included from day one, it becomes an integral part of the day's lesson, not just an afterthought. The benefits of creating a caring classroom environment extend to every part of the school community: teachers, students, parents, and other staff. When topics such as relationships and emotional reactions are incorporated into lessons throughout the day, it can positively affect how students learn.

Using strategies to help build self-esteem and promote a caring, collaborative classroom connects you to the heart of your students. Establishing a strong foundation and building positive relationships with students are keys to creating a bridge where students can flourish and feel great about who they are and who they will become. Being a caring teacher is a blend of attitude and action. No strategy can substitute a genuine caring teacher who provides students with warmth, trust, respect, and authentic relationships. These relationships will provide a solid foundation for your school community to thrive.

CHAPTER 8

Fostering Empathy in the Classroom

> *"Happy, calm students learn best."*
>
> *–Daniel Goleman,*
> Emotional Intelligence

Empathy, the ability to understand perspectives and feelings other than your own, is an essential skill for all children to master, and it is an important teaching strategy in establishing a caring classroom that promotes social-emotional learning.

kindness
safety
consideration
gentle
thoughtful
loving genuine respect
share time listen connect
caring
empathy trust understanding
humanity
friendly
compassion

KEY CONCEPTS

- What does empathy look like in the classroom?

- How do teachers build a climate of empathy?

- What are some strategies for children to learn to share values and differences?

- How do teachers connect feelings, thoughts, and behaviors in their lessons?

- What are some tools for children to understand their own emotions and feelings and those of others?

- What are ways that we can demonstrate caring?

INTRODUCTION

Teaching empathy in the classroom is about focusing on teaching students, *not* content. Empathy is at the core of education. The term *empathy* is used to describe a wide range of experiences in the classroom and can be defined as the ability to tune into other people's emotions and/or imagine what they might be thinking or feeling. Simply put, empathy as it is explained to children means understanding and responding with caring to what others think and feel. It is seeing the world through another person's eyes.

When we show empathy, we understand the perspectives of another, and we can sense their emotions and feelings. For example, you can teach even the youngest children to refrain from bullying and be more respectful of others by helping them understand how kids that are bullied might feel and how they would feel if they were bullied.

This expression of care for another is not an innate ability but rather a skill that needs to be taught, nurtured, and modeled in a caring classroom community. Because empathy is the ability to understand and share the feelings of another, it is at the core of everything that makes a classroom or school a caring, responsive, inclusive place to be. Empathy demonstrates that students can relate to one another and shows that they are self-aware and can deal with their own feelings as well as tuning in to the emotions and feelings of others. This chapter provides teachers with practical tools and techniques to encourage compassion in kids and to develop kinder, more compassionate students.

What Does the Research Say?

Empathy is certainly gaining attention as a vital component of SEL and as a way to reduce bullying in schools. When a child learns to understand and share the feelings of another, that student can have better relationships, closer friendships, and stronger classroom communities. Research has found that students who have high levels of empathy tend to also display increased classroom engagement, higher academic achievement, and better communication skills (Jones et al., 2014). Furthermore, empathy reduces aggression and boosts prosocial behaviors (Eisenberg et al., 2010) and may be one of the best antidotes to bullying and racism in schools (Santos et al., 2011).

Some experts claim that we are not born empathetic (Heyes, 2018). Before students can empathize, they need to be able to understand their own emotions and those of others. Children who can recognize and name feelings tend to be better adjusted emotionally and are more outgoing in their relationships with others and more sensitive to their own needs (Goleman, 1995). Besides the inclination of achieving more academically, such students are also more resilient and more in tune with their executive functions (Gottman & DeClaire, 1997). However, researchers also warn that the emphasis of online learning in our digitally focused world may be reducing students' abilities to carefully perceive human emotions and thereby limit their empathetic capacities (Uhls et al., 2014).

Furthermore, educating the heart and educating the mind do not have to be mutually exclusive. Many collaborative practices support empathy education *and* academic growth. For instance, studies have found that cooperative learning structures and strategies not only boost empathy skills such as active listening for feelings of others and perspective taking (Dean et al., 2012), but also enhance academic growth. Conflict resolution helps students work together to solve their problems, and jigsaw-style activities help students learn from one another and care about one another's opinions and beliefs (Walker & Crogan, 1998).

What happens when kids feel more secure and in tune with their own and others' emotions? They are more likely to reach out to others and get involved when they see someone who may need sympathy or help (Barnett, 1987; Kestenbaum et al., 1989; Waters et al., 1979). Children who are better at regulating their own emotions tend to display greater empathetic concern for others (Song et al., 2017). Therefore, it makes sense to devote time in class for these strategies that support "emotional coaching."

Research shows that teaching SEL in the classroom through the lens of empathy also has positive long-term effects into adulthood. Therefore, teaching kids about empathy, kindness, and compassion for others is a must for teachers and schools today more than ever. But where do we start? We need to teach our students to be in touch with and recognize their own emotions, not just to react to them. We also need to help our students realize the impact their emotions and actions have on others. We are all humans and share similar feelings and concerns and deserve to be treated with dignity and respect. Empathy makes our students better people.

BENEFITS OF EMPATHY IN EDUCATION

As educators, we need to recognize the pivotal place that empathy has among other skills like collaboration, time management, and critical thinking. All these skills are important to prepare our students for their future and present lives. However, as Henry Ford contended more than a century ago, "If there is any one secret of success, it lies in the ability to get the other person's point of view and see things from his angle as well as your own." So, how can we support our students to embody a skill that is rooted in feelings and emotions instead of facts and figures?

Building Positive Classroom Culture

With the ever-increasing diversity of students entering our classrooms, it is more important than ever to build a positive classroom culture. Empathy is at the core of our own feelings and those of others. Empathy helps students build friendships based on positive relationships and respect. Furthermore, taking time to model empathy and incorporate empathy throughout the curriculum can also develop more positive student–teacher relationships.

Every student in the classroom should be valued and respected as part of the community. Teachers need to emphasize being inclusive, caring, and open as part of the classroom community. Therefore, teachers should work together with the students to establish classroom *norms* (conditions needed to work together), including how everyone will treat each other. Have students vote on these for agreement and then keep these norms posted and visible to all.

Strengthening a Sense of Community in the Classroom

Consider a broader definition of empathy that includes understanding another's feelings without having their experience. This sets our students up to deepen relationships with others from different cultures and/or different socioeconomic backgrounds. The effects of a strong sense of community extend beyond the four walls of the classroom, and these deeper relationships build trust.

Empowering Students to Lead the Way

Students must first understand the power of empathy in their relationships with others, then be taught the tools and skills to be able to empathize in order to make everyone feel valued. As teachers, we need to equip our students to be the future leaders of our communities and beyond. Remember, educating for empathy is not just about a one-time lesson on kindness and identifying feelings. It requires ongoing, embedded work guided by a broader understanding of the competencies, strategies, and practices that cultivate these traits and tuning in to students' needs. Look for smiles, engagement, joy, and even tears, because lessons in empathy are all around us.

Other Considerations

The first step to developing empathy is **emotional literacy,** or the ability to read or recognize your own emotions and the emotions of others so that you can figure out what they are feeling and respond appropriately. By tuning in and noticing what others are feeling, you have accomplished the first step toward developing empathy. In fact, according to Borba (2016) and other researchers, this emotional literacy is associated with children who are kinder and more resilient and students who are better adjusted emotionally.

The following section describes other aspects of emotional literacy that teachers need to consider to better support students and their feelings.

Making Connections: Emotional Literacy   Before students can empathize with one another, they need to be able to recognize and identify specific emotions. How do we do this? Empathy continues to thrive in classrooms that foster face-to-face connections and nurture meaningful interactions and engagement. This can start with simply looking at your classroom setup and how your furniture is arranged. Does it encourage communication in small clusters so that students can easily share ideas and discuss lessons?

Do you teach your students how to "read" and identify emotions in others? Even young children can do this with a morning ritual of showing them a chart of emotions, and they can point to the facial expression that describes how they are feeling. For older children, I let them provide their own "Morning Weather Report" by having them identify which of the following they are feeling:

- Sunny

- Stormy

- Foggy

- Cloudy

- Unsettled

These "emotional check-ins" can also be done with sticky notes that the students sign and put on a poster that labels the feelings they are experiencing. This is an excellent way for the teacher to quickly "take the temperature" of the group before lessons begin and to identify who might need a little more attention or support that day. To increase sensitivity, students can share with a partner how they are feeling.

Moral Identity: Inner Value System   A student's inner value system can help to inspire empathy, develop their character, and increase their compassion. The key here is to model these skills and values in our own actions, before we expect them to be reflected by students. Consider working with the students to create a class motto, mantra, or slogan to boost unity and a sense of belonging. Some samples include these phrases: "I am here for you," "We help each other," "Throw kindness like confetti." Ask, "What do we stand for? How are we expected to behave?" What matters most is not a poster on the wall but how the teacher models these actions in their everyday interactions with students. Students look to teachers for more than just academic learning and they will pick up on your behaviors.

Perspective Taking: Stepping Into Another's Shoes   Perspective taking, or stepping into another's shoes, helps students understand others and their feelings. Posing a simple question such as, "How would you feel if this happened to you?" can help even the youngest of students learn how to stretch their perspectives and understand the feelings of others.

Moral Imagination Through Books   Teacher read-alouds of certain fictional books can enhance empathy with students and help students feel connected with the characters and prompt empathetic feelings. For instance, in sharing *Dumbo,* you can use puppets or role-play to point out how the crows were making fun of Dumbo. Take an opportunity to pause and discuss feelings and how students might react if they were in the same situation.

Self-Regulation: Keeping Emotions in Check   Emotions drive behavior, behavior drives attention, and attention drives learning. Activating children's natural body rhythms and emotions helps regulate their nervous systems and readiness for learning. Regulating feelings starts by modeling for children how to recognize their stressors before they feel overwhelmed. Try using "cool-down corners," or stress boxes (filled with fidgets, stress balls, and other small manipulatives). Another technique, previously described in this book, is "belly breathing."

Practicing Kindness   Being kind is a great way to help students tune in to other people's feelings and needs. Acts of kindness remind kids to notice others and comfort them. Practicing kindness can also change a child's self-image to see themselves as kinder individuals. Learning by doing is important in the classroom. Consider starting the morning out with smiles, special class handshakes, "high 5's," fist bumps, and eye contact. Making these simple gestures part of your daily classroom routines provides great reinforcers for both the senders and receivers. You could also instruct the students to chart their good deeds daily. Challenge them to do three kind things a day and keep track of these to increase the positive interactions.

Developing Change-Makers   Encouraging children to help one another can foster greater empathy and help them see that they can make a difference and make positive changes to be role models to others. *Every* student has the power to make their world a better place. You can implement a classroom service project, depending on the age and the ability level of your students. Examples include bringing toys to a local shelter or planting a school vegetable garden and delivering their harvest to a local soup kitchen. Students need to see the positive effects of their actions and realize that they *do* make a difference by their actions.

Cultivating Collaborative Classrooms　　Empathy is a "we" trait, not a "me" trait. We need to teach our children to keep their hearts open and not be selfish. Working together on common goals can help students to do this. Conflict-resolution activities and role-play scenarios can help students learn to care about one another. The use of jigsaw-like learning activities promotes working together to solve problems.

Ingredients for Effective Empathy Education　　There are seven essential factors for effective empathy education, outlined in the following sections. Including each of these in all empathy-related instruction will ensure that students are equipped to fully understand the concepts of empathy.

Meaningful　　Empathy education needs to be real and authentic, touching the hearts and minds of the students through modeling and integration in the school day.

Student Centered　　Put the students at the center of all you do—always. Remember, as educators teach children, *not* content.

Integrated　　Competencies of empathy need to be interwoven and infused into your curriculum and interactions throughout the day, not just appended as an add-on.

Ongoing　　When you integrate empathy into your classroom routine, it becomes a continual focus and not a one-time lesson.

Respectful Relationships　　Classroom culture that embraces empathy should emphasize relationships that are respectful and caring.

Internalized　　Our goal as educators is to go from teaching empathy strategies to the students authentically adopting empathy as a way of life, with lifelong habits, having internalized these competencies.

Empathetic School Leaders　　Principals and other school administrators need to be integral to the pervasive implementation of empathy across the school culture. Therefore, empathy needs to be modeled, expected, and at the core of the school's mission and vision.

Teaching the Language of Empathy　　Helping a student be able to describe and name their feelings is not just a strategy reserved for the youngest children. As students mature, their feelings also develop and become multidimensional and more complicated. Without the explicit teaching and nurturing of empathy, it will not develop on its own.

It is important to provide your students with a "wardrobe of words" to express their empathy with each other. They need to listen actively to each other and be responsive as well as empathetic in face-to-face conversations. Empathetic people actively listen to others, not to "fix them" but to *feel* what they are feeling.

Figure 8.1 provides some sentence starters that might be helpful to share with your students so that they can respond to each other more empathetically.

Empathy Sentence Stems

- What I heard you say is _____.

- If I understand you correctly _____.

- I am thankful that you shared this with me even though _____.

- From where I stand, it seems _____.

- I can hear how _____ you are feeling now.

- It sounds like you are feeling _____.

- I can see how important this is to you because _____.

- Your expression seems to say _____.

Figure 8.1. Empathy sentence stems.

STRATEGIES FOR YOUR CLASSROOM

Empathy Discussion Questions

Teachers need to be role models and demonstrate to students the power of empathy in relationships. As teachers model how to be positive when learning, students reflect more optimistic and confident learning behaviors. As educators, it is important that we are empathetic toward our students. If we are not empathetic, we cannot understand the needs or feelings of the diverse students we serve. The following discussion starters will help develop a greater sense of empathy in the classroom. It is important to let every student's voice be heard. The perspectives and ideas of each child in the classroom should be recognized and valued.

- What is empathy?
- Why is it important to show empathy toward others?
- What does it mean to "put yourself in someone else's shoes"?
- Think of a time when you hurt someone's feelings. Describe what happened.
  - How did you know you hurt the person's feelings?
  - How did you feel about the situation?
  - Did you do anything to make the situation better?
- Are there times when students don't show empathy for each other?
- What would school be like if everyone showed empathy toward each other all the time?

Five Steps to Cultivate Empathy

Teach students the following five steps to consider when interacting with a friend or family member:

1. Watch and Listen: What is the other person saying, and what does their body language convey?
2. Remember: When did you feel the same way?
3. Imagine: How does the other person feel? How would you feel in that situation?
4. Ask: Ask what the person is feeling.
5. Show You Care: Let them know that you care through your words and actions.

Let Every Voice Be Heard

The unique perspective of each child in the classroom needs to be recognized and celebrated. We need to nurture students who are interdependent and assume responsibility for their own learning.

Provide Tools to Recognize Their Own Emotions

Students need to be able to identify their own feelings first before they can show empathy to others. Sharing with them an "emotional vocabulary" is a great place to start. For younger students, this can be done with a chart of faces showing various emotions. A well-developed "feeling vocabulary" can help our students distinguish between feelings and give them ways to better communicate with others and engage in conversations about the impact of those feelings.

Celebrate Positive Responses

Keep your "radar" tuned in to student actions to catch a student being empathetic toward a classmate. For example, when you hear a student speaking to another in a way that shows kindness, be sure to point out and describe what the student has done. With this positive reinforcement, you will see empathy increase in your classroom.

Situation Cards

Copy and cut out "Situation Cards for Empathy" from the Resources section (Appendix A). Ask the children how would they feel in this situation and how would they react to this child based on these feelings.

Get to Know Your Students Better

It is important to discover the qualities that make your students unique. Find out what interests them, their favorites, their hobbies, their strengths, passions, and dreams. Encourage them to share these with others in the class.

Get in Tune With Global and Community Issues

Sharing real-world issues with children can help provide valuable lessons on empathy. You can empower students to stand up for people being treated unfairly so they learn how even the smallest acts of kindness can make a big difference in the lives of others. When we set aside time for our students to focus in on the hardships of others, it boosts their level of compassion and empathy.

Press the "Pause" Button for Reflection

Taking time for reflection is a powerful tool for developing empathy. Educators must teach students how to reflect on their actions and feelings and the impact they have on others. In my experience, I found that using reflective journals with my older students in which they were asked to write responses from prompts related to empathy was a very successful exercise. Here are some questions to get you started:

- What was an important conversation you had today? Why was it important?
- How did you show kindness today?
- Write about a hard time you had this week. Why did you think that was?
- What is something you learned today from a classmate?
- How would you feel if someone called you names today or picked on you?
- How would you feel if you saw someone calling another classmate names or picking on them?
- What could you do to help someone else in class today? How would you help and why?

- What would it be like if you did not have a safe place to live?

- What would you do if you found out that a classmate did not have enough food to eat at home?

Activities for Teaching Empathy Skills

Teachers who embrace empathy do it less through *what* they teach than *how* they teach. Empathy needs to be acquired gradually over time through modeling and experience. The following sections contain strategies to infuse empathy throughout your school day:

Labeling Feelings   It is important to help children develop a language of feelings and kindness that they can use in specific situations. For instance, ask children how they would feel in these sample situations:

- If they see someone being bullied

- If they were being bullied themselves

- If they bullied someone

Talk about how bullying can lead to very strong feelings such as anger, fear, and loneliness. It is okay to feel these feelings, but it is never okay to intentionally hurt someone.

Feelings Pantomime   Have the kids form a circle and then pantomime their feelings. As they do this, ask them to look around the circle and see how others are feeling. Ask them how did *joy, anger, sadness* feel in their body?

Random Acts of Kindness   Explain that *kindness* is the opposite of *bullying* because it helps others feel *good* instead of *bad.* Have children share something nice they did for someone else and how it made them feel. Have the students plan to do one "random act of kindness" that day and share about it during circle time at the end of the school day. You could ask:

- How did the act of kindness make you feel? (ask both givers and receivers)

- How do you think you would feel if you did an act of bullying instead of kindness?

Helping Others Feel Better   Spend time discussing with your children what they can do to help others feel better.

- How can you tell how someone else feels?

- How do we know when someone is feeling bad or feeling left out?

- How can we cheer someone up who feels bad?

You need to demonstrate empathy in your interactions to model and guide the students. Even the smallest interactions can demonstrate empathy, such as positive use of eye contact and keeping uncomfortable conversations private or discreet.

You can also engage the children in role-playing situations to practice how to react when a fellow student is feeling hurt and how to help that classmate feel better.

- Instruct students to work as partners.

- Ask one in each pair to pretend that they have been bullied or feel bad and the other child pretends to be a bystander to help the child feel better.

- Have the pairs of students switch roles and repeat the role play from a different perspective.
- Spend time discussing their feelings in both roles as a group.

The Golden Rule Talk with the students about the Golden Rule: "Do to others as you would want them to do to you." Ask them if bullies are caring about other children's feelings and treating them the way that they would want to be treated. Have them discuss examples of bullying and their reactions to them.

Empathy Award Students will identify a person who has demonstrated empathy. Have them give you a brief description of the person and why they think this person deserves the award. What have they learned about empathy from their winner? Display the "Empathy Award" (Figure 8.2) posters on a bulletin board for all to see.

- Extension activity: Write a thank you note to your Empathy Award winner, thanking that person for the empathy that he or she has shown toward you or others.

Writer's Notebook Having students express their feelings in writing can be an excellent tool for children to develop the skills to express empathy. The purpose of the writer's notebook is to express personal reflections around feelings and think about how our feelings impact our decisions and interactions with others. To get your students started, place a feeling word at the top of the paper, have the children illustrate that feeling, and then have them write about a time they felt that way and what they did. See the Resources section of this book (Appendix A) for additional ideas for your students to get in touch with their feelings through writing.

Start a "Caught You" Board This is a special, interactive bulletin board where you acknowledge when you caught a student demonstrating empathy—showing compassion, being patient, and so forth. Students can also use it to show their appreciation and acknowledgment for acts of kindness with each other.

Modeling Helpfulness

Show pictures, tell stories, or use puppets or props to model examples of how children and adults can show they care about others' feelings and help each other. Discuss how showing kindness and caring about each other makes both the giver and the receiver feel better and happy instead of sad or mad.

Happiness Boards

Encouraging students to share vulnerabilities and dreams is a way to get them to show and learn empathy. Happiness boards are a useful tool for helping students share these personal details. Students create collages of positive memories, hopes, and dreams by cutting pictures out of magazines. First, ask students to make a list of memories or moments that made them feel proud. Next, have them create a list of dreams or goals they have for their life. Finally, ask them to think of people they admire and write down what makes those people special. Teachers can also create their own happiness board as a model for the students. Display the collages around the classroom and have the students do a gallery walk to look at each other's posters. Discuss with them the similarities and connections they see between their own happiness board and that of their classmates.

Empathy

Character Award

For understanding how others are feeling!

Congratulations!

_____
Name

_____
Signed

_____
Date

Figure 8.2. Empathy character award.

Using Reading to Cultivate Empathy

Reading stories with lively and diverse characters can be a powerful way to build community in the classroom. It is a time that students from diverse backgrounds can gather to share experiences around a book. The characters, setting, and the story can provide students with experiences that they have not experienced themselves yet. When reading books that cultivate empathy, set the purpose for the reading and ask the students to notice the characters' actions, infer their feelings, and try to understand the decisions they make.

Bring Empathy to Readers' Workshop   Ask students to listen to the read-aloud story (see the Children's Books to Support Social-Emotional Learning in Appendix B for suggested, age-appropriate titles) and write down what feelings the characters are experiencing. Then have the students break into small groups to discuss the events that led the characters to experience those feelings. Help students make connections to the times that they have experienced those feelings in the past and predict what the characters in the story might do next. Figure 8.3 provides questions to ask when reading stories to cultivate empathy.

Reading fictional stories and books helps kickstart the children's imagination to think about what the characters are feeling. The questions in Figure 8.3 are designed to be used as a launch pad to a discussion about empathy.

Other Creative Strategies to Promote Empathy

It is important to teach our students how to be empathetic both in and out of the classroom through creative activities that teach them to manage emotional and social situations. The following sections contain some ideas to consider:

Construction Paper Exercise   Instruct the children to select their favorite color of construction paper. Ask them to write down positive adjectives that describe the paper and how it makes them feel. Then ask them to crumple, rip, or step on the paper. This now becomes a visual, tactile exercise and a learning opportunity as they realize that when they are rude or unkind to others (like the paper) it has a lasting impact. Discuss their feelings after the activity.

Video Clips   Use brief video clips of children's favorite television shows or movies to teach empathy to even the youngest of students. Viewing these clips allows children to experience what's happening with other people's feelings, even if they are fictional characters. An example of this is the film *Wonder*, which has led to many meaningful discussions in classrooms as children share their thoughts and feelings. Using video clips helps the children learn how to communicate openly and honestly about real-life situations in a risk-free way.

Empathy Maps   This is a powerful strategy to promote deeper understanding of how our words and actions connect to our thoughts and feelings. Children create Empathy Maps that are divided into four sections: Think, Feel, Say, Do. To model this, you can draw a large circle on the whiteboard or poster and label it "our class." Then divide it into quadrants: think, feel, say, do. Give each student four sticky notes to write down the following:

- One emotion they sometimes feel
- A thought they connect to that emotion
- An action they take when they have that feeling
- Something they might say

Empathizing With Characters

- Would you have done the same thing as _____ when _____?

- If you were in the same situation as _____, what would you do _____?

- Do any of the characters remind you of yourself or someone you know? Why?

- Do the characters seem believable?

- Can you relate to the challenges they are facing? In what ways?

- What do you wish you could ask the main characters? Why?

- How do the characters develop and change throughout the story?

- What events caused these changes?

- If you were in this story, what would your relationship be to the main character? Why?

- Have any of the events from this story happened to you? How did you react?

- Can you relate to the main character of the story? Why or why not?

- Who is your favorite character of the story? Why?

- Which character do you feel you know the best? Why?

- If you could ask the main character a question, what would you ask? Why?

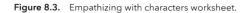

Figure 8.3. Empathizing with characters worksheet.

Leave the chart or the board up and have students add to it as they think of new emotions and feelings.

Role-Play Exercises   Using role-play situations and case studies allows students to learn about how other people are thinking and feeling. Role-play exercises allow them to empathize with various individuals and help students learn to view differences with respect and begin to develop a growth mindset.

Listening Circle   This community-building activity provides your students with an opportunity to hear different perspectives about feelings to build a sense of empathy. Ask the class the following questions:

- Who do you look up to most and why?

- What advice would you give yourself today? Why?

Balloon Bonanza   For this hands-on activity, bring balloons to school and pass out one balloon to each student. Ask the students to blow up their balloon and then each write their name on it. Next, students should toss the balloons around and then create a batch of balloons in the center of the classroom. You then mix the balloons up and give the students 5 minutes to find the balloon with their name on it. In my experience with this activity, the students ran around, looking frantically, but as the time ran out, nobody had found their own balloon. I then told them to take the balloon closest to them and give it to the person whose name was on it. In less than 2 minutes everyone had their own balloon back. I closed this session by explaining to them, "Balloons are like happiness. No one will find it looking for theirs only. However, if everyone cares about each other's, they will find theirs as quickly as possible."

Empathy Book Trailers   Sharing stories is a powerful and positive way to promote empathy. After reading a book of their choice, students can create a brief book trailer to promote it with their peers. Ask the students to focus on the experiences of one of the main characters in the book by synthesizing events in the character's life. Help students make the connection with empathy for the character as they create deeper understanding of their own feelings and thoughts for others.

SUMMARY

Like other facets of SEL, empathy requires practice over time. It certainly is possible for all students to cultivate empathy skills, but doing so requires slow and steady work. Look all around you for inspiration and focus on the importance of face-to-face conversations and learn valuable lessons from each other. It is not about a one-time lesson or having a guest speaker. Keep in mind integrating the following ingredients for effective empathy education:

- *Meaningful.* Empathy education needs to be "real"—authentic, touching the hearts and minds of the students through modeling and integration in the school day.

- *Student centered.* Put the students at the center of all you do—always. Remember, we teach children, *not* content.

- *Integrated.* Competencies of empathy need to be woven in and infused into your curriculum and interactions throughout the day, not just an add-on.

- *Ongoing.* When you integrate empathy into your classroom routine it becomes a continual focus, not just a one-time lesson.

E – Everybody needs kindness

M – Model caring

P – Put yourself in their shoes

A – Ask how you can help

T – Treat others with respect

H – Helpful and honest

Y – You feel better and they fell better

- *Respectful relationships.* Classroom culture that embraces empathy should emphasize relationships that are respectful and caring.

- *Internalized.* Our goal is to go beyond strategies for promoting empathy to having the children adopt empathy as a way of life, with lifelong habits of internalizing these competencies.

- *Empathetic school leaders.* The administrative staff needs to be integral to the pervasive implementation of empathy across the school culture. Therefore, empathy needs to be modeled, expected, and at the core of the school's mission and vision.

    Empathy needs to be infused throughout the school day and woven into all lessons.

Cultivating empathy and focusing in on connections is the right work for our schools given the world we live in today. The result? Students develop awareness of others' emotions and how to respond to them. Our students will have greater academic success, confidence and self-worth, and joy when they practice these principles and learn to live empathetically with each other.

CHAPTER 9

Relationships

Strengthening Bonds

> "No significant learning can occur without a significant relationship."
>
> –Dr. James Comer, Leave No Child Behind

Think about one of your favorite teachers in elementary school. What made them so special to you? The relationships that teachers make with their students can be everlasting memories and maybe even life changing. This chapter will help you learn more about the importance of teacher–student relationships and how to foster more positive interactions in your classroom. These relationship-building strategies are very quick and easy to implement and will leave a lasting impact on your students.

KEY CONCEPTS

- Why is it important to foster relationships in the classroom?
- What strategies can teachers use to develop positive relationships with students?
- How can teachers monitor equitable response opportunities?
- What is the connection between positive relationships and student achievement?
- What are ways to provide student voice and choice in learning?

INTRODUCTION

Spending time on lessons about identity and belonging with your students helps them appreciate differences, both in themselves and in their peers. Teacher–student relationships also matter when teaching your SEL skills to your students. It is not enough just to engage socially with your students—you need to go deeper and start to engage with them about their curiosities, interests, and hobbies. It is also important to show respect for their culture and affirm their worthiness, which will also foster a growth mindset. Sometimes I feel that teachers don't understand the impact that their relationship with each student has on that student's sense of well-being, identity, and belonging to the classroom community. So, how can teachers improve their relationships with students? In one word, the answer is *empathy*. Based on results of several recent studies, researchers have found that teachers who foster a sense of empathy for and with their students are able to promote positive student behavior and engagement.

Keys to Building Relationships in the Classroom

The secret to inspiring and transforming students and fostering positive relationships resides in the power of building a collaborative community in the classroom.

Make Connections With Students   What would a classroom be like without connections? Without robust relationships? Relationships need to go beyond just rapport and regular check-ins with your students; fostering connections needs to be pervasive throughout the curriculum. Create a classroom environment in which children become intrinsically motivated to thrive.

Inject Passion Into Your Content!   Bring your lessons to life! You have the power to captivate, motivate, intrigue, and engage your students. Don't hold back when putting pizzazz in your lessons! This also involves providing opportunities for collaboration so that students can share in your enthusiasm about the topic with each other.

Build Respect and Trust   Building trust begins with small steps. Students appreciate their teachers' emotional honesty. Stories stick and facts fade. Tell them some personal anecdotes about yourself so that you become "more real." React to challenges and issues that come up during the day with honest emotions and then make your reactions known to the children by clearly explaining your thought process.

Model Your Emotions: Empathy, Kindness, and Compassion   Students will be watching you throughout the day to ascertain how you react to certain situations. Consider your reactions from a student's perspective. Remember, even small acts of kindness will build trust and community. As you model compassion, be your authentic self.

Tune In to Student Strengths   It is important to tune in to student strengths as you integrate differentiated instruction to meet the unique needs of your learners. Promoting a student's strengths and gifts helps to boost their confidence and participation in your lessons. Combining diverse strengths in groups supports student achievement and relationships as they learn from one another.

Determine How Students Learn Best   Tune in to your students to understand their preferred learning style: auditory, visual, or kinesthetic. The important thing to remember is to teach utilizing multimodality instruction so that you can appeal to the learning styles of all your students.

Expect Success and a Growth Mindset   Don't let your students slip into the mode of "learned helplessness." Instill in them through your actions and words that can-do spirit! Promoting a growth mindset requires modeling. You need to feel confident and competent as well—students are looking to you as a role model.

View Mistakes as Learning Opportunities   Remember the "power of *yet*." When they say, "I can't do this; this is too hard; I don't get it," answer them with that important refrain: *yet*. ("You can't do this yet, but you will succeed with more hard work!") Your students need to know that mistakes are viewed as powerful learning opportunities and a vital part of the process. Make a habit of recognizing effort and attitude of students.

What Does the Research Say?

Many studies have examined the power of positive relationships with students. In addition, research also indicates that building relationships with students improves student achievement (Marzano et al., 2010). Thompson (1998) stated, "The most powerful weapon available to teachers who want to foster a favorable learning climate is a positive relationship with our students" (p. 6).

Similarly, Canter and Canter (1997) made the case that most people recall classes in which they did not try hard because they didn't like their teachers. This demonstrates how important it is to have positive relationships with our students and to put your heart into your lesson plans. In fact, be more purposeful and focus as much on getting to know and guiding your students as you do on teaching academic concepts (Pattison et al., 2011).

Furthermore, students who have had negative relationships with adults may have a hard time trusting their teachers (Varga, 2017). In contrast, students benefit and are motivated when their teachers create a safe and trustful learning environment (Reis da Luz, 2015). Therefore, it makes sense that developing positive student–teacher relations can have a ripple effect and is one of the most effective ways to develop a positive classroom environment.

Positive student–teacher connections can help students develop important self-regulation skills that are critical to their social-emotional development and learning how to reach their personal and academic goals (Reis da Luz, 2015). Beyond academic success, at-risk students whose teachers work with them in respectful, caring ways are more likely to develop socially appropriate behavior (Hall & Hall, 2003). Kohn has found that "children are more likely to be respectful when important adults in their lives respect them" (1996, p. 111).

Because these relationships can give students the guidance and support they need to succeed in the classroom and beyond, it is vital to nurture relationships in school. And don't forget to share your own stories with your students ("stories stick, facts fade"). As previously stated, studies suggest that telling personal anecdotes and making storytelling an integral part of your curriculum to connect with your students build teacher–student relationships (Mello, 2001).

STRATEGIES FOR YOUR CLASSROOM

Strategies for Daily Integration

Teachers acknowledge that building strong relationships is a vital part of the educational process. In fact, it may be the first and most important step in getting students to learn. Integrating relationship-building strategies into the daily routine of school helps to increase student motivation, reduce behavioral outbursts, and create an environment where students are motivated to be successful.

Hold Morning Meetings   Procedures, routines, and daily rituals are so important when creating a more cohesive classroom community. These times should be dedicated to giving your students voice, fostering relationships, and giving students greater ownership of their environment. These check-ins are predictable ways for students to celebrate together what is working and how they are feeling, and to share appreciations and gratitude greetings.

Here is a sample agenda for a morning meeting to get you started:

- Norms (review):
  - Give everyone a voice.
  - If it's not your turn to talk . . . take time to listen.

- ○ Look at the speaker with your eyes.
- ○ Have fun . . . respectfully.
- Greetings—class slogan chanting and salutes
- Morning "weather report"—how are you feeling?
- News of the Day
- Poem/Passage
- Be a goal getter—how are you going to make today successful?

Start the Day With a Check-In   During your morning meeting, take time for students to check in with their feelings and with each other. As the teacher, you also need to model this practice and let your students know how you're feeling.

Share Morning Messages   Posting a morning message is a great way to "hook" your students as soon as they arrive. This procedure can be built into your morning meeting structure. Answering an open-ended question is inclusionary and welcoming to the students. It is also important for them to practice their speaking and listening skills. In this way, students can share what's important to them and support each other as well. Here are some examples of my favorite morning message ideas to connect with students:

- What makes you special?
- How will you grow this week?
- What can you change to be more productive?
- If you had a superpower, what would it be and how would you change the world?
- What is your focus this week?
- What will you choose to do today to make it a success? How will you decide what to do?
- What is meaningful to you in the world around you?
- Where do you travel in your dreams?
- What do you see when you look up at the sky?
- How can you be a good friend today?
- What makes you feel proud of yourself?
- What makes you feel loved?
- What makes you happy in this time and place?
- What is important to you?
- What do you like about your classmates?

Allow for Positive Talk Time   Be sure to allow plenty of opportunities throughout the school day for structured and unstructured "talk time." This could be as simple as bouncing ideas off one another or discussing issues or problems. These important "brain breaks" also help to boost students' speaking and listening skills.

You can also build in opportunities for "turn-and-talk" times as well as partner sharing throughout the day. During "turn-and-talk" students turn to a nearby learning partner and share their ideas about a topic for a brief period before whole class discussion resumes. This provides time for students to share in a risk-free way their opinions and beliefs about a topic with a trusted peer. Understanding and confidence are increased as they are able to bounce ideas off each other. This is a great way to hit the reset button and create a state change for greater student engagement.

Pause for Reflective Writing   Please press the "pause" button during your busy day to give your students time to reflect, free-write, and journal on a regular basis. Make this a calming, soothing break from your busy schedule. Consider playing soft, classical music in the background to promote greater reflection. Provide a menu of writing prompts to get them started (see Appendix A for sample journal prompts).

Conduct Closing Community Circles   Instruct students to reflect on the day together at the end of the day by forming a circle. Check in with the students about how they are feeling and what went well for them, and share some acts of kindness from the "kindness bucket" (see Chapter 7).

Here are some prompts you can use to get a discussion going and to reflect during this time:

- Something new they learned

- A wondering they have

- A goal for the next day

- A closing song

- A closing game

"Ah-Ha's," Appreciations, and Apologies   Students form a circle and randomly share an "ah-ha" they had (key learning), appreciation (what they are grateful for), or apology (someone from whom they want to ask forgiveness). This is a powerful and positive process to culminate your school day.

Classroom Cheers   It is fun to use cheers to acknowledge an individual or group or to add energy to the close of the school day. Here are some sample cheers to start with; then you could ask students to come up with their own:

- *Alligator:* Stretch both arms straight out in front as if to make alligator jaws; at the signal, do one big clap.

- *Sparkle:* Raise hands to shoulder level, palms facing out. Wiggle fingers as you lower hands, imitating a sparkling movement.

- *Firecracker:* Similar to "Sparkle," have the children pretend they are exploding fireworks with their bodies (noise or no noise).

- *High 5:* Do high 5's around the circle, in partners.

- *Invent Your Own:* The best cheers will be the ones the students create. Have them design cheers that relate to the purpose of the cheer.

- *Round of Applause:* Clap while moving your hands around in a circle.

Whisper Wishes   As a closing activity, all children whisper a wish into their hand. Once everyone has whispered, count to three and release them together. This is a fun way to finish off the week. As a variation, this activity can be used for sharing by having each student in the circle share their wish.

Strategies for Progress Monitoring

Progress monitoring is an important tool for supporting the unique learning needs of all students. It provides a means of seeing each student's real-time learning outcomes and helps teachers adjust instruction as needed. Furthermore, monitoring student progress also gives teachers the opportunity to reflect on their own teaching and determine how effective their instruction is. This promotes relationship building with the students as they become more aware of their own performance and abilities.

Self-Monitoring   Have kids be "goal getters" and start each day by setting their own learning goals. You can have them respond to this prompt: "Today would be a success for me if _____." Discuss the importance of making sure the goals are realistic and attainable in the day. Have them jot these goals on sticky notes and share with a learning partner. Then, at the end of the day, students can revisit their goals and share whether they achieved them or not.

- Another way to exercise personal goal setting is for each student to track their own personal progress (academic, emotional, social) through a chart or bar graph (e.g., sight words that they know how to read). This gives them greater ownership of their learning.

- Instruct students to revisit and adjust their goals often to monitor their progress by asking the following:
  - Am I meeting my goals?
  - How do I want to grow today?
  - What do I need to work on next?

"Rose and Thorn" Student Check-In   This is a quick strategy to add to your morning meeting during which the students share their "roses" (good news) during check-in as well as their "thorns" (negative news). Some examples of roses could be as simple as "It is sunny outside," or "I got my homework done." Some sample thorns might be "I feel tired," or "My cat is sick." Each student in turn shares their rose and thorn—and don't forget, the teacher does, too. Consider the needs of your students before deciding whether to share roses and thorns aloud. Some classrooms may benefit from private journaling.

Strategies for Group Work

The ability to work productively in pairs and small groups is an important life skill even for the youngest students. We do not want to assume that the children already have these important relationship skills. Therefore, use activities that guide and model how to negotiate, develop leadership skills, and make use of students' individual strengths to contribute to a group. Teams promote social skills. Getting along with different types of people is essential to prepare them to be college and career ready. Cooperative learning promotes taking turns as well as taking responsibility.

For various units or lessons, create small groups. Provide the opportunity for some "get to know each other" activities (see the Resources section of this book [Appendix A] for ideas). If the team will be together for a while, have them create a team name and/or a cheer or slogan for their team. This creates a sense of identity, some bonding, and some fun.

Work in Partnerships   Provide multiple opportunities for your students to work with a learning partner. This helps the kids to learn to cooperate and collaborate with others. Alternate between assigning groups/partners and random pairs. Make sure that these groupings are flexible and changeable and not based on ability.

Group Salutes   This is a quick, low-prep yet high-impact technique to build a sense of community in the classroom. A salute is a gesture or recognition of respect when people meet or say goodbye. It can be a social or physical gesture that two or more students share at the beginning or end of a group/partner experience or activity. As an activator at the beginning of a lesson, it can help break the ice and engage the students with one another. If used at the end of a lesson as a summarizer, it can bring a sense of closure or be a tool of transition.

- Opening Salutes

  - Share your favorites: ice cream, food, book, movie, hobby.

  - Welcome your partner with a high 5—"Glad you're here!"

  - Say hello in another language.

  - Act out (pantomime) a greeting for your partner.

  - Share your birthday with your learning partner.

- Closing Salutes

  - Close the lesson with "Thank you for working with me."

  - Say goodbye in another language.

  - Ask them to share with their partner one word that summarizes what they learned/ how they feel.

  - Affirm your partner with "Good job, partner!" or "We did it!"

Group salutes can also involve physical interactions such as handshakes, fist bumps, high 5s, waves, dance move, or hand claps. They provide an excellent technique to signal time for transitioning into another lesson or topic. Keep the salutes brief, fresh, fun, and age appropriate.

Build Solidarity and Collaboration With Teams   Consider providing alternative seating arrangements so that children are arranged in pods/teams of small groups of four to six students in each. Increase team spirit by asking the teams to come up with a team name, slogan, and poster. This promotes a feeling of belonging and solidarity. It also reduces stress because individuals learn how to share their ideas with others, and they learn from each other. It is advisable to keep the teams for about 6 to 10 weeks and then to change their members so these groups do not become fixed.

Build It With Buddies   This team-building strategy is fun and flexible. Divide the students into teams, give each team equal amounts of a certain material, such as pipe cleaners, Lego blocks, dried pasta, minimarshmallows, toothpicks, or modeling clay. Then, ask each team to create some kind of structure within a specific time period. You can vary the task, the time, or the goal (e.g., tallest, strongest, longest, fastest).

Peer Mediation and Managing Conflict   Take time out for problem solving and positive conflict resolution. How can disputes be settled in a safe, private, and confidential setting?

You can designate a peer coach or student ambassador and work with them about strategies for conflict resolution to share with their peers. Create a poster for all to see such as the one in Figure 9.1.

Peacemakers Versus Peacebreakers   Gather your students together during your morning meeting or closing community circle to discuss what it means to be a "Peacemaker" with their peers. Create an anchor chart with students' brainstormed ideas for all to see, such as in Figure 9.2.

Then ask the students to think about the opposite: What would "Peacebreakers" do? It is important to have them be aware and to share the actions that interfere with building positive relationships. You should also make an anchor chart (see Figure 9.3) for posting about "Peacebreakers" to remind students about the actions that are negative.

Strategies for Community Building

A classroom community is formed when students come together as a class to work toward the common goal of learning. Fostering a caring classroom community helps students feel valued and connected to the teacher and the other students in the class. Recent studies have shown that children who feel a sense of identity within a group are better adjusted and more successful in school (Nickerson et al., 2019). As children progress developmentally, their group interaction skills become more fine-tuned as well. There are many benefits for developing close classroom communities; they

- Fill students' need for belonging

- Provide a way for all students to feel included

- Allow students to form and maintain positive relationships

- Teach students important social skills, such as collaboration and responsibility toward others

The Name Story   What's in a name? In pairs, students tell the story of their name, answering questions such as: Who gave you your name? What does your name mean? Are there any nicknames that you use? What do you like most about your name? Students learn things about each other and the differences that make us unique.

If You Know Me   This is usually done with partners, sometimes in writing, other times verbally. One person starts and completes this sentence frame: "If you knew me, you would know . . ." Without comment, the other person then completes the same sentence frame, sharing an interesting fact about themselves. This is an interesting and interactive way for children to find out about each other and build stronger relationships. See Figure 9.4.

Overcoming Obstacles   This is a variation on the classic team-building game called Minefield. Arrange a fun obstacle course of common classroom objects and divide students into teams. One partner is blindfolded while the other partner guides them using verbal clues only to avoid the obstacles in their pathway. Then they switch roles. You can also ask the students to use only certain words or clues to make it more challenging. Before completing this exercise, confirm that students feel comfortable being blindfolded. Ensure that all students understand they have an easy way to opt out of being blindfolded if it makes them uncomfortable.

Acts of Kindness   This lesson is designed for students to share ways that they have acted with kindness and caring toward others. Begin by providing an explanation about feeling

Peaceful Conflict Resolution

Respect the right to disagree.

Express your real concerns.

Share common goals and interests.

Open yourself to different points of view.

Listen carefully to all proposals.

Understand the major issues involved.

Think about probable consequences.

Imagine several possible alternative solutions.

Offer some reasonable compromises.

Negotiate mutually fair cooperative agreements.

–Robert E. Valett

Figure 9.1. Peaceful conflict resolution poster.

Peacemakers

- Share

- Are kind

- Work hard

- Help others

- Say "I'm sorry"

- Raise hands

- Walk, not run

- Listen

- Clean up

- Take care of thing

Figure 9.2. Peacemakers poster.

Peacebreakers

- Are messy

- Talk out of turn

- Throw things

- Are too loud

- Are unkind

- Run in the hallways

- Hit and kick others

- Don't listen

- Don't take care of things

Figure 9.3. Peacebreakers poster.

Student Survey

What are your favorite things to do in your spare time?

_____

What kind of books do you like to read?

_____

What are some places you would like to visit?

_____

What foods do you like to eat?

_____

What are some things you know a lot about?

_____

What do you like most about school?

_____

What is your favorite hobby?

_____

It's a sunny day. What are you going to do?

_____

What things are you curious about?

_____

Figure 9.4. Student survey.

grateful and have a discussion. Then, ask the students to close their eyes and visualize someone they have been kind to or helped. Ask them how this made them feel, as well as what the other person said or did in response. Then ask students to open their eyes and share what they visualized. Have them draw a picture of what they visualized and write a caption to go with it. Older students can also write a short paragraph about it. To extend this lesson and explore more of the feelings that come from showing kindness to others, students could be encouraged to write about times when they have shown kindness to others, why they did, and how they felt, in a gratitude journal.

Friendly Hands   This is a community-building art project that also integrates writing skills. Start this activity with a brief discussion about kindness, patience, and being a friend, and brainstorm sentences that describe ways to be friendly to others. Next, pair up the students to work together. They trace each other's hands, then cut out and design their own handprint with a friendly message written on it. Finally, glue all the students' work (handprints) together. These hands are then placed on a bulletin board to create a beautiful example of how to be friendly to others.

Food Gratitude   Ask the class to brainstorm as many different kinds of fruits as they can. Then, have them vote on which fruit is their favorite. Next, guide students through a visualization to think about all the people who made it possible for them to be able to enjoy this fruit. In other words—what did it take to get it from the tree, the field, and so forth to their mouth? In small groups, students share their visualization and jot down the images on chart paper, including all the people needed to produce the fruit. As students draw, have them think about and discuss how they would show gratitude to everyone, and instruct them to add this to the chart. As a treat, on the following day, bring in some of the fruit that the students selected.

Buddy Up With a "Big Brothers/Sisters Class"   There are many ways that students and teachers can create a community of learners in a school. One way to quickly build relationships between students is to create Buddy Classrooms. These are classrooms composed of students from different grade levels who meet on a regular basis. This buddy system helps to promote friendship and better support of learning, behavioral, and social needs, and can help foster a greater sense of belonging and a more inclusive school experience (Anderson et al., 2020; Hughes, 2011).

Students find it easier to share relationships with a partner class of peers who are older or younger. Why? The big kids feel important, and the little ones feel special. The older students become role models for these younger students. As a result, there are SEL gains on both sides. See the Resources section of this book (Appendix A) for additional ways of how "buddy classes" can support your students. Creating a community of learners in a school can be done in many ways to help promote positive relationships among students.

Conduct Interview Projects   Consider having your students pretend they are news reporters and give them a chance to interview each other throughout the school year about topics important to them: for example, their culture, family traditions, favorite foods, hobbies, current events, or favorite book. Model how to conduct an interview. Make sure to discuss how interviews are more than just a casual conversation. Interviews will teach your children focused listening and conversational skills. It is also an excellent tool for them to find out what they have in common with each other as well as the differences that make them unique.

Find Out About Me Game   This game can be played in partners at the beginning of the day or modified to meet your schedule of activities.

Materials Needed
- Game board

- One die

- Player game pieces (one per player)—buttons can be used

How to Play
- All players put their game piece on START.

- First player rolls the die and moves that many places.

- The player answers the question on the space they land on.

- Next player rolls, moves, and answers question.

- The first player who gets to the final square is the winner!

Find Out More About Me Board Game Questions
- What is your favorite animal? Why?

- What is your favorite hobby?

- When you grow up, what do you want to do?

- What kinds of books are your favorite?

- What is a place would you like to visit?

- What is your favorite movie?

- What are you most proud of?

- What flavor of ice cream do you like best?

- If you had a magic wand, what would you wish for?

- What is your favorite color?

- What do you like best about your family?

- What is your favorite holiday?

- If you had $1,000, how would you spend it?

- It is rainy outside. What are you going to do?

- What subject in school do you like the best? Why?

- What is your favorite time of year? Why?

- What food do you like to eat?

- What three words describe you best?

- What is your favorite place to be?

- What are the most interesting places you have visited?

- It's a sunny day, what will you do?

- What makes a friend special?

- What is your favorite game to play?

- What do you hope to learn about tomorrow?

- What does kindness mean to you?

- What are you grateful for?

- What is your favorite part of the day?

"Me Bag" Students get to choose three objects from their home that are special to them in some way and bring them in to share with the class. It's more fun if the teacher models this first by bringing in three items that are special to them. This activity gets interesting and personal when the teacher/student describes why the object is important to them and what it represents. For example, a photograph, a paintbrush, or a seashell are all things that may have special meaning attached to them. This can be done as a total class activity with a few children sharing each day. It can also be done in partners, taking turns sharing with each other. The next step is to ask, "Why is this important to you?"

"Two Facts and a Fib" This is a fun way for students and their teacher to get to know each other. As usual, teachers model this activity first for the students by writing down three statements about themselves. It is more interesting if the truths are rather "unbelievable," and the fib is something that is probable or "believable." The following are some examples: "I was a cheerleader in high school," "I was born in New York City," "I can play the piano." This is a flexible structure that can be done in pairs, in small groups, or by the whole class. An adaptation of this activity is to instruct students to write their facts and a fib on an index card and return the index card to the teacher. The teacher then chooses an index card at random, and the rest of the students can guess which of their classmates wrote these statements (adapted from Kagan, 1994).

Windowpane Activity: "This Is Me!" In this activity, students get to practice their speaking, listening, and writing skills while they get to know each other better. You can use the "This Is Me" activity sheet (Figure 9.5) or create your own prompts in a new "windowpane" by folding a standard, letter-size sheet of paper in fourths, putting a different prompt in each quadrant for students to respond to. It is a quick-write activity, depending on the age and ability level of the students.

Strategies to Use During Instruction

The following sections include strategies that can be used during content instruction. The strategies can be seamlessly infused into lesson plans and adapted depending on the subject matter being taught.

Maximize the Lessons in Storytime Think about lessons you can glean from interactive read-alouds that boost relationships and SEL with your students. One of the most helpful strategies for integrating SEL can be through interactive teacher read-alouds. In addition, reading aloud helps students learn how to use language to make sense of the world, and it improves their information-processing skills, vocabulary, and comprehension. Reading aloud also targets the skills of audio learners. Using literature to target SEL skills is quite simple. Teachers can read the text as they normally would, and then pause along the way to highlight any issues or critical skills that arise. This is a unique opportunity to spark

This Is Me

My favorite subject at school is . . .	Here is a picture of my family . . .
I am happiest when . . .	**My favorite book is . . .**

Figure 9.5. This is me worksheet.

rich discussions and to teach core values. The following are sample questions that can be asked:

- How do you think the characters feel?
- How might they be understood or misunderstood by others in the story?
- What are some ways the character could handle the situation they're presented with?

See Appendix B for a list of children's books to support SEL.

The Wonder of Words   Help children develop their "feeling" vocabulary by giving them new words and positive phrases to express themselves. Provide sample self-talk sentence stems to build resilience and overcome any sense of learned helplessness, shifting to a positive growth mindset. Figure 9.6 includes sample sentence stems (these can be reproduced on a large poster so that all can see, and you can point out to your students how to use affirmations for themselves and others).

Call-and-Response Affirmations   To start or end your lesson, ask students to repeat after you a set of affirmations, in a call-and-response way. For example:

Teacher: "I am lovable."

Class: "I am loveable!"

Teacher: "I am good enough."

Class: "I am good enough!"

Teacher: "I am strong."

Class: "I am strong!"

Repeat a second or third time if you want. Once this becomes part of your classroom routines, invite students to lead the call and response. Ask them to come up with their own positive affirmations over time.

Practice Role-Play Situations   This is a way for the students to put themselves in somebody else's shoes to help them understand troubling situations and respond to other people's feelings. Role playing can be particularly effective in acting out potential bullying situations. (Please refer to character role-playing cards in the Resources section of this book [Appendix A].) Often when put in a position to act out a situation, students learn about their own emotions (how do I feel about this situation?), how to control the feelings of the character (what would this person say or do?), and consider the perspective of someone other than themselves. For this exercise, two students can role-play an argument and then switch roles to truly feel the other's perspective.

"Learning Line-Up"   An alternative activity is to have the students form two parallel lines facing each other. This structure is called a "Learning Line-Up." Students stand in their line, facing a partner. One line is designated as the "movers" and the other line the "shakers." The teacher instructs students to share their answer to a prompt; the students then take turns of 60 seconds each to share with the student directly across from them. After the time signal is given, the "movers" move up the line by one person and the "shakers" shake/dance in place waiting for their new partner to arrive. The teacher repeats a shout-out for a different prompt to share this time and the students share with their new partner.

The Wonder of Words!

- I am an amazing person.
- I did my very best!
- I will have an awesome day.
- It's okay to keep learning new things.
- Today I will be happy.
- Today I will spread kindness.
- I will make a difference.
- I am ready and willing to learn.
- I will make good choices.
- I am an important person.
- I have people who love me.
- I can make my dreams come true.
- I matter a lot and make a difference.
- I am loveable and capable.
- I am one of a kind.
- I help other people feel better.
- I accept myself for who I am.
- I can get through tough times.
- I want to do my best every day.
- I'm going to keep trying and not give up.
- I am relaxed and calm.
- I choose my attitude and feelings.
- I've got that "can-do" feeling.
- I will think positively.
- Today I will be confident and strong.
- Today is a new beginning.
- I am thankful for today.
- I get better and smarter every day.
- I forgive myself for my mistakes.
- Challenges help me become stronger.
- I will do better next time.

Figure 9.6. The wonder of words poster.

Emotional Expression Through Art   Sometimes students have feelings and/or problems that they have difficulty expressing in words. However, artistic expression is a way for children to share the issues they are having. Art also provides students with a tool to explore topics from a different perspective.

Strategies for the Classroom Environment

The classroom environment is one of the most important factors affecting student learning. Positive and productive learning environments are key to children's academic, emotional, and social success in school. Unfortunately, positive learning environments don't just happen—they must be consciously created. There are multiple components that contribute to making a positive learning environment for students. These caring classroom communities should offer an overall sense of safety, where risk taking and open conversations are encouraged, trust and respect are fostered, and positive interactions are the norm.

"Positive Pitches" Poster   Figure 9.7 is an example to use to display "positive pitches" so that your students become more aware of the power of the words we use and the impact they have on ourselves and others in the classroom.

Create a "Bucket of Kindness"   I suggest reading the book *Have You Filled a Bucket Today?*, which is a picture book and story about the impact and power of words of kindness. Then create your own "kindness bucket" for the classroom. Have the students decorate it and then, using index cards, have them write positive pitches and words of kindness, appreciation, and gratitude. Students continue to write these random messages of kindness throughout the week to fill up the bucket. At the end of the week, as part of your closing community circle, spend a few minutes reading some of the messages of kindness to share with the students.

Buddy Bench   A buddy bench provides a way for students to signal that they are feeling sad or lonely during recess and want support and/or a friend. You can use an existing bench near the playground or have the students design and paint the bench and work together to ensure the bench is used properly. Explain to students that if someone does not have a friend to play with, they can sit on the buddy bench, and another student will come and sit with them and help that student. This positive project was created based on students' ideas and desire to help others.

Create a "Cool-Down Corner" or "Peace Place" in the Classroom   Look at your classroom through a new lens: is there a get-away space that can be created for students to retreat to when they are feeling stressed-out? It is important to create a special place in your classroom for kids to take a break and to calm themselves down when they are feeling frustrated or angry. This special space might include comfortable pillows, stuffed animals, small manipulatives and stress balls, a fish tank, serene photographs of nature, headphones to block the noise, or journaling materials.

Create Social-Emotional Learning Anchor Charts   In your caring classroom, you want to create "wallpapers of wonder" to reinforce positive messages and themes that support SEL and to promote better relationships. Here are some possible topics to consider:

• What does kindness look like?

• How do you spell R-E-S-P-E-C-T?

In Our Classroom, We Use "Positive Pitches" to Promote Learning

We say . . .	Instead of . . .
• How can I improve?	I'm no good at this.
• I like a challenge!	I'll stay with what I know.
• Learning takes time.	This is too hard.
• Have I done my best work?	I'm all done.
• Let me try a different way.	I give up.
• How can we learn from each other?	They are smarter than me.
• My attitude is important.	My abilities are stuck.
• Mistakes are part of learning.	I failed . . . so that's it.

Figure 9.7. Positive pitches poster.

- Be a goal getter and a problem solver.

- Own your learning/progress monitoring.

- What does success look like?

"I Am" Poster   There are many variations on this activity. For instance, students may choose to create a poster, a poem, a song, or a slideshow about themselves. It might be helpful to provide students with some prompts such as the worksheet in Figure 9.8 to get them started. For sharing these with the class, you can hang the posters and allow students to do a gallery walk or use some of the sharing methods provided throughout this chapter to share in pairs, in small groups, or as a whole class.

Power Cards   Power cards provide a visual reminder of appropriate and desired behaviors exhibited by a person or a character that the student admires. For example, design a poster of "Super Girl" or "Super Boy" and then have the children brainstorm positive qualities that this character has. Super Girl and Super Boy use words of kindness, help others, follow directions, listen well.

Classroom Roles and Responsibilities   Assigning various "resource managers" and classroom jobs teaches responsibility and gives students greater ownership in their classroom. It boosts their confidence in a job well done and is a great confidence builder.

SUMMARY

Teachers need to build a strong sense of community in their classrooms to foster better student–student relationships as well as student–teacher relationships. Creating and strengthening bonds between and among students is not a one-time event or lesson. Building relationships and mutual respect among peers is fostered over time and throughout the day. Finding ways to design learning experiences that tap into what your students value is the key to making your classroom more student centered. In caring, collaborative classrooms, students know that every voice matters, and each student has the opportunity to be heard every single day. Doing daily check-ins with your students also provides them the opportunity to practice responsive listening, taking turns, and following group norms.

In this chapter, many strategies have been presented to show you ways to reach your students, help them achieve, create a caring classroom environment, and build positive relationships with them. As researchers have demonstrated, building strong relationships with students can promote their academic and social development and reduce behavior problems. What are some important tips to keep in mind when implementing these techniques?

- *Try to Personally Connect With Students.* Although your day is already busy and packed with responsibility, try to spend personal time every week with each of your students—especially those students who might struggle or feel that their voices aren't being heard. Keep these conversations positive, pleasant, and upbeat, not punitive. For example, you could ask about what's going on in their life, how they are feeling, or what they are going to do on the weekend. This will help foster a stronger connection and help them develop socially.

- *Keep an Eye Out for Something to Comment On.* In other words, "catch them being good" and make a point of commenting on it. You can also comment on one of their interests, their hobbies, or favorite sports team. The bottom line is that students feel happier when their teacher shows a genuine interest in them.

"I Am" Poster Prompts

- I am happy when _____.

- I wonder _____.

- I get scared when _____.

- I like _____ because _____.

- I worry about _____ because _____.

- In the future, I want to be _____.

- I am sad when _____.

- I wish that I could _____.

- I was surprised when _____.

- My friends like me because _____.

Figure 9.8. "I am" poster prompts.

- *Share Your Stories.* It is important to reveal yourself to students through personal stories. Maybe you could share an incident that happened to you in school in which you showed resilience and succeeded so that they understand that challenges are a natural part of life. In other words, let students inside your world—it will really make a difference and makes you more relatable and accessible to students. Be real with them and let students see you make mistakes and grow from those mistakes.

- *Be Interested in Students' Interests.* This is a special way to connect with your students. Our students have many interests and hobbies, and when you show you care about what they are interested in, a sense of respect and connection is developed, even for the hard-to-reach students.

- *Participate in Student Events.* Make sure you are there to cheer them on in the school play or concert, to recognize and celebrate their talents beyond the classroom. You can attend their sporting events. This has the added benefit of giving you something to talk about with them: "That was a great hit you made in baseball practice today."

- *Take Care of You.* Please take these strategies one step at a time. It is so important to take care of yourself and your stressors first and foremost. If you are not ready for the day, then you are not ready to support the emotional well-being of your students. Take time for your own emotional stability—walk with a friend, attend a yoga class, use a mindfulness app to meditate, eat well, and be healthy. Don't forget to breathe. Know where your own emotions are and get support if needed.

Additional Resources

A1   GROUPS 174

A2   SEL Sentence Stems to "Spark" Quick-Writes 175

A3   Focus on Your Feelings 176

A4   Reacting to My Feelings 177

A5   Brain Breaks/State Changes 178

A6   Ask a "Question of the Day" to Get Started 179

A7   Strategies to Promote "Buddy Classrooms" 180

A8   Thank You Notes Made Easy! 181

A9   Preparing to Write Your Thank You Notes 182

A10   Recipe for a Thank You Note 183

A11   Reframing Praise for a Growth Mindset 184

A12   Sample Role-Play Cards 185

A13   Empathy Situation Cards 186

A14   Feelings Illustrations 187

A15   "I Can Change It" coloring sheet 189

A16   Brainpower coloring sheet 190

A17   Boss of My Mind coloring sheet 191

A18   I Can't Do It Yet coloring sheet 192

Get along

Respect

Offer your ideas

Use quiet voices

Participate actively

Stay on task

The Social-Emotional Learning Toolbox by Kathy Perez. Copyright © 2022 by Paul H. Brookes Publishing Co., Inc. All rights reserved.

SEL Sentence Stems to "Spark" Quick-Writes

Sparks for self-awareness:

- What are five words that best describe you?
- What are some ways that you showed kindness?
- What does it mean to be a good student?
- I am most successful when . . .

Sparks for cultivating identity:

- I'm the kind of friend who . . .
- I'm the kind of student who . . .
- I'm the kind of classmate who . . .
- I'm the kind of reader who . . .

Sparks for self-management:

- What goals do I have for myself this week (month)?
- What interests/hobbies do I love to do?
- What is my favorite subject in school?
- What challenges will I need to work harder on or get support for?

Sparks for connecting with emotions:

- A time I felt happiest was when . . .
- I get frustrated when . . .
- When I'm angry I sometimes . . .
- Sometimes I get scared when . . .

Focus on Your Feelings

Name: _____

Date: _____

Instructions: Finish the following statements with specific examples of things in your life that make you feel stressed, upset/mad, sad, or scared.

I feel stressed when _____

_____

_____

I feel happy when _____

_____

_____

I feel upset/mad when _____

_____

_____

I feel sad when _____

_____

_____

I feel scared when _____

_____

_____

Reacting to My Feelings

Name: _____

Date: _____

Instructions: Fill in the following statements/situations with your *first* and *automatic* reaction to feeling stressed, upset, sad, or scared. Don't worry that your reaction is good or bad, or what others will think of your reaction . . . just answer how you would really react.

Situation 1 – Feeling stressed

When I am feeling stressed out because _____

I usually _____

Situation 2 – Feeling angry/mad

When I am feeling upset or angry because _____

I usually _____

Situation 3 – Feeling sad

When I am feeling sad because of _____

I usually _____

Situation 4 – Feeling scared

When I am feeling scared because _____

I usually _____

Brain Breaks/State Changes

Focused brain breaks and state changes are important for student engagement and to increase productivity. They are easy to implement and help the children refocus so they can return to work feeling centered and ready to learn!

- Stomp feet
- Tell a story
- Just jump!
- Do the "wave"
- Make it rain
- Tell a joke/riddle
- Show a brief video clip
- Make faces
- Change where you stand in the room
- Do a cross-lateral "break chant"
- Pantomime a feeling
- Do a magic trick
- Rock, paper, scissors
- Ball toss, bean bag, Frisbee toss
- Role-play learning
- Take a deep breath
- Partner re-teach
- Sing/whistle
- Play Simon Says
- Stand still
- Mix and mingle—to music
- Special gestures
- High 5
- Invent ways to shake hands
- Touch/find objects
- Repeat after me
- Music
- Read slogans
- Stretch break
- Change expressions
- Visualization
- Synectics – show object
- Change seats
- Touch/find objects
- Lazy 8s, thumbs in circle
- Get in animal teams
- Repeat what was said
- Story starters
- Invisible pictures
- Rhyme time

- "Focus ball" breathing
- Teach quick sign language words
- Cruise on an imaginary skateboard
- Do the partner shuffle
- Add a quick yoga move
- Do some facial gymnastics
- Take a doodle break
- Clap on, clap off
- Spread your wings (in slow motion)
- Toss a "hot potato" for quick response
- Celebrate with a silent cheer
- Sound effects
- Knock, knock
- Drumbeats on the desk
- Point to something
- Secret bag—can you guess?
- Squiggle story
- Rise and fall
- Stir the pot
- Do the Cha-Cha Slide
- Hold your breath for a minute
- Call and response
- Teach them clapping games
- Jump rope
- Hop on, hop off
- Vote with your body
- Pass the motion
- Puppets
- Hit the wall with beanbags
- Try a cat/cow pose
- Try boom, snap, clap
- 3-2-1 blastoff rocket
- Brainstorm
- Pretend you are popcorn
- Flowers blooming
- Scream, pause, silence
- Change tonality
- Float like a jellyfish
- Do sound effects

Ask a "Question of the Day" to Get Started

(Questions can be changed based on the age and background of your students)

- What do you dream about?
- What are your strengths? How can you use them to make the world a better place?
- What do you complain about?
- What is your favorite word? Why?
- What is one thing you wish that I knew about you?
- What is your favorite movie? Why?
- What does success look like?
- Who is your favorite famous person? Why?
- What is one of your fears?
- What is one of your talents?
- The Beatles sang, "All You Need Is Love." Do you agree or disagree? Why?
- What kind of music do you like to listen to?
- Is trust important? Why or why not?
- Where do you see beauty in the world?
- If you could pick any job to do when you grow up, what would it be? Why?
- What do you like to do for fun with yourself? With friends? With family?
- What are you thankful for? Why?
- If you could change anything in this world, what would it be? Why?
- What do you do when you are angry?
- What is your favorite place at home? Why?
- What do you feel like when you are lost?
- Who is your favorite superhero? Why?
- If you could visit anywhere in the world, where would you go? Why?
- What sounds do you like? Why?
- What bothers you?

- If you were outside all day, what would you do?
- What memory makes you happy?
- What makes you awesome?
- What do you like best about our classroom?
- What would you like to change in our classroom?
- What makes someone smart?
- What do you like to play?
- If you wrote a book, what would it be about?
- Who is your hero? Why?
- If you owned a store, what would you sell? Why?
- Tell me about a time you were brave.
- What makes a true friend?
- What makes you laugh?
- What do you look forward to? Why?
- What makes you feel loved? Why?
- What kind of weather do you like best? Why?
- If you could name yourself, what would you be called?
- What do you do after school?
- What is your superhero name and what is your power?
- How do you solve problems?
- How do you show others that you care?
- What are your favorite smells? Why?
- If you could do anything today—what would you do? Why?
- Who is your favorite character in a movie? Why?
- Pretend you just arrived at the beach for the first time. What would you do first?
- What are you most proud of?

Strategies to Promote "Buddy Classrooms"

There are many powerful ways these classroom connections can become even more powerful for your school. Here are some successful strategies to consider for use in buddy classrooms:

Reading Buddies—Have older students read to younger students and vice versa. This builds rapport and provides positive modeling. Together they can create book discussions, posters, and more to share with their peers.

Art Projects—Another activity that both age groups can participate successfully in is to create art projects together.

Science or History Project Teammates—The use of cross-age peers can be used throughout the content areas. Why not have them create a hands-on science experiment that buddies can work on together? Buddies can also partner up to do a history project together; older students can help research historical people, places, or events.

Sharing Good News—Take time out of your shared time together to celebrate the "good news" of their buddy class. Develop ways to cheer them on or create class salutes.

Obstacle Course—Get the kids outside and have the older class set up a fun obstacle course for the younger class to navigate or vice versa. The other team cheers them on.

Technology Teammates—It is challenging to keep up with the latest tech tools. Have the "buddy partners" explore these innovative technology tools together while learning new software or hardware; teams can then share out their project.

Writing Stories—Students can write a story together, then share out to the whole class. Younger students can dictate the story to their older partner who will be the scribe and write it down. Both students can help develop the story together.

Assembly Partners—Why not have them make connections throughout the school day? During school assemblies, older students can sit with their younger buddy partners; modeling is key here.

Creating Buddy Class Logo, Team Name, and Saying—Fostering a special team atmosphere and partnership by each buddy classroom can be a positive force. Invite the teams to create a logo or develop a chant and have an inspirational saying associated with the team.

Playground Pals—Older students are placed with younger students to teach them how to use the playground equipment; older students can help oversee games and activities outside and model and teach the younger students.

Buddy "Brain Breaks"—When a student needs a break from the classroom or other activity, a buddy partner can walk with them in a designated area or participate in another form of a "brain break" together.

Breakfast Buddies/Lunch Buddies—Buddy partners can eat with each other for breakfast or lunch in the school cafeteria.

Reward Reinforcement—A classroom can earn points to spend more time with their buddy classroom; as a variation, both classrooms can attain a certain goal and then they get to do something fun together.

Thank You Notes Made Easy!

There is so much kindness in our world! People spend time with us, teach us new things, help improve our life, or even give us gifts. It's important to celebrate and appreciate the kindness of others. One way to do that is to write a thank you note. A thank you note is a hands-on way to show your appreciation for a gift or someone's act of kindness.

Brainstorm with your students some characteristics of meaningful thank you notes:

- Have positive words and phrases
- Are hand-written
- Reflect who you are
- Are personalized
- Discuss what the person did and what it means to you

What do you include in a thank you note?

- Greeting
- Description of what you are thankful for
- Explanation of why you like what you received or what the person did for you
- Sign off
- Signature

Preparing to Write Your Thank You Notes

WHO do you want to write a thank you note to?

_____

_____

WHAT did this person do that you are thankful for?

_____

_____

HOW did this person's kindness make you feel?

_____

_____

In WHAT way is your life a little better because of this person's kindness or gift?

_____

_____

Recipe for a Thank You Note

GREETING

Start your thank you note with a friendly greeting.

_____,

SAY THANK YOU

Begin your thank you note with a sentence about what you are thankful for. Be specific.

_____

_____

ADD DETAILS

Describe exactly why you appreciate the person's gifts or acts of kindness. Add details.

_____

_____

EXPLAIN

Tell them how the person's gift or effort made you feel.

_____

_____

CLOSING

Choose a friendly way to finish your note of thanks. Don't forget your signature!

_____,

_____

REVIEW AND IMPROVE YOUR DRAFT.

SEND OR DELIVER!

Reframing Praise for a Growth Mindset

Instead of . . .	I would say . . .	Why would this be better?
Great job! You are really smart about this!	Excellent! Your effort and trying new strategies have really paid off.	
Some of these problems are really hard. Just do your best.	Some of the problems may be challenging. Try them even if you are not sure because mistakes will help you learn. When you take time to think hard about a problem, that's when real learning happens!	
You tried your hardest, and that's all you can do.	Don't worry if you don't understand something right away. Focus on next steps. What should they be?	
You are such a good writer!		
You need to revise this.		
These seem too hard for you. Maybe you should work on an easier page.		
You made a lot of mistakes on this page.		
This certainly is not your best subject, is it?		
I'm so proud of you for getting 100%.		
You don't know how to do this, do you?		
You are such a good writer!		
You just don't get it, do you?		
Don't you know this already?		

The simple word *yet* can change negative statements into positive ones, promoting growth, according to Dweck.

This linguistic trick works especially well with sentences that include *can't* or *don't*, because it reverses the negative connotation.

See for yourself by adding *yet* to the end of these sentences:

- I can't solve these problems in math . . . YET.
- I don't understand opposites . . . YET.
- I don't know the answer to this question . . . YET.

When you catch yourself using similar sentences, keep this simple strategy in mind and share it with students.

Sample Role-Play Cards

- You were assigned a partner for group work that you don't like. What would you do?

- A stack of books toppled down in your classroom and a classmate told the teacher that you knocked them down. What would you do?

- Your friends are teasing a kid in your class who just got new glasses. What would you do?

- You just saw a friend of yours stealing candies from another kid's desk. What would you do?

- During a test, you notice that the kid sitting next to you is copying all your answers. What would you do?

- You see somebody who is new to your school at recess. You notice that he is all alone and looking sad. What would you do?

- You notice that someone is being teased in the lunchroom about being "fat" and she starts to cry. What would you do?

- They are choosing teams to play basketball for PE. One child is left and both team captains do not want that kid on their team and say so. What would you do?

Empathy Situation Cards

Situation cards	Empathy
he received a gift from his brother	he is going to the movies this afternoon
his friend did not want to play with him	he wants a new toy
she is waiting for Grandma to visit	she drew a very pretty picture
his ice cream fell off his cone	she has been in the hot car for 1 hour alone
her birthday party is today	she is hungry and wants dinner now
he scraped his elbow	he is meeting a new friend

SURPRISED

SCARED

SAD

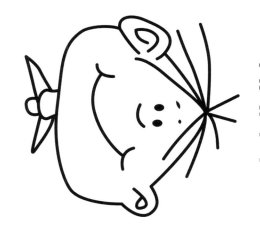

HAPPY

(continued)

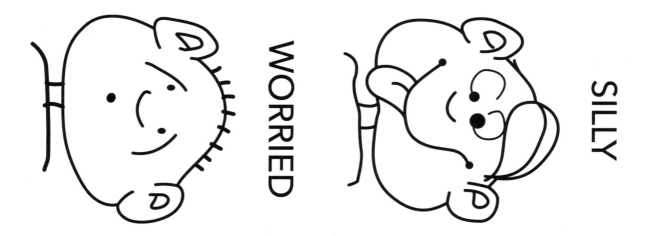

WORRIED

SILLY

CALM

ANGRY

I Can't Do It Yet But I WILL

Children's Books to Support Social-Emotional Learning

CHILDREN'S BOOKS: FOCUS ON CARING

Grades K-2

Clifford's Good Deeds by Normal Bidwell

Corduroy by Don Freeman

Swimmy by Leo Lionni

Rainbow Fish to the Rescue by Marcus Pfister

Alexander and the Windup Mouse by Leo Lionni

Big Al and Shrimpy by Andrew Clements

The Mitten Tree by Candace Christianson

Wilfrid Gordon McDonald Partridge by Mem Fox

A Mother for Choco by Keiko Kasza

Now One Foot, Now the Other by Tomie dePaola

Knots on a Counting Rope by Bill Martin, Jr.

The Giving Tree by Shel Silverstein

Grades 3-5

Angel Child, Dragon Child by Michele Maria Surat

Horton Hears a Who! by Dr. Seuss

Beach and Blue by Sarah Kilborne

Oliver Button Is a Sissy by Tomie dePaola

Ferdinand by Munro Leaf

Mufaro's Beautiful Daughters by John Steptoe

More Random Acts of Kindness by Conari Press

The Roughfaced Girl by Rafe Martin

Through Grandpa's Eyes by Patricia MacLachlan

Pink and Say by Patricia Polacco

CHILDREN'S BOOKS: FOCUS ON FEELINGS AND KINDESS

I believe children of any age enjoy exposure to picture books. Illustrations along with text lead to more complex analyses, and reading between the lines provides opportunities for different interpretations for older children while promoting freedom of expression in regards to feelings and emotions. Therefore, this book list (and subsequent lists) is not delineated by grade levels.

The Butter Battle Book by Dr. Seuss

It's Okay to Be Different by Todd Parr

Horace and Morris but Mostly Dolores by James Howe

Hey Little Ant by Phillip M. Hoose

A Sick Day for Amos McGee by Phillip C. Stead

Bear Feels Sick by Karma Wilson

The Name Jar by Yangsook Choi

Swimmy by Leo Lionni

Stand Tall, Molly Lou Mellon by Patty Lovell

My Name Is Yoon by Helen Recorvit

Amos & Boris by William Steig

Those Shoes by Maribeth Boelts

Last Stop on Market Street by Matt de la Peña

The Spiffiest Giant in Town by Julia Donaldson

Sam and the Lucky Money by Karen Chinn

Each Kindness by Jacqueline Woodson

The Sneetches by Dr. Seuss

The Invisible Boy by Trudy Ludwig

Enemy Pie by Derek Munson

How to Heal a Broken Wing by Bob Graham

The Kindness Quilt by Nancy Elizabeth Wallace

The Lion and the Mouse by Jerry Pinkney

The Ugly Duckling by Hans Christian Andersen

The Hundred Dresses by Eleanor Estes

Somebody Loves You, Mr. Hatch by Eileen Spinelli

Earrings! by Judity Viorst

BOOKS TO TEACH OLDER CHILDREN EMPATHY

Out of My Mind by Sharon M. Draper

Wonder by R.J. Palacio

365 Days of Wonder: Mr. Browne's Book of Precepts by R.J. Palacio

The One and Only Ivan by Katherine Applegate and Patricia Castelao

Brown Girl Dreaming by Jacqueline Woodson

Bridge to Terabithia by Katherine Paterson

El Deafo by Cece Bell

Inside Out and Back Again by Thanhhà Lai

My Side of the Mountain by Jean Craighead George

The Family Under the Bridge by Natalie Savage Carlson and Garth Williams

Island of the Blue Dolphins by Scott O'Dell

Where the Red Fern Grows by Wilson Rawls

I Hadn't Mean to Tell You This by Jacqueline Woodson

Fish in a Tree by Lynda Mullaly Hunt

Same Sun Here by Silas House and Neela Vaswani

Sunborn Rising: Beneath the Fall by Aaron Safronoff

Hannah Coulter by Wendell Berry

Jayber Crow by Wendell Berry

Paperboy by Vince Vawter

The Boy on the Wooden Box: How the Impossible Became Possible . . . On Schindler's List by Leon Leyson

One Came Home by Amy Timberlake

Tasting the Sky: A Palestinian Childhood by Ibtisam Barakat

Persepolis: The Story of a Childhood by Marjane Satrapi

READ-ALOUDS FOR TEACHING GROWTH MINDSET

Are you talking with your students about persistence and overcoming failure this year? An easy way to encourage growth mindset is through engaging, purposeful read-alouds. These growth mindset read-alouds can help guide your conversation.

How to Catch a Star by Oliver Jeffers

Best for: Grades PreK–2

Whistle for Willie by Ezra Jack Keats

Best for: Grades PreK–2

Everyone Can Learn to Ride a Bicycle by Chris Raschka

Best for: Grades PreK–3

Flight School by Lita Judge

Best for: Grades PreK–3

A Splash of Red: The Life and Art of Horace Pippin by Jen Bryant

Best for: Grades K–3

Rosie Revere Engineer by Andrea Beaty

Best for: Grades 1–3

Emmanuel's Dream by Laurie Ann Thompson

Best for: Grades K–4

Nadia: The Girl Who Couldn't Sit Still by Karlin Gray

Best for: Grades 1–4

Brave Irene by William Steig

Best for: Grades 1–4

Drum Dream Girl: How One Girl's Courage Changed Music by Margarita Engle and Rafael Lopez

Best for: Grades 1–4

Hana Hashimoto, Sixth Violin by Chiere Uegaki

Best for Grades 2–5

Ruby's Wish by Sharin Yim Bridges

Best for Grades 2–5

RECOMMENDED BOOKS FOR CHILDREN WITH ANXIETY

What to Do When You Worry Too Much: A Kid's Guide to Overcoming by Dawn Huebner and Bonnie Matthews

A Little Spot of Anxiety by Diane Alber

David and the Worry Beast by Anne Marie Guanci and Caroline Attia

Is a Worry Worrying You? by Ferida Wolff

Sea Otter Cove by Lori Lite

Little Mouse's Big Book of Fears by Emily Gravett

A Boy and a Bear: The Children's Relaxation Book by Lori Lite

Don't Panic, Annika by Juliet Clare Bell and Jennifer E. Morris

Wemberly Worried by Kevin Henkes

Wilma Jean the Worry Machine by Julia Cook

What to Do When You're Scared and Worried: A Guide for Kids by James J. Crist

When My Worries Get Too Big! A Relaxation Book for Children Who Live With Anxiety by Kari Dunn Buron

CHILDREN'S PICTURE BOOKS THAT TEACH ACCEPTANCE AND EMPATHY

The Sneetches by Dr. Seuss

Chrysanthemum by Kevin Henkes

One by Kathryn Otoshi

The Butter Battle Book by Dr. Seuss

Amazing Grace by Mary Hoffman

It's Okay to Be Different by Todd Parr

Horace and Morris by Mostly Dolores by James Howe

Hey, Little Ant by Phillip M. Hoose

A Sick Day for Amos McGee by Phillip C. Stead

Bear Feels Sick by Karma Wilson

Resources for Continued Learning

WEB SITES

Mindful Schools
http://mindfulschools.org

The Greater Good Science Center at UC-Berkley
http://greatergood.berkeley.edu/

The Guardian Teacher Network Resources
http://www.theguardian.com/teacher-network

Mindfulness in Schools Project
http://mindfulnessinschools.org/

The Center for Mindfulness at the University of Massachusetts
http://umassmed.edu/cfm/index.aspx

Mindful Magazine
http://mindful.org

The Mindsight Institute (UCLA)
http://www.drdansiegel.com

BOOKS

Full Catastrophe Living by Jon Kabat-Zinn

Search Inside Yourself by Chade-Meng Tan

Finding the Space to Lead by Janice Marturano

The Mayo Clinic Guide to Stress-Free Living by Amit Sood, MD

10% Happier by Dan Harris

A Mindful Nation by Congressman Tim Ryan

Mindfulness: An Eight-Week Plan for Finding Peace in a Frantic World by Mark Penman and Danny Williams

Mindful Teaching and Teaching Mindfulness by Deborah Schoeberlein David and Suki Sheth

The Way of Mindful Education by Daniel Rechtschaffen

The Mindful Brain by Dan Siegel

The Mindfulness Revolution edited Barry Boyce

ARTICLES

Black, D. S., Milam, J., & Sussman, S. (2009). Sitting-meditation interventions among youth: A review of treatment efficacy. *Pediatrics, 124*(3), 532.

Burke, C. A. (2010). Mindfulness-based approaches with children and adolescents: A preliminary review of current research in an emergent field. *Journal of Child and Family Studies, 19*(2), 190.

Rampel, K. (2012). Mindfulness for children and youth: A review of the literature with an argument for school-based implementation. *Canadian Journal of Counseling and Psychotherapy, 46*(3), 201–220.

Trauma-Informed Resources

ONLINE RESOURCES

Attachment and Trauma Network
https://www.attachmenttraumanetwork.org/

National Childhood Traumatic Stress Network
https://www.nctsn.org/

Association for Treatment and Training in the Attachment of Children (ATTACh)
https://attach.org/

A Forever Family
https://www.foreverfamily.org/

Child Trauma Academy
https://www.childtrauma.org/

BOOKS

The Heart of Learning and Teaching: Compassion, Resiliency, and Academic Success by Ray Wolpow, PhD, Mona M. Johnson, EdD, CDP, Ron Hertel, BS, and Susan O. Kincaid, PhD

Reaching and Teaching Children Who Hurt: Strategies in Your Classroom by Susan E. Craig, PhD

Lost at School by Ross W. Greene, PhD

Helping Traumatized Children Learn by Massachusetts Advocates for Children

Help for Billy by Heather Forbes, LCSW

TRAUMA-SENSITIVE CLASSROOM STRATEGIES

MindUP—A research-based training program that teachers social and emotional learning skills that link cognitive neuroscience, positive psychology, and mindfulness awareness training utilizing a brain-centric approach. (https://mindup.org/)

Sound Discipline—A web site for both parents and educators about the practice of Positive Discipline. Offers free newsletter articles and resources. (https://www.sounddiscipline.org/)

FuelEd Schools—Training in social/emotional competency and teaching empathy, as well as exploring teachers' attachment styles. (https://www.fueledschools.org/)

ARTICLES

Dorado, J., & Zakrzewski, V. (2013). How to help a traumatized child in the classroom. *Greater Good Magazine*. https://greatergood.berkeley.edu/article/item/the_silent_epidemic_in _our_classrooms

Gindis, B. (1998). Navigating uncharted waters: School psychologists working with internationally adopted post-institutionalized children. *Communiqué*, Part 1, *27*(1), 6–9; Part 2, *27*(2), 20–23.

Smith, L. B. (2008). *Oil and water: The attachment disordered child in school.* http://www .attachmentnewengland.com/oil_water.pdf

Glossary

cognitive flexibility   The brain's ability to switch between thinking about two different ideas or to think about multiple concepts at the same time.

cognitive regulation   Attention control, inhibitory control, working memory and planning, and cognitive flexibility.

coping   An individual's ability to effectively deal with difficult circumstances.

declarative memory   A type of long-term memory, also referred to as explicit memory, that involves conscious memory of specific facts and/or events.

emotional intelligence   The ability to manage one's feelings and interact positively with other people.

emotional literacy   The ability to read or recognize one's own emotions and the emotions of others to determine what others are feeling and to respond appropriately.

emotional processes   Knowledge of emotions and expression, emotion and behavior regulation, and empathy or perspective taking. See **empathy**.

emotional self-regulation   The ability to manage your emotional responses. We often cannot control the things that we experience, but we can learn to control our response to them.

empathy   The ability to understand perspectives and feelings other than your own.

episodic memory   A type of long-term memory that involves conscious memory of multiple previous experiences within the context of time, place, emotions, and so forth.

The Every Student Succeeds Act (ESSA), 2015   The primary law for K–12 public education in the United States to ensure public schools provide quality education for all students.

executive functioning (EF)   Neurological processes involved in mental control and self-regulation. See **self-regulation**.

feedback   Providing specific responses to a student's performance of a task as a basis for improvement.

fixed mindset   The belief that one's abilities are innate and/or unchangeable.

formative assessment   Providing ongoing feedback to monitor student learning and/or help students identify strengths and weaknesses and set goals.

growth mindset   The belief that an individual can improve their abilities through effort and perseverance.

implicit memory   One of the two main types of long term memory (see also declarative memory), implicit memory is obtained and used unconsciously; it may affect one's thoughts and behaviors.

impulse control   An individual's ability to resist sudden, forceful urges to do something that may cause harm to oneself or others.

interpersonal skills   The ability to understand social cues, conflict resolution, and prosocial behavior.

learned helplessness   Occurs when an individual feels that they have no control over their situation, so they begin to behave in a helpless manner. This inaction can lead one to miss opportunities for relief or change in a situation. Learned helplessness has also been associated with depression, anxiety, phobias, and other psychological conditions.

long-term memory   The brain's ability to store information for an extended period of time. Divided into two types of memory: see **declarative memory** and **implicit memory**.

mindfulness   A mental state and/or practice achieved by focusing one's awareness on the present moment and acknowledging and accepting feelings, thoughts, and physical sensations.

motivation   A willingness or desire of an individual to do or achieve something.

procedural memory   Part of the long-term memory responsible for knowing how to complete tasks, also called motor skills.

relationship skills   The ability to initiate and sustain positive connections with peers, teachers, families, and other groups.

resilience   One's ability to recover from or adjust easily to unfortunate circumstances or change.

responsible decision making   The ability to make choices that consider the well-being of oneself and others.

self-awareness   The capacity to reflect on one's own feelings, values, and behaviors.

self-management   A set of skills that includes self-motivation, goal setting, personal organization, self-discipline, impulse control, and use of strategies for coping with stress.

self-motivation   An individual's ability to take action to pursue goals and complete tasks.

self-regulation   An individual's ability to control one's thoughts, emotions, and behaviors and manage disruptive impulses in pursuit of long-term goals.

semantic memory   The brain's ability to retain general factual knowledge and concepts that allow individuals to assign meaning to information and engage complex cognitive processes as recognizing objects and using language.

sensory memory   The ability for the brain to briefly retain information from each of the five senses (sight, hearing, smell, taste, and touch) beyond the occurrence of the stimulus for recoding into another memory or for comprehension of stimulus.

short-term memory   The brain's system for temporarily storing and managing information needed to complete complex cognitive tasks such as learning, reasoning, and comprehension.

social awareness   The ability to view situations from another perspective, respect the social and cultural norms of others, and celebrate diversity.

social-emotional learning (SEL)   A set of social, emotional, behavioral, and character skills that support success in school, the workplace, relationships, and the community. SEL includes instruction to address behavior, discipline, safety, and academics to help children become self-aware, manage their emotions, build social skills, form relationships, and make positive decisions.

Study Guide

This study guide is designed to extend your understanding and application of the information shared in *The Social-Emotional Learning Toolbox: Practical Strategies to Support All Students* written by Dr. Kathy Perez.

You can use this study guide before or after you have read the book, or as you finish each chapter. The guide can serve as a catalyst for conversation for your professional learning community (PLC) group at your school site, use it as a launchpad to learning for a teacher book club, or as a personal study guide for you to make the text-to-self connections.

Most of the questions in this study guide are ones you can think about on your own, or you might consider pairing with a colleague to share or form a study group with others who are interested in fostering social-emotional learning (SEL) in their classrooms.

HOW TO START AND FACILITATE AN EDUCATOR STUDY GROUP

- Ask each group member to order a copy of *The Social-Emotional Learning Toolbox: Practical Strategies to Support All Students*.

- Determine the specific date, time, and place for your group to meet.

- Assign a discussion leader or decide to rotate the role.

- Let the group decide how often you will meet (e.g., weekly, biweekly, monthly).

- Ask participants to read the chapter-to-be-discussed prior to meeting. Use the questions provided to facilitate group discussion or create your own.

CHAPTER 1: MAKING THE CASE FOR SOCIAL-EMOTIONAL LEARNING

- Is SEL part of your district or school's strategic plan? Why or why not?

- How do you define "social-emotional learning"?

- In what ways could you improve communication and understanding around SEL in your school district?

- Does the phrase, "Educating the mind without educating the heart is no education at all" (Aristotle) resonate with you? What might happen if this was a banner hanging over your school's front door?

- What is the biggest challenge you are facing in implementing SEL in your classroom or school? What can you do to overcome that challenge?

- What would it take to weave SEL into the daily routine of your classroom?

CHAPTER 2: SOCIAL-EMOTIONAL
LEARNING AND THE SELF: EMOTIONAL INTELLIGENCE

- How would you define "emotional intelligence"?

- Why are emotions an important part of a classroom's culture?

- What strategies have you used to teach emotional intelligence? Are you seeing a positive change in students' behavior as a result of those strategies?

- How can teachers expand students' feeling vocabularies?

- Which students are you reaching? Not reaching? Why?

- What can educators do to help our digital-driven students understand feelings?

- Which strategies described in the book will you begin to implement in your classroom? Why? How?

- What do you do in your classroom to boost your students' self-confidence and self-expression?

CHAPTER 3: SELF-REGULATION: HELPING
YOUR STUDENTS UNDERSTAND THEIR EMOTIONS

- In what ways do you help your students develop coping skills?

- Describe a positive classroom structure that supports self-regulation. What would it look like? Feel like? Sound like?

- What do you feel are the most important skills to teach your students to support self-regulation?

- How would you use a "calm-down corner" or "peace place"? What would it look like?

- What are the most important goals for fostering self-regulation with your students?

- How do you model self-regulation skills and your reactions to situations throughout the school day?

- What does "lesson mastery, not lesson mystery" mean to you?

- How would you rank your classroom regarding stress levels on a scale of 1 (lowest ranking) to 10 (highest ranking)? If you have a low score, how can you enhance that? If you had a high score, to what do you attribute that? Share your thoughts with others.

CHAPTER 4: DEVELOPING EXECUTIVE FUNCTION SKILLS IN STUDENTS

- When you were a child, what executive function skills were most difficult for you and why?

- What are some tools or techniques that you use to help students develop executive function skills? Which ones do you want to try next that were described in this chapter?

- What are your thoughts on the effectiveness of mindfulness in helping students with executive function skills? Share these thoughts with others.

- What would be an effective first-step in implementing strategies for students to learn executive function skills in your classroom?

- Research states that self-control is a better predictor of adult wealth, health, and happiness than grades—do you agree or disagree? Why?

- Are you noticing a change in your student's attention and retention? If so, to what do you attribute this change?

CHAPTER 5: MINDFULNESS IN THE CLASSROOM

- How will you start implementing mindfulness in your classroom? Which strategies resonated with you from the book?

- What are some ways that you could use stories as a launchpad to learning about mindfulness? Do you have favorite books that you use? Share with others.

- What breathing exercises do you find most useful?

- How can you use visualization to enhance mindfulness and be a catalyst for meditation?

- What are your favorite ways to calm down your students? What techniques from the chapter were most meaningful to you? Why?

- What will you do to "choose your own path to mindfulness"?

CHAPTER 6: SUPPORTING A GROWTH MINDSET

- Respond to this quote: "A growth mindset is not a declaration, it's a journey" (Carol Deck). What does this mean to you?

- How are you helping students develop a growth mindset?

- What does "the power of yet" mean to you?

- What are your favorite strategies shared in this chapter that you are ready to implement? Where will you start?

- How do you use music to "set the tone" in your classroom?

- Which of the myths about growth mindset did you find most surprising? Why?

- How do you handle learned helplessness? What do you do for the student who just gives up?

- How do you practice self-care as a teacher?

- How do you celebrate student successes?

- How we praise students helps define who they are and the type of people they believe themselves to be. Describe how you use praise in your classroom.

CHAPTER 7: SOCIAL-EMOTIONAL LEARNING AND RELATIONSHIPS: HOW TO CREATE A CARING, POSITIVE CLASSROOM ENVIRONMENT

- Describe the "conditions we need to work together" (classroom norms) that you have found most successful. How do you remind the students about these norms?

- What is most important in the process of developing procedures and routines?

- Describe how you set the tone for the day. If you have a morning meeting, what are the components of that meeting?

- What do you do to promote a culture of kindness in your classroom? Which strategies from this chapter do you want to try?

- Why are flexible groups important in a SEL classroom?

- What are some ways that group your students?

- How do you create an environment that supports small groups?

- How do you develop your student's collaborative skills?

- How do you create "caring mindsets"?

- What three words do you think students would use to describe your classroom? What words do you hope they would verbalize?

CHAPTER 8: FOSTERING EMPATHY IN THE CLASSROOM

- What practices are you implementing to support empathy development with your students?

- What strategies suggested in this chapter will you implement?

- What are your thoughts about this statement: "Every child has the potential to become a changemaker if we provide the right experiences and proven strategies"? How do educators reach students who have not had the right experiences and best strategies?

- What are some common pitfalls to educational programs that attempt to teach empathy?

- How can we teach empathy habits to students so that they internalize them?

- Which teaching practices do you use to enhance your students' perspective-taking abilities? Why are these important to developing empathy?

- What are some techniques you use to share the language of empathy?

CHAPTER 9: RELATIONSHIPS: STRENGTHENING BONDS

- What are the implications of the statement: "No significant learning can occur without a significant relationship" (Dr. James Comer)?

- Do you agree that "talk time matters"? How do you provide opportunities for children to share in partners and teams?

- What are the significant distinctions between "peacemakers" and "peacebreakers"?

- What strategies for conflict resolution have you found to be most successful? Why? Share with others.

- What strategies have you found to be most successful in promoting collaboration with your students? Which techniques suggested in this chapter will you try?

- What do you consider to be the most important keys to building relationships in the classroom?

- What self-care strategies do you use for your mental well-being?

References

Alexander, J. (2019). *Building trauma-sensitive schools: Your guide to creating safe, supporting learning environments for all students.* Paul H. Brookes Publishing, Co.

Andersen, J. F., Norton, R. W., & Nussbaum, J. F. (1981). Three investigations exploring relationships between perceived teacher communication behaviors and student learning. *Communication Education, 30*(4), 377–392.

Anderson, K. L., Weimer, M., & Fuhs, M. W. (2020). Teacher fidelity to Conscious Discipline and children's executive function skills. *Early Childhood Research Quarterly, 51,* 14–25.

Barkley, R. A. (2012). *Executive functions: What they are, how they work, and why they evolved.* New York: Guilford Press.

Barnett, M. A. (1987). Empathy and related responses in children. In N. Eisenberg & J. Strayer (Eds.), *Empathy and its development* (pp. 146–162). Cambridge University Press.

Bear, G. G., Whitcomb, S. A., Elias, M. J., & Blank, J. C. (2015). SEL and schoolwide positive behavioral interventions and supports. In J. A. Durlak, C. E. Domitrovich, R. P. Weissberg, & T. P. Gullotta (Eds.), *Handbook of social and emotional learning.* Guilford Press.

Berman, S., Chaffee, S., & Sarmiento, J. (2018). *The practice base for how we learn: Supporting students' social, emotional, and academic development.* The Aspen Institute, National Commission on Social, Emotional, & Academic Development.

Bierman, K. L., Greenberg, M. T., & Abenavoli, R. (2017). *Promoting social and emotional learning in preschool: Programs and practices that work.* Pennsylvania State University, Edna Bennet Pierce Prevention Research Center.

Bierman, K. L., & Motamedi, M. (2015). SEL programs for preschool children. In J. A. Durlak, C. E. Domitrovich, R. P. Weissberg, & T. P. Gullotta (Eds.), *Handbook of social and emotional learning.* Guilford Press.

Birnie, K., Speca, M., & Carlson, L. E. (2010). Exploring self-compassion and empathy in the context of mindfulness-based stress reduction (MBSR). *Stress and Health, 26*(5), 359–371.

Blackwell, L. S., Trzesniewski, K. H., & Dweck, C. S. (2007). Implicit theories of intelligence predict achievement across an adolescent transition: A longitudinal study and an intervention. *Child Development, 78*(1), 246–263.

Blad, E. (2016). Mindset is a key factor in student success. *Education Week, 35*(37), 1–3.

Blair, C., & Diamond, A. (2008). Biological processes in prevention and intervention: The promotion of self-regulation as a means of preventing school failure. *Development and Psychopathology, 20*(3), 899–911.

Bluestein, J. (2012). *The art of setting boundaries, (2012)* https://www.educationworld.com/a_curr/bluestein -setting-student-boundaries.shtml

Borba, M. (2016). *Unselfie: Why empathetic kids succeed in our all-about-me world.* Simon and Schuster.

Brandt, R. (1992). On building learning communities: A conversation with Hank Levin. *Educational Leadership, 50*(1), 19–23.

Brooks, R., & Goldstein, S. (2001). *Raising resilient children: Fostering strength, hope, and optimism in your child.* Contemporary Books.

Brophy, J. (1981). Teacher praise: A functional analysis. *Review of Educational Research, 51*(1), 5–32.

Bryk, A. S., & Driscoll, M. E. (1988). *The high school as community: Contextual influences and consequences for students and teachers.* Office of Educational Research and Improvement.

Canter, L., & Canter, M. (1997). *Assertive discipline for today's classrooms.* Solution Tree Press.

Carlana, M. (2019). Implicit stereotypes: Evidence from teachers' gender bias. *The Quarterly Journal of Economics. 134*(3), 1163–1224.

Carnegie Council on Adolescent Development. Task Force on Education of Young Adolescents. (1989). *Turning points: Preparing American youth for the 21st century.* Carnegie Corporation of New York.

CASEL. (2021). *The CASEL Guide to Schoolwide SEL Essentials.* https://schoolguide.casel.org/uploads /sites/2/2019/09/2021.6.15_School-Guide-Essentials.pdf

CASEL (n.d.) *Equity and SEL.* https://schoolguide.casel.org/what-is-sel/equity-and-sel/.

Casenhiser, D., Shanker, S., & Stieben, J. (2012). *Understanding the nature of self-regulation.* Milton & Ethel Harris Research Initiative, York University.

Catalano, R. F., Berglund, M. L., Ryan, J. A., Lonczak, H. S., & Hawkins, J. D. (2004). Positive youth development in the United States: Research findings on evaluations of positive youth development programs. *The Annals of the American Academy of Political and Social Science, 591*(1), pp. 98–124.

Cherng, H. S. (2017). If they think I can: Teacher bias and youth of color expectations and achievement. *Social Science Research*. 66, 170–186.

Cheyney, K., Wang, J., & Bettini, E. (2013). Make every word count: Using language as a bridge to self-regulation in early childhood settings. *Dimensions of Early Childhood, 41*(2), 11–17.

Chiesa, A., & Serretti, A. (2009). Mindfulness-based stress reduction for stress management in healthy people: A review and meta-analysis. *The Journal of Alternative and Complementary Medicine, 15*(5), 593–600.

Cleaver, S. (2013). What is social emotional learning? *education.com.* www.education.com/magazine /article/social-emotional-learning

Collaborative for Academic, Social, and Emotional Learning. (2015). *2015 CASEL Guide: Effective social and emotional learning programs - Middle and high school edition.*

Collaborative for Social and Emotional Learning. (2013). *2013 CASEL guide: Effective social and emotional learning programs—Preschool and elementary school edition.* http://www.casel.org/preschool-and -elementary-edition-casel-guide

Comer, J. (2004). *Leave no child behind: Preparing today's youth for tomorrow's world.* Yale University Press.

Condon, P., Desbordes, G., Miller, W. B., & DeSteno, D. (2013). Meditation increases compassionate responses to suffering. *Psychological Science, 24*(10), 2125–2127.

Conley, C. S. (2015). SEL in higher education. In J. A. Durlak, C. E. Domitrovich, R. P. Weissberg, & T. P. Gullotta (Eds.), *Handbook of social and emotional learning.* Guilford Press.

Coplan, S., & Masuda, D. (2015). Adding mindset to the order set: Changing the way we change. *Journal of Healthcare Information Management, 28*(1), 8–10.

Damasio, A. R. (1994). *Descartes' error: Emotion, rationality and the human brain.* Putnam.

Dawson, P., & Guare, R. (2009). *Smart but scattered: The revolutionary "executive skills" approach to helping kids reach their potential.* Guilford Press.

Dean, C. B., Hubbell, E. R., Pitler, H., & Stone, B. (2012). *Classroom instruction that works: Research-based strategies for increasing student achievement* (2nd ed.). Association for Supervision and Curriculum Development (ASCD).

DeBacker, T. K., Heddy, B. C., Kershen, J. L., Crowson, H. M., Looney, K., & Goldman, J. A. (2018). Effects of a one-shot growth mindset intervention on beliefs about intelligence and achievement goals. *Educational Psychology, 38*(6), 711–733.

de La Riva, S., & Ryan, T. G. (2015). Effect of self-regulating behaviour on young children's academic success. *International Journal of Early Childhood Special Education, 7*(1), 68–92.

Denham, S. A. (1998). *Emotional development in young children.* Guilford Press.

Desbordes, G., Negi, L. T., Pace, T. W., Wallace, B. A., Raison, C. L., & Schwartz, E. L. (2012). Effects of mindful-attention and compassion meditation training on amygdala response to emotional stimuli in an ordinary, non-meditative state. *Frontiers in Human Neuroscience, 6*, 292.

Dessemontet, R. S., & Bless, G. (2013). The impact of including children with intellectual disability in general education classrooms on the academic achievement of their low-, average-, and high-achieving peers. *Journal of Intellectual and Developmental Disability, 38*(1), 23–30.

Dewey, John. (1938) *Experience and education.* Touchstone Press.

Doolittle, J. (2006). *The sustainability of positive behavior supports in the schools.* ProQuest.

Duane, A., Casimir, A.E., Mims, L.C., Kaler-Jones, C., & Simmons, D. (2021). Beyond deep breathing: A new vision for equitable, culturally responsive, and trauma-informed mindfulness practice. *Middle School Journal, 52*(3), 4–14.

Duncan, G. J., Dowsett, C. J., Claessens, A., Magnuson, K., Huston, A. C., Klebanov, P., & Sexton, H. (2007). School readiness and later achievement. *Developmental Psychology, 43*(6), 1428–1432.

Durlak, J. A., & Weissberg, R. P. (2011). Promoting social and emotional development is an essential part of students' education. *Human Development, 54*(1), 1–3.

Durlak, J. A., Weissberg, R. P., Dymnicki, A. B., Taylor, R. D., & Schellinger, K. B. (2011). The impact of enhancing students' social and emotional learning: A meta-analysis of school-based universal interventions. *Child Development, 82*(1), 405–432.

Durlak, J.A., Weissberg, R.P., & Pachan, M. (2010). A meta-analysis of after-school programs that seek to promote personal and social skills in children and adolescents. *American Journal of Community Psychology, 45*, 294–309.

Dweck, C. S. (2008). *Mindset: The new psychology of success.* Random House Digital.

Dweck, C. (2015). Carol Dweck revisits the growth mindset. *Education Week, 35*(5), 20–24.

Dweck, C. (2016). What having a "growth mindset" actually means. *Harvard Business Review, 13*, 213–226.

Dweck, C. S., Chiu, C. Y., & Hong, Y. Y. (1995). Implicit theories and their role in judgments and reactions: A word from two perspectives. *Psychological Inquiry, 6*(4), 267–285.

Dweck, C. S., & Master, A. (2009). Self-theories and motivation. In K. R. Wenzel & A. Wigfield (Eds.), *Handbook of motivation at school* (pp. 123–140). Routledge.

Eisenberg, N., Eggum, N. D., & Di Giunta, L. (2010). Empathy-related responding: Associations with prosocial behavior, aggression, and intergroup relations. *Social Issues and Policy Review, 4*(1), 143–180.

Elias, M. J., Leverett, L., Duffell, J. C., Humphrey, N., Stepney, C. T., & Ferrito, J. J. (2016, March). *How to implement social and emotional learning at your school.* Edutopia.

Elias, M. J., Nayman, S. J., Duffell, J. C., & Kim, S. A. (2017). Madam Secretary, help us improve social-emotional learning. *Phi Delta Kappan, 98*(8), 64–69.

Elias, M. J., Zins, J. E., Weissberg, R. P., Frey, K. S., Greenberg, M. T., Haynes, N. M., Kessler, R., Schwab-Stone, M. E., & Shriver, T. P., et al. (1997). *Promoting social and emotional learning: Guidelines for educators.* Association for Supervision and Curriculum Development (ASCD).

Emmerling, R. J., Shanwal, V. K., & Mandal, M. K. (2008). *Emotional intelligence: Theoretical and cultural perspectives.* Nova.

Farrington, C. A., Roderick, M., Allensworth, E., Nagaoka, J., Keyes, T. S., Johnson, D. W., & Beechum, N. O. (2012). *Teaching adolescents to become learners: The role of noncognitive factors in shaping school performance: A critical literature review.* Consortium on Chicago School Research.

Flook, L., Goldberg, S. B., Pinger, L., & Davidson, R. J. (2015). Promoting prosocial behavior and self-regulatory skills in preschool children through a mindfulness-based kindness curriculum. *Developmental Psychology, 51*(1), 44–45.

Froh, J. J., Sefick, W. J., & Emmons, R. A. (2008). Counting blessings in early adolescents: An experimental study of gratitude and subjective well-being. *Journal of School Psychology, 46*(2), 213–233.

Furrer, C., & Skinner, E. (2003). Sense of relatedness as a factor in children's academic engagement and performance. *Journal of Educational Psychology, 95*(1), 148–152.

García, E., & Weiss, E. (2017). Education inequalities at the school starting gate: Gaps, trends, and strategies to address them. Economic Policy Institute. https://www.epi.org/publication/education-inequalities-at-the-school-starting-gate/#epi-toc-24

Gardner, H. (1993). *Multiple intelligences: The theory in practice.* Basic Books.

Gehlbach, H. (2017). How teachers can find the time for social-emotional learning. *Education Week, 37*(10), 24–25.

Genesee, F., Lindholm-Leary, K., Saunders, W., & Christian, D. (2005). English language learners in U.S. schools: An overview of research findings. *Journal of Education for Students Placed At Risk, 10*(4), 363–385.

Gibbs, J. (1995). *TRIBES: A new way of living and being together.* Center Source Systems, LLC.

Gifford-Smith, M. E., & Brownell, C. A. (2003). Childhood peer relationships: Social acceptance, friendships, and peer networks. *Journal of School Psychology, 41*(4), 235–284.

Glasser, W. (1988). *Choice theory in the classroom.* Harper Collins.

Goldin, P. R., & Gross, J. J. (2010). Effects of mindfulness-based stress reduction (MBSR) on emotion regulation in social anxiety disorder. *Emotion, 10*(1), 83.

Goldstein, S. (2002). Continuity of ADHD in adulthood: Hypothesis and theory meet reality. In S. Goldstein & A. T. Ellison (Eds.), *Clinicians' guide to adult ADHD: Assessment and intervention* (pp. 25–46). Academic Press. https://doi.org/10.1016/B978-012287049-1/50004-9

Goldstein, S., & Naglieri, A. (2014). *Handbook of executive functioning.* Springer-Verlag.

Goleman, D. (1995). *Emotional intelligence: Why it can matter more than IQ.* Bantam Books.

Goleman, D. (1998). The emotional intelligence of leaders. *Leader to Leader, 1998*(10), 20–26.

Goleman, D. (2017). *What makes a leader?* (Harvard Business Review Classics). Harvard Business Press.

Goleman, D., & Cherniss, C. (2001). *The emotionally intelligent workplace: How to select for, measure, and improve emotional intelligence in individuals, groups, and organizations.* Jossey-Bass.

Goleman, D., & Gurin, J. (Eds.). (1995). *Mind body medicine: How to use your mind for better health.* Consumer Reports Book.

Goodenow, C. (1993). Classroom belonging among early adolescent students: Relationships to motivation and achievement. *The Journal of Early Adolescence, 13*(1), 21–43.

Gottfried, M. A. (2009). Excused versus unexcused: How student absences in elementary school affect academic achievement. *Education Evaluation and Policy Analysis, 31*(4), 392–415.

Gottman, J., & DeClaire, J. (1997). *The heart of parenting: How to raise an emotionally intelligent child.* Simon & Schuster.

Gottman, J. M., & DeClaire, J. (1997). *The heart of parenting: How to raise an emotionally intelligent child.* Simon & Schuster.

Grant, H., & Dweck, C. S. (2003). Clarifying achievement goals and their impact. *Journal of Personality and Social Psychology, 85*(3), 541–544.

Green, A. L., Cohen, D. R., & Stormont, M. (2019). Addressing and preventing disproportionality in exclusionary discipline practices for students of color with disabilities. *Intervention in School and Clinic, 54*(4), 241–245.

Gullotta, T. P. (2015). After-School Programming and SEL. In J. A. Durlak, C. E. Domitrovich, R. P. Weissberg, & T. P. Gullotta (Eds.), *Handbook of social and emotional learning.* Guilford Press.

Hall, P. S., & Hall, N. D. (2003). Building relationships with challenging children. *Educational Leadership, 61*(1), 60–63.

Hallinger, P., & Murphy, J. F. (1986). The social context of effective schools. *American Journal of Education, 94*(3), 328–355.

Hamre, B. K., & Pianta, R. C. (2001). Early teacher–child relationships and the trajectory of children's school outcomes through eighth grade. *Child Development, 72*(2), 625–638.

Hawkins, J. D., Kosterman, R., Catalano, R. F., Hill, K. G., & Abbott, R. D. (2008). Effects of social development intervention in childhood 15 years later. *Archives of Pediatrics & Adolescent Medicine, 162*(12), 1133–1141.

Hawkins, J. D., Smith, B. H., & Catalano, R. F. (2004). Social development and social and emotional learning. In J. E. Zins, R. P. Weissberg, M. C. Wang, & H. J. Walberg (Eds.), *Building academic success on social and emotional learning: What does the research say?* (pp. 135–150). Teachers College Press.

Hawkins, S. M., & Heflin, L. J. (2011). Increasing secondary teachers' behavior-specific praise using a video self-modeling and visual performance feedback intervention. *Journal of Positive Behavior Interventions, 13*(2), 97–108.

Haycock, K. (2014). Achievement among English language learners: Where are we? What can we do? https://1k9gl1yevnfp2lpq1dhrqe17-wpengine.netdna-ssl.com/wp-content/uploads/2013/10/ga.atlanta.EL_.pdf.

Hehir, T., Grindal, T., & Eidelman, H. (2012). Review of special education in the Commonwealth of Massachusetts. Boston, MA: Massachusetts Department of Elementary and Secondary Education. http://www.doe.mass.edu/sped/hehir/2012-04sped.pdf

Heyes, C. (2018). Empathy is not in our genes. *Neuroscience & Behavioral Reviews, 95,* 499–507.

Higgins, A., Power, C., & Kohlberg, L. (1984). Student judgments of responsibility and the moral atmosphere of high schools: A comparative study. In W. Kurtines & J. L. Gewirtz (Eds.), *Morality, moral behavior and moral development: Basic issues in theory and research* (pp. 74–106). Wiley-Interscience.

Hoge, E. A., Bui, E., Marques, L., Metcalf, C. A., Morris, L. K., Robinaugh, D. J., & Simon, N. M. (2013). Randomized controlled trial of mindfulness meditation for generalized anxiety disorder: Effects on anxiety and stress reactivity. *The Journal of Clinical Psychiatry, 74*(8), 786–792.

Hong, J. (1999). Structuring for organizational learning. *The learning organization.*

Hong, Y., Chiu, C., & Dweck, C. S. (1995). Implicit theories of intelligence: Reconsidering the role of confidence in achievement motivation. In M. H. Kernis (Ed.), *Efficacy, agency, and self-esteem* (pp. 197–216): Plenum Press.

Howell, J., & Reinhard, K. (2015). *Rituals and traditions: Fostering a sense of community in preschool.* NAEYC.

Hughes, J. N. (2011). Longitudinal effects of teacher and student perceptions of teacher-student relationship qualities on academic adjustment. *The Elementary School Journal, 112*(1), 38–60.

Humphrey, N., Lendrum, A., Wigelsworth, M., & Greenberg, M. T. (Eds.). (2020). *Social and emotional learning.* Routledge.

Immordino-Yang, M. H., & Damasio, A. (2007). We feel, therefore we learn: The relevance of affective and social neuroscience to education. *Mind, Brain, and Education, 1*(1), 3–10.

Jagers R. J. (2016). Framing social and emotional learning among African American youth: Toward an integrity-based approach. *Human Development, 59*: 1–3.

Jha, A. P., Krompinger, J., & Baime, M. J. (2007). Mindfulness training modifies subsystems of attention. *Cognitive, Affective, & Behavioral Neuroscience, 7*(2), 109–119.

Johnson, D. W., Johnson, R. T., & Stanne, M. B. (1989). Impact of goal and resource interdependence on problem-solving success. *The Journal of Social Psychology, 129*(5), 621–629.

Jones, D.E., Greenberg, M., & Crowley, M. (2015). Early social-emotional functioning and public health: The relationship between kindergarten social competence and future wellness. *American Journal of Public Health, 105*(11), 2283–2290.

Jones, S., Bailey, R., Brush, K., & Kahn, J. (2018). *Preparing for effective SEL implementation.* Harvard Graduate School of Education Easel Lab. https://www.wallacefoundation.org/knowledgecenter/Documents/Preparing-for-Effective-SEL-Implementation.pdf

Jones, S., Brush, K., Bailey, R., Brion-Meisels, G., McIntyre, J., Kahn, J., & Stickle, L. (2017). *Navigating SEL from the inside out: Looking inside & across 25 leading SEL programs: A practical resource for schools and OST providers (elementary school focus).* Harvard Graduate School of Education Easel Lab.

Jones, S. M., & Bouffard, S. M. (2012). Social and emotional learning in schools: From programs to strategies. *Social Policy Report, 26*(4), 1–33.

Jones, S. M., & Kahn, J. (2017). *The evidence base for how we learn: Supporting students' social, emotional, and academic development.* Consensus Statements of Evidence from the Council of Distinguished Scientists. Aspen Institute.

Jones, S. M., Weissbourd, R., Bouffard, S., Kahn, J., & Ross, T. (2014). *How to build empathy and strengthen your school community.* Harvard Graduate School of Education.

Kabat-Zinn, J. (2009). *Wherever you go, there you are: Mindfulness meditation in everyday life.* Hachette.

Kagan, S. (1994). *Cooperative learning* (Vol. 2). Cooperative Learning Press.

Katz, M. (2011, February). Classroom strategies for improving working memory. *Attention Magazine*, 6–9.

Katz, M. (2014). Executive function: What does it mean? Why is it important? How can we help? *The Special EDge*.

Kerman, S., & Martin, M. (1980). *TESA: Teacher expectations and student achievement*. Teacher handbook. Phi Delta Kappa.

Kern, L., & Clemens, N. H. (2007). Antecedent strategies to promote appropriate classroom behavior. *Psychology in the Schools, 44*(1), 65–75.

Kestenbaum R., Farber, E. A., & Sroufe, L. A. (1989). Individual differences in empathy among preschoolers: Relation to attachment history. *New Directions for Child and Adolescent Development, 8*, 51–64.

Kiger, L. L. (2017). Growth mindset in the classroom. Empowering Research for Educators. *EdSurge News, 1*(1), 4.

King, R. B., McInerney, D. M., & Watkins, D. A. (2012). How you think about your intelligence determines how you feel in school: The role of theories of intelligence on academic emotions. *Learning and Individual Differences, 22*(6), 814–819.

Kohn, A. (1996). *Beyond discipline: From compliance to community*. Association for Supervision and Curriculum Development (ASCD).

Kovalik, S., & Olsen, K. D. (1998). How emotions run us, our students, and our classrooms. *Nassp Bulletin, 82*(598), 29–37.

Kovalik, S., & Olsen, K. (1994). *ITI: The model. Integrated thematic instruction*. Books for Educators.

Ladd, G. W., & Burgess, K. B. (2001). Do relational risks and protective factors moderate the linkages between childhood aggression and early psychological and school adjustment? *Child Development, 72*(5), 1579–1601.

Laevers, F. (2000). Forward to basics! Deep-level-learning and the experiential approach. *Early Years, 20*(2), 20–29.

Laevers, F. (2015). *Making care and education more effective through wellbeing and involvement. An introduction to experiential education*. Research Centre for Experiential Education, University of Leuven.

Lightfoot, S. L. (1984). *The good high school*. Basic Books.

Linder, R. (2021). Enhancing social awareness development through multicultural literature. *Middle School Journal, 52*(3), 35–43.

Litman, J. A. (2007). Curiosity as a feeling of interest and feeling of deprivation: The I/D model of curiosity. *Issues in the psychology of motivation*, 149–156.

Littman, E. (2017). Never enough? Why your brain craves stimulation. In *Additide: Inside the ADHD mind* (pp. 6–9). CHADD.

Lund, M. K., Hillis, A., Green, J., & Mofield, E. (2021). Mindsets matter for equitable discipline: Aligning beliefs to practice among middle grade educators. *Middle School Journal. 52*(3), 15–24.

Lutz, A., Slagter, H. A., Dunne, J. D., & Davidson, R. J. (2008). Attention regulation and monitoring in meditation. *Trends in Cognitive Sciences, 12*(4), 163–169.

Marzano, R. J., Pickering, D., & Pollock, J. E. (2001). *Classroom instruction that works: Research-based strategies for increasing student achievement*. Association for Supervision and Curriculum Development (ASCD).

Marzano, R. J., Pickering, D. J., & Heflebower, T. (2010). *The highly engaged classroom: The classroom strategies series*. Marzano Research Laboratory.

Maslow, A. (1943). A theory of human motivation. *Psychological Review, 50*(4), 370–396.

McMillan, D. W., & Chavis, D. M. (1986). Sense of community: A definition and theory. *Journal of Community Psychology, 14*(1), 6–23.

Merolla D. M., & Jackson, O. (2019). Structural racism as the fundamental cause of the academic achievement gap. *Sociology Compass.*13:e12696.

Merrell, K. W., & Gueldner, B. A. (2010). *Social and emotional learning in the classroom: Promoting mental health and academic success*. Guilford Press.

Meyers, D., Gil, L., Cross, R., Keister, S., Domitrovich, C. E., & Weissberg, R. P. (in press). *CASEL guide for schoolwide social and emotional learning*. Chicago: Collaborative for Academic, Social, and Emotional Learning.

Mikulincer, M., Shaver, P. R., Gillath, O., & Nitzberg, R. A. (2005). Attachment, caregiving, and altruism: Boosting attachment security increases compassion and helping. *Journal of Personality and Social Psychology, 89*(5), 817–840.

Muhammad, A. (2009). *Transforming school culture: How to overcome staff division*. Solution Tree Press.

Mustard, J. F., & Rowcliffe, P. I. P. P. A. (2009). The long reach of early childhood. *Our Schools, Our Selves*, 149.

National Center for Educational Statistics (NCES). (2018a). 2018 Digest of Educational Statistics Table 104.20. https://nces.ed.gov/programs/digest/d17/tables/dt17_104.20.asp?current=yes

National Center for Educational Statistics (NCES). (2018b). 2018 Digest of Educational Statistics Table 221.20. https://nces.ed.gov/programs/digest/d16/tables/dt16_221.20.asp?current=yes

National Center for Educational Statistics (NCES). (2018c). 2018 Digest of Educational Statistics Table 222.90. https://nces.ed.gov/programs/digest/d17/tables/dt17_222.90.asp?current=yes

National Commission on Social, Emotional, and Academic Development. (2019). *From a nation at risk to a nation of hope: Recommendations from the National Commission on Social, Emotional, & Academic Development*. The Aspen Institute.

Nickerson, A. B., Fredrick, S. S., Allen, K. P., & Jenkins, L. N. (2019). Social emotional learning (SEL) practices in schools: Effects on perceptions of bullying victimization. *Journal of School Psychology, 73*, 74–88.

Nikolajeva, M. (2015). *Children's literature comes of age: Toward a new aesthetic*. Routledge.

Oberle, E., Domitrovich, C. E., Meyers, D. C., & Weissberg, R. P. (2016). Establishing systemic social and emotional learning approaches in schools: A framework for schoolwide implementation. *Cambridge Journal of Education, 46*(3), 277–297.

Ortner, C. N., Kilner, S. J., & Zelazo, P. D. (2007). Mindfulness meditation and reduced emotional interference on a cognitive task. *Motivation and Emotion, 31*(4), 271–283.

Parrish, N. (August 22, 2018). How to teach self-regulation. George Lucas Foundation. *Edutopia.*,

Pattison, P., Hale, J. R., & Gowens, P. (2011). Mind and soul: Connecting with students. *Journal of Legal Studies Education, 28*(1), 39–66.

Paunesku, D., Walton, G. M., Romero, C., Smith, E. N., Yeager, D. S., & Dweck, C. S. (2015). Mind-set interventions are a scalable treatment for academic underachievement. *Psychological Science, 26*(6), 784–793.

Pianta, R. C., & Stuhlman, M. W. (2004). Teacher-child relationships and children's success in the first years of school. *School Psychology Review, 33*(3), 444–458.

Prince, K., & Prince, K. (2017, October 17). Why the increased focus on social-emotional learning? Education Domain. www.inacol.org/news/why-the-increased-focus-on-social-emotional-learning

Prince, K., Saveri, A., & Swanson, J. (2017). The future of learning: Redefining readiness from the inside out. KnowledgeWorks Foundation. www.knowledgeworks.org/redefining-readiness

Purkey, W. N., & Novak, J. M. (1996). *Inviting school success: A self-concept approach to teaching, learning, and democratic practice*. Wadsworth.

Putnam, R. D., & Feldstein, L. (2009). *Better together: Restoring the American community*. Simon & Schuster.

Reis da Luz, F. S. (2015). *The relationship between teachers and students in the classroom: Communicative language teaching approach and cooperative learning strategy to improve learning* [Master's thesis]. https://vc.bridgew.edu/theses/22/

Rempel, K. (2012). Mindfulness for children and youth: A review of the literature with an argument for school-based implementation. *Canadian Journal of Counselling and Psychotherapy, 46*(3).

Roemer, L., Williston, S. K., & Rollins, L. G. (2015). Mindfulness and emotion regulation. *Current Opinion in Psychology, 3*, 52–57.

Rufo, J.M., & Causton, J. (2022). *Reimagining special education: Using inclusion as a framework to build equity and support all students*. Paul H. Brookes Publishing, Co.

Ryff, C. D., Love, G. D., Essex, M. J., & Singer, B. (1998). Resilience in adulthood and later life. In *Handbook of aging and mental health* (pp. 69–96). Springer.

Saarni, C. (1999). *The development of emotional competence*. Guilford Press.

Salovey, P., & Mayer, J. D. (1990). Emotional intelligence. *Imagination, Cognition and Personality, 9*(3), 185–211.

Santos, R. G., Chartier, M. J., Whalen, J. C., Chateau, D., & Boyd, L. (2011). Effectiveness of school-based violence prevention for children and youth: A research report. *Healthcare Quarterly (Toronto, Ont.), 14*, 80–91.

Scott, J., Moses, M.S., Finnigan, K.S., Trujillo, T., & Jackson, D.D. (2017). *Law and order in school and society: How discipline and policing policies harm students of color, and what we can do about it*. National Education Policy Center. http://nepc.colorado.edu/publication/law-and-order

Schaps, E., & Solomon, D. (1990). Schools and classrooms as caring communities. *Educational Leadership, 48*(3), 38–42.

Schonert-Reichl, K. A., & Lawlor, M. S. (2010). The effects of a mindfulness-based education program on pre-and early adolescents' well-being and social and emotional competence. *Mindfulness, 1*(3), 137–151.

Schunk, D. H., & Zimmerman, B. J. (Eds.). (2012). *Motivation and self-regulated learning: Theory, research, and applications*. Routledge.

Sedlmeier, P., Eberth, J., Schwarz, M., Zimmermann, D., Haarig, F., Jaeger, S., & Kunze, S. (2012). The psychological effects of meditation: A meta-analysis. *Psychological Bulletin, 138*(6), 1139.

Shanker, S. (2009). *Developmental pathways: Scaffolding for early learners*. Paper presented at the meeting of the Milton & Ethel Research Initiative, York University, Toronto, Canada.

Shanker, S. (2013). *Calm, alert, and learning*. Pearson Canada.

Sheldon, S. B., & Epstein, J. L. (2004). Getting students to school: Using family and community involvement to reduce chronic absenteeism. *School Community Journal, 14*(2), 39–56.

Shonkoff, J., & Phillips, D. (2000). *From neurons to neighbourhoods: The science of early childhood development*. National Academies Press.

Simmons, D.N. (2019). You can't be emotionally intelligent without being culturally responsive: Why family and consumer sciences must employ both to meet the needs of our nation. *Journal of Family & Consumer Sciences, 111*(2), 7–16.

Simmons, D. (2021). Why SEL alone isn't enough. *Educational Leadership, 78*(6), 30–34.

Sizer, T. (1984). *Horace's compromise: The dilemma of the American high school*. Houghton Mifflin.

Sklad, M., Diekstra, R., Ritter, M.D., Ben, J., & Gravesteijn, C. (2012). Effectiveness of school-based universal social, emotional, and behavioral programs: Do they enhance students' development in the area of skill, behavior, and adjustment? *Psychology in the Schools, 49*(9), 892–909.

Snel, E. (2013). *Sitting still like a frog: Mindfulness exercises for kids (and their parents)*. Shambhala.

Solomon, D., Watson, M., Battistich, V., Schaps, E., & Delucchi, K. (1992). Creating a caring community: Educational practices that promote children's prosocial development. In F. K. Oser, A. Dick, & J.-L. Patry (Eds.), *Effective and responsible teaching: The new synthesis* (pp. 383–396). Jossey-Bass.

Song, J. H., Colasante, T., & Malti, T. (2018). Helping yourself helps others: Linking children's emotion regulation to prosocial behavior through sympathy and trust. *Emotion, 18*(4), 518–524.

Song, Y., & Shi, M. (2017). Associations between empathy and big five personality traits among Chinese undergraduate medical students. *PloS one, 12*(2), e0171665.

Sroufe, L. A., Egeland, B., Carlson, E., & Collins, W. A. (2005). Placing early attachment experiences in developmental context: The Minnesota longitudinal study. In K. E. Grossmann, K. Grossmann, & E. Waters (Eds.), *Attachment from infancy to adulthood: The major longitudinal studies* (pp. 48–70). Guilford Press.

Sun, K. L. (2015). *There's no limit: Mathematics teaching for a growth mindset* [Unpublished doctoral dissertation, Stanford University].

Thapa, A., Cohen, J., Gulley, S., & Higgins-D'Alessandro, A. (2013). A review of school climate research. *Review of Educational Research, 83*(3), 357–385.

Thompson, J. G. (1998). *Discipline survival kit for the secondary teacher*. University of Minnesota, Center for Applied Research in Education.

Tsujimoto, S. (2008). The prefrontal cortex: Functional neural development during early childhood. *The Neuroscientist, 14*(4), 345–358.

Uhls, Y. T., Michikyan, M., Morris, J., Garcia, D., Small, G. W., Zgourou, E., & Greenfield, P. M. (2014). Five days at outdoor education camp without screens improves preteen skills with nonverbal emotion cues. *Computers in Human Behavior, 39*, 387–392.

U.S. Department of Education. *Chronic absenteeism in the nation's schools*. https://www2.ed.gov/datastory/chronicabsenteeism.html

Varga, M. (2017). *The effect of teacher-student relationships on the academic engagement of students*. http://hdl.handle.net/11603/3893

Vega, V. (2012, 2017). *Social and emotional learning research review*. https://www.edutopia.org/sel-research-learning-outcomes

Veldman, M. A., Doolaard, S., Bosker, R. J., & Snijders, T. A. B. (2020). Young children working together. Cooperative learning effects on group work of children in Grade 1 of primary education. *Learning and Instruction, 67*, 10130

Walker, I., & Crogan, M. (1998). Academic performance, prejudice, and the jigsaw classroom: New pieces to the puzzle. *Journal of Community & Applied Social Psychology, 8*(6), 381–393.

Walls, J. (2021). Tensions in care and control in the middle school classroom: Lessons for equitable social-emotional learning. *Middle School Journal, 52*(3), 25–34.

Waters, E., & Sroufe, L. A. (1983). Social competence as a developmental construct. *Developmental Review, 3*(1), 79–97.

Waters, E., Wippman, J., & Sroufe, L. A. (1979). Attachment, positive affect and competence in the peer group: Two studies in construct validation. *Child Development, 50*, 821–829.

Wehlage, G., Smith, G., & Lipman, P. (1992). Restructuring urban schools: The new futures experience. *American Educational Research Journal, 29*(1), 51–93.

Weissberg, R. (2016). Why social and emotional learning is essential for students. *Edutopia*.

Wentzel, K. R. (1999). Social-motivational processes and interpersonal relationships: Implications for understanding motivation at school. *Journal of Educational Psychology, 91*(1), 76–79.

Wiggins, G. P., & McTighe, J. (2005). *Understanding by design*. Association for Supervision and Curriculum Development (ASCD).

Willard, C. (2006). *Child's mind: Mindfulness practices to help our children be more focused, calm, and relaxed*. Parallax Press.

Willey, K. (2017). *Breathe like a bear: 30 mindful moments for kids to feel calm anytime anywhere*. Rodale Press.

Williams, J. (2017). Social emotional learning: What it is and why it matters. *Professional Educator, 17*(2), 11–15.

Williford, A. P., & Wolcott, C. S. (2015). SEL and student-teacher relationships. In J. A. Durlak, C. E. Domitrovich, R. P. Weissberg, & T. P. Gullotta (Eds.), *Handbook of social and emotional*. Guilford Press.

Willis, J. (2010). The current impact of neuroscience on teaching and learning. *Mind, brain and education: Neuroscience implications for the classroom*, 45–68.

Willis, J., & Willis, M. (2020). *Based strategies to ignite student learning: Insights from neuroscience and the classroom*. Association for Supervision and Curriculum Development (ASCD).

Wilson, D. B., Gottfredson, D. C., & Najaka, S. S. (2001). School-based prevention of problem behaviors: A meta-analysis. *Journal of Quantitative Criminology, 17*(3), 247–272.

Wisneski, D. B., & Goldstein, L. S. (2004). Questioning community in early childhood education. *Early Child Development and Care, 174*(6), 515–526.

Yeager, D. S., Romero, C., Paunesku, D., Hulleman, C. S., Schneider, B., Hinojosa, C., Trott, J. et.al. (2016). Using design thinking to improve psychological interventions: The case of the growth mindset during the transition to high school. *Journal of Educational Psychology, 108*(3), 374–378.

Yoder, N. (2013). *Teaching the whole child: Instructional practices that support social and emotional learning in three teacher evaluation frameworks.* Washington, DC: American Institutes for Research Center on Great Teachers and Leaders

Zadra, J. R., & Clore, G. L. (2011). Emotion and perception: The role of affective information. *Wiley Interdisciplinary Reviews: Cognitive Science, 2*(6), 676–685.

Zimmerman, B. J., & Schunk, D. H. (2008). An essential dimension of self-regulated learning. *Motivation and self-regulated learning: Theory, research, and applications,* 1.

Zins, J. E., Weissberg, R. P., Wang, M. C., & Walberg, H. J. (Eds.). (2004). *Building academic success on social and emotional learning: What does the research say?* Teachers College Press.

Index

*Page numbers followed by *f* indicate figures.

Academic learning and social-emotional learning, 7
Acceptance, children's picture books that teach, 197
ACEs, *see* Adverse childhood experiences
Activities for sharing feelings, 16–27
    classroom curiosity questions, 29*f*
    face the feelings, 17, 21, 187–188*f*
    feeling cubes, 24, 25*f*
    feeling with your feet, 24
    feelings balloons, 23–24, 23*f*
    good things, 30
    "If You're Happy and Know It" . . . remixed!, 24, 26
    mirror, mirror, on the wall, 27, 28*f*
    plastic egg faces, 24
    puppets and feelings, 24
    questions, 18*f*, 19*f*, 20*f*
    role-play, 21–22
    Simon Says, 22–23
    sing it with feeling!, 24
    stepping up to learning, 30, 31*f*
    teaching feeling words, 26
    Which emotion am I?, 27
Adverse childhood experiences (ACEs), 37
"Ah-Ha's," 153
Animal sounds partners, 126
Anxiety
    exercise and movement and, 48
    mindfulness and, 72
    recommended books for children with, 196
Apologies, 153
Art, emotional expression through, 167
Ask a "Question of the Day" to Get Started, 179*f*
Attention and concentration, mindfulness
    and, 72

Backpack luggage tag, 65, 67*f*
Balloon bonanza, 145
Balloon breathing, 77, 78*f*
Be the sky, 82, 84
Beautiful Oops, 103
Birthday line-up, 127
Board games, 68
Body-breathing, 48
Boss of My Mind coloring sheet, 191*f*
Brain Breaks/State Changes, 178*f*
Brain development
    growth mindset and, 96
    mindfulness and, 72–73
Brain massage, 80–81
Brain plasticity, 89
Brainpower coloring sheet, 190*f*
Breathe Like a Bear, 77

Breathing buddies, 61, 77, 79
Breathing for mindfulness, 74, 76–77
Breathing rings, 79
Bucket-filler activities, 122–123, 167
Buddy bench, 167
Buddy Classrooms, 161, 180*f*

Call-and-response affirmations, 165
Candy bar wrapper partners, 126
Card games, 68
Caring, children's books focused on, 193
Caring coupon books, 124
Caring/kindness circle, 123
CASEL (Collaborative for Academic, Social, and
    Emotional Learning), 2, 3
    on social-emotional learning (SEL) and equity, 8
"Caught You" board, 141
Celebrating student successes, 117
"Celebrating Success" files, 106
Change-makers, developing, 135–136
Checking in with feelings anchor chart, 40, 41*f*
Children's books
    for children with anxiety, 196
    focused on caring, 193–194
    focused on feelings and kindness, 194
    to teach older children empathy, 195
    for teaching growth mindset, 195–196
Child's Mind, 85
Class meetings, 9, 17
Classroom cheers, 153
Classroom curiosity questions, 29*f*
Classroom environment, 109
    conditions needed to work together in, 115
    creating a learning environment for small
        groups in, 126–128
    cultivating gratitude in, 125–126
    cultivating kindness in, 122–125
    empathy and building a positive, 133
    getting to know each other and, 119–120, 121*f*
    giving students a voice in, 118–119
    importance of procedures and routines in, 112, 114*f*
    integrating cooperative learning in, 115–116
    introduction to, 110–112
    relationship skills and, 167–169
    research on, 110–112
    supporting the whole child in, 116–118
    working together rules for, 113*f*
Classroom roles and responsibilities, 169
Classroom strategies
    classroom environment, 112–128
    emotional intelligence, 16–30

Classroom strategies—*continued*
    empathy, 138–145
    executive functioning (EF), 55–68
    growth mindset, 95–108
    mindfulness, 73–85
    self-regulation, 37–48
    social-emotional learning (SEL), 9–10
    teacher-student relationships, 151–169
    trauma-sensitive, 201–202
Classroom structures and social-emotional
        learning (SEL), 7
Clench and calm, 82
Closing community circles, 153
Cognitive flexibility, 65
Cognitive regulation, 4
Comic strip teams, 127
Committee for Children, 2
Community, classroom, 119–120, 121*f*
    empathy and, 134
    strategies for building, 156–163
Community-building questions, 27, 30
Compassion, 72
Compliments, 118–119
Conflict management, 155–156, 157*f*
Construction paper exercise for empathy, 143
"Cool-down corner," 42, 44*f,* 167
Cooperative learning, 115–116
Coping strategies, 10, 40

Daily check-in, 40, 152
Daily schedules, 69
Dance party!, 81
"Doodle and Do" mindset messages, 106
Doodling or drawing, 82

Eating practice, mindful, 84–85
EF, *see* Executive functioning
Emotional intelligence
    classroom strategies for, 16–30
    defined, 14
    five components or elements of, 16
    four dimensions of, 15
    importance of sharing feelings for, 16
    introduction to, 13–16
    journal writing and, 16
    research on, 14–16, 15*f*
Emotional literacy, 134
Emotional planner, 39
Emotional processes, 4
Emotional regulation, 64–65
    mindfulness and, 72
Emotional resiliency, 2
Emotional self-regulation, *see* Self-regulation
Emotional vocabulary, 26, 40, 138–139,
        165, 166*f*
Empathy, 16
    activities for teaching, 140–141
    awards for, 141, 142*f*
    benefits of, 133–137, 138*f*
    books to teach older children, 195

children's picture books that teach, 197
classroom strategies for, 138–145
defined, 131, 132
discussion questions on, 138
five steps to cultivate, 138
happiness boards and, 141
ingredients for effective education in, 136, 145–147
introduction to, 132–133
mindfulness and, 72
modeling helpfulness and, 141
other creative strategies to promote, 143–145
research on, 132–133
situation cards for, 186*f*
teaching the language of, 136, 137*f*
using reading to cultivate, 143, 144*f*
Empathy maps, 143
Empathy Situation Cards, 186*f*
Equity and social-emotional learning (SEL), 8–9
Every Student Succeeds Act (ESSA), 1
Executive functioning (EF)
    classroom strategies for, 55–68
    controlling impulses and, 61
    creating a positive environment for, 68–70
    defined, 51
    emotional regulation and, 64–65
    games and activities to use to teach, 65
    importance of, 54
    introduction to, 51–53
    memory and, 63–64
    mindfulness and, 72
    organization and planning skills and, 56–59
    organization worksheet, 59, 60*f*
    research on, 54–55
    sustained attention and, 59–61
    teaching behavioral expectations and, 61
    time management and, 61, 63
    to-do checklist for students, 56, 58*f*
    tracking checklist for, 57*f*
Exercise and movement
    anxiety and, 48
    mindfulness and, 77
Exit tickets, growth mindset, 105
Expectations
    growth mindset, 107
    making clear, 37
    managing, 47
    teaching behavioral, 61

Face the feelings, 17, 21, 187–188*f*
Fast response games, 68
Feedback, 10
    growth mindset and, 107–108
Feeling barometer, 40
Feeling cubes, 24
"Feelin' Good" journal, 17
Feeling with your feet, 24, 25*f*
Feelings, children's books focused on, 194
Feelings balloons, 23–24, 23*f*
Feelings pantomime, 140
Feelings word wall, 42, 43*f*
Fidget box manipulatives, 59

Find out about me game, 161–163
Five-finger gratitude, 81–82, 83f
Fixed mindset, 87–88
    research on, 89–90
Fixed-ability grouping, 107, 126
Focus on Your Feelings, 176f
Follow the leader guided meditation, 80
Food gratitude, 161
Formative assessment, 10
    growth mindset and, 107–108
Free-writes, 82
"Fresh-Start Reframing," 106
Friendly Fridays, 117
Friendly hands, 161
From a Nation at Risk to a Nation at Hope, 5
"Fun Facts" cards, 120

Games
    find out about me, 161–163
    gratitude, 126
    for teaching executive functioning (EF), 65–68
Girl Who Never Made Mistakes, The, 103
Golden Rule, 141
Good things activity, 30
Goodness awards, 96
Gratitude, cultivating, 125–126, 153
Gratitude journals, 46
Group salutes, 120, 155
Group work
    creating a learning environment for, 126–128
    growth mindset and, 96, 105
    relationship skills for, 154–156
    see also Cooperative learning
GROUPS poster, 174f
Growth assessments, 102
Growth mindset
    being a growth mindset teacher and, 100–107
    celebrating and tracking, 106
    classroom strategies for, 95–108
    versus fixed mindset, 87–90
    fresh start reframing of, 106
    helping students develop, 95–98
    heroes of, 106
    music and, 103, 105
    phrases to encourage, 91, 92f
    quotes for kids on, 107
    read-alouds for teaching, 195–196
    rephrasing for, 93f, 184f
    research on, 89–90
    scaffolding instruction for, 98–100
    simple drawings for expressing, 106
    student choice and voice and, 106–107
    teaching practices checklist for, 94f
    teaching practices to promote, 107–108
    techniques for teaching students about, 100
    unpacking myths about, 92–95
    worksheet, 103, 104f
Guess My Rule, 68
Guessing games, 65
Guided imagery, 81
Guided meditations for mindfulness, 79–80

Happiness boards, 141
Have You Filled a Bucket Today?, 167
Helpfulness, modeling of, 141
Helping hands, 117–118
Heroes, mindset, 106
Hierarchy of needs, 110

"I Am" mirror wall, 103
"I Am" poster, 169, 170f
"I Believe You Can" statements, 105–106
"I Can Change It" coloring sheet, 189f
I Can't Do It Yet coloring sheet, 192f
Identification of stressors by students, 45
If you knew me, 156
"If You're Happy and Know It" . . . remixed!, 24, 26
Impulse control, 2, 61
Inner value system, 135
Interpersonal skills, 4
Interview projects, 161

Journal writing, 16, 17
    empathy and, 141
    and free-writes for mind-body connections, 82
    gratitude journals, 46
    reflective writing, 153

Kindness, 140, 156, 161
    children's books focused on, 194
    cultivating, 122–125
    practicing, 135

Labeling feelings, 140
Learned helplessness, 96
"Learning Line-Up," 165
Letter to future self, 117
Lightbulb worksheet, 98, 99f
Listening circle, 145
Long-term memory, 63–64

Management of emotions, 15, 15f
Managing mistakes, 98
Mantra, mindfulness, 79
"Me Bag," 163
"Me Posters," 117
Meditation
    guided, 79–80
    walking, 84
Memory, 63–64
Mental health and well-being, mindfulness and, 72
Mind jiggle jars, 84
Mind-body connection, 47–48
    journaling and free-writes for, 82
Mindful breathing with a pinwheel, 45
Mindful eating practice, 84–85
Mindfulness
    breathing and, 74, 76–77
    breathing buddies and, 61, 77, 79

Mindfulness—*continued*
  checking your personal weather report and, 74–76
  choosing your own path to, 85–86
  classroom strategies for, 73–85
  defined, 71
  developing brain and, 72–73
  getting started with, 73–74
  guided meditations for, 79–80
  introduction to, 71–73
  mantra for, 79
  other activities for, 80–85
  research on, 72
  resources for continued learning on, 199–200
  using stories as a springboard for, 74
Mindfulness mantra, 79
Minefield, 156
Mirror, Mirror, on the Wall, 27, 28*f*
Misconceptions about social-emotional learning, 7–9
Modeling of helpfulness, 141
Moral identity, 135
Moral imagination, 135
Morning Centers, 39
Morning greetings, 116, 152
Morning meetings, 151–152
Morning mood message, 39
Most Magnificent Thing, The, 103
Motivation, 16
Movement and exercise, 48
Music and growth mindset, 103, 105

Name story, 156
Nature, getting outside in, 48
Navigating SEL from the Inside Out, 4

1-2-3-4 breathing, 76
Open your heart, 81
Opposite partners, 127
Organization and planning skills, 56–59
Outcomes, social-emotional learning (SEL), 6–7
Own Your Learning, 101*f*

Parent/family role in social-emotional learning (SEL), 7
Peace place, 42, 167
Peacemakers *versus* peacebreakers, 156, 158–159*f*
Peer mediation, 155–156
People Bingo, 120, 121*f*
Perceiving emotion, 15, 15*f*
Personal weather report, 74–76
Perspective taking, 135
Pick a pair, 127
Picture books
  teaching about feelings using, 46
  that teach acceptance and empathy, 197
Plastic egg faces, 24
Playing card teams, 127
Pom-pom bucket fillers, 123
Positive interdependence, 116
"Positive Pitches" poster, 167, 168*f*
Positive self-talk, 118
Power cards, 169

Praise, 95, 184*f*
Preparing to Write Your Thank You Notes, 182*f*
Pretzel breathing, 79
Prevention pointers, 61, 62*f*
Previewing changes to plans, 69
Progress monitoring, 154
Puppets and feelings, 24
Puzzle pieces, 127

Questions
  to ask kids, 18*f*
  classroom curiosity, 29*f*
  of the day, 117, 179*f*
  empathy discussion, 138
  getting to know you, 19*f*
  tell me about yourself, 20*f*

Random acts of kindness, 123–124, 140
RAS, *see* Reticular activating system
Reacting to My Feelings, 177*f*
Read-alouds, 163
  for teaching growth mindset, 195–196
Reading
  children's books to support SEL, 193–197
  for cultivating empathy, 143, 144*f*
Recipe for a Thank You Note, 183*f*
Reflection, 139–140
Reflective writing, 153
Reframing Praise for a Growth Mindset, 184*f*
Relationship skills, 3*f*, 4, 27, 30, 69–70
  classroom environment strategies, 167–169
  community building strategies, 156–163
  daily integration strategies, 151–154
  group work strategies, 154–156
  introduction to, 149–151
  progress monitoring and, 154
  research on, 151
  strategies to use during instruction, 163–167
Repeating of instructions for games, 68
Reporter and recorder, 118
Research
  on classroom environment, 110–112
  on emotional intelligence, 14–16, 15*f*
  on empathy, 132–133
  on executive functioning (EF), 54–55
  on growth mindset, 89–90
  on mindfulness, 72
  on self-regulation, 35–37, 49*f*
  on social-emotional learning (SEL), 3–5, 3*f*, 4*f*
  on teacher-student relationships, 151
Resilience, 45
  growth mindset and, 90
Respect, 69
Responsible decision making, 3*f*, 4
Reticular activating system (RAS), 55
Rhyming partners, 126
Rhythm, 47
Role-play, 21–22, 165, 185*f*
  empathy and, 145
"Rose and Thorn" student check-in, 154
Routines and procedures, 69, 112, 114*f*

Sample Role-Play Cards, 185*f*
Scaffolded instruction, 98–100
SCAN breathing, 76–77
SEL, *see* Social-emotional learning
SEL Sentence Stems to "Spark" Quick-Writes, 175*f*
SELF breath, 79
Self-awareness, 3, 3*f*, 16
    teaching relationship skills and, 27, 30
Self-esteem, 92
Self-management, 3*f*, 4
Self-monitoring, 154
Self-motivation, 95
Self-regulation, 16, 33–34
    boosting emotional vocabulary for, 40
    building a positive environment for, 37–39
    building resilience for, 45
    classroom checklist for, 38*f*
    classroom strategies for, 37–48
    defined, 34
    empathy and, 135
    gratitude journals and, 46
    importance of, 35
    introduction to, 34
    managing expectations and, 47
    mind-body connection and, 47–48
    preparing a safe, calming classroom for, 40–45
    research on, 35–37, 49*f*
    starting the day off right for, 39
    teaching, 35*f*
    using picture books to teach about feelings, 46
Self-talk, positive, 118
Sensory memory, 63–64
Shared responsibility, 70
Sharing the joy, 124
Sharing your own feelings first, 42
Short-term memory, 63–64
"Shout-outs," 120
Simon Says, 22–23, 68
Sing it with feeling!, 24
Singing bowl, 42, 45
Sitting Still Like a Frog, 74
Situation cards, 139
Snowball toss, 120
Social awareness, 3, 3*f*
Social skills, 16
Social-emotional learning (SEL), 1–2
    anchor charts, 167, 169
    children's books to support, 193–197
    common misconceptions about, 7–9
    defined, 2
    Every Student Succeeds Act (ESSA) and, 1
    glossary of terms in, 203–205
    impact of, 6–7
    importance of, 5–7
    key features of effective programs for, 4–5, 4*f*
    positive class culture and, 10
    research on, 3–5, 3*f*, 4*f*
    simple ways to integrate, 11*f*
    study guide for, 207–211
    teachable moments and, 9–10

Stepping up to learning, 30, 31*f*
Sticky note brainstorming, 118
Storytelling
    to communicate feelings, 36
    empathy and, 145
    as springboard for mindfulness, 74
Storytime lessons, 163
Strategies to Promote "Buddy Classrooms," 180*f*
Stress detectors, 37
Stress reduction and mindfulness, 72
Stretch to the sky!, 81
Student survey, 156, 160*f*
Study skills, 37, 39
Sustained attention, 59–61

Talk time, positive, 152–153
Teachable moments, 9–10
Teachers sharing feelings, 42
Team-building strategies, 155
Thank you notes, 125, 181–183*f*
Thank You Notes Made Easy!, 181*f*
Thinking out loud, 69
"This is Me!," 163, 164*f*
Tibetan singing bowl, 42, 45
Time management, 61, 63
Trauma-informed resources, 201–202
Tuning in to the heart, 81
"Two Facts and a Fib," 163
2-week thankful challenge, 125–126

Understanding by Design, 111
Understanding of emotions, 15, 15*f*
Using emotions to facilitate thought, 15, 15*f*

Valentine buddies, 127
Venn diagram, 120
Video clips, 143
Vocabulary, emotional, 26, 40, 138–139, 165, 166*f*
Voice, student, 118–119, 138

Walking meditation, 84
Wallace Foundation model, 4
Weekly report, 65, 66*f*
Welcome doors, 116–117
"What Is Social Emotional Learning?," 5
Which emotion am I?, 27
Whisper wishes, 153–154
Whole child, supporting the, 116–118
Windowpane activity, 163
Windowpane strategy, 96, 97*f*
Wonder of words, 165, 166*f*
Word family teams, 127
Word wall, feelings, 42, 43*f*

Your Fantastic Elastic Brain: Stretch It, Shape It, 103